Educational Technology
Expanding Our Vision

Educational Technology
Expanding Our Vision

R C Krishnamurthy

AUTHORSPRESS

Worldwide Circulation through Authorspress Global Network
First Published 2003
Reprinted 2004, 2005, 2006
Second Enlarged Edition 2007
Reprinted 2008
by Authorspress

E-35/103, Jawahar Park
Laxmi Nagar, Delhi-110092

e-mail: authorspress@yahoo.com

Typeset in NewCenturySchlbk by Chitra Computers

Educational Technology: Expanding our Vision
ISBN 81-7273-230-9

Printed in India at Tarun Offset, Delhi.

Preface

We are facing a time of "information evolution". In the ever-changing world filled with new technology, our teachers and students require the right information, from the right sources, today. Technology offers the opportunity to change the roles that teachers and students have traditionally played. With technology dispensing information, teachers are free to coach and facilitate students learning. With technology monitoring, students can become active learners, working to effectively acquire new skills as they solve problems. If the goal of creating high-performance learning organisations is to be realised, the reinvention of education has to incorporate these new tools.

Educational access to information and communications technologies (ICTs) tools, applications, networks, and media worldwide has grown dramatically. Education is facing a significant challenge in preparing students and teachers for our future 'knowledge-based' society at a time when most teachers are not trained to use ICTs and the majority of existing school buildings, even in the most developed countries, are not equipped to integrate the new information and communication technologies.

The new digital ICTs in education today encompass a wide range of rapidly evolving technologies, including hardware, software and applications. They can integrate multiple media into single educational applications; they are interactive and include the capacity to control, manipulate, and contribute to the information environment; they are flexible, offering freedom from rigid scheduling and from barriers of time and location; through connectivity, they provide access to every other person on the planet who has an internet account, to hundreds of thousands of information archives, and to millions of web pages. A wide range of initiatives are taking place all over the world, at all levels of education, showing a potential for further developments which looks almost unlimited.

Leading change and implementing technology often go hand in hand. The key to success in both is a thorough, inclusive planning process. A new vision of technology's place in education is required if teachers and students are to develop the skills necessary to meet the challenges of a high-tech society. Today, technology changes too rapidly to allow school leaders the luxury of planning for the future. Those involved in planning must understand the role of technology in education. Efforts need to address the uses of technology as tools that can help staff and students realise educational and managerial goals. Besides government, NGOs, educational planners and school administrators have major roles in promoting school reforms and accelerate technology use by serving as visionaries, catalysts, and publishers of pertinent information and knowledge.

The fundamental purpose of the book is to provide a comprehensive analysis of the elements and processes that need to be considered in the context of increasing access to information and communication technologies, at all levels of education, as any other walks of life. The author hopes that the work will help educational leaders, policy-makers, administrators and teachers, who are grappled with the complexity of establishing strategic priorities in a complex and dynamic environment, to make clear and dynamic vision of educational technology, we should have in this era of information dissemination.

R.C. Krishnamurthy

Contents

1

Education, Technology and Change

While basic skills such as reading and writing will likely remain at the core of the curriculum, the abilities built on this foundation continue to change with our society. As people seek to adjust to these changes, to find their footing in this continually evolving context, they turn to education for assistance and for reassurance about the future. As they enter the work force, adults have seen the need for more and better education for themselves. The result has been increased expectations of our education system, particularly as indicated by levels of student achievement. Parents and community members working in the shifting economic environment are turning to schools to provide education for students which will equip them for a more internationally competitive workplace in which skilled workers are the norm.

Nations around the world are experiencing dramatic shifts in their political, economic and social structures. With the end of the Cold War, the political agenda which had provided the basis for American foreign policy and many domestic issues as well was suddenly gone. As we have tried to redefine our role in the international arena, Indians have begun to see ourselves in a new world, one demanding a greater understanding of many cultures and histories. We have also begun to focus more on our domestic policies, looking at how we can reform our education, health care, welfare, campaign finance and other systems. Much of this is in response to dramatic shifts in our economy and social fabric that are demanding new policies.

Meanwhile, national economies are becoming increasingly internationalised with greater movement of capital, products, technology and information. This brings Indian industry into direct competition with industries from around the world. Standards for skills, products and worker knowledge are derived not only from our domestic agenda, but from our needs for competing in this international arena.

The very concept and expectations of work and career have changed dramatically in the past twenty years. The nation's economic shifts have social parallels. There are shifts in family structure, increased child poverty, inadequacy of social welfare and social service programs, and what some have called a decreased sense of civic responsibility. All of these combine to exacerbate existing inequities in our society, reflected vividly in the education system. In our daily lives, we are inundated with information. From the news media to advertising to the world wide web, the amount of information available to individuals in today's society is staggering. This has prompted some to say that we are moving beyond the information age into the knowledge age. They point out that we are already well immersed in the information age and that what we really need is a way to sift and sort this information, a way to gauge what is useful and what is not.

The defining characteristic of the knowledge age is perpetual change. Unlike previous transformations, the transformation to the knowledge age is not a period of change, followed by stability. It will usher in an epoch of continuous change on an accelerating time cycle. This means that the kinds of knowledge that will serve each individual and our society as a whole are constantly evolving. In order to lead change effectively, it is crucial to understand personal and organisational change styles. The resources in this section provide questions and inventories that can help you begin to understand your and your organisation's change styles.

Systemic change is an approach which involves players from throughout the system in considering all parts of an organisation or group, how change in one area affects another, and how to coordinate change in a system so that it furthers the shared goals and visions. It is closely linked to the concept of continuous improvement, in which people work in a specific process to keep improving their results.

In the field of education, systemic change practices offer tools that can help educators and leaders to remain effective in the rapidly changing context. A system in education can range in size from the classroom to the state level. Educators have been addressing change for a long time, and very intensively for the past 15 years. Our reform efforts have dealt with practically every instructional issue one-at-a-time – and still we persist in our belief that schools are not performing as well as we would like and are in need of additional reforms. Many disgruntled educators have come to call new efforts in this parade of reform programmes the "flavour of the month".

Systemic change offers an opportunity to enact change while moving beyond thinking about individuals and individual organisations, single problems and single solutions. It entails thinking about systems – policy systems, education systems, social service systems, information systems, technology systems. It is a cyclical process in which the impact of change on all parts of the whole and their relationships to one another are taken into consideration. In the contexts of schools, it is not so much a detailed prescription for improving education as a philosophy advocating reflecting, rethinking, and restructuring.

Systemic change entails working with stakeholders throughout the system to:

i) Create a vision of what you want the system to look like and accomplish.

ii) Take stock of the current situation.

ii) Identify strengths and weaknesses of the current system in light of the vision.

iv) Target several priority items for improvement.

v) Establish a plan for addressing these priority items and for measuring success.
vi) Assess progress regularly and revise actions as needed.
vii) Take stock again and use feedback to revisit vision and begin cycle again when the action cycle is completed.

A big benefit to be gained from the systemic change approach is involvement of players from throughout the system from the start of the initiative. When stakeholders from all functional areas of the organisation focus on how the future could be different from the past, when they draw out the implications of these changes for their organisational mission, goals, structure, functioning, and implementation plans, they are more likely to want to make the resulting plan work.

In a 1989 study in US researchers found that schools that used systemic change practices outperformed traditional schools by 30 per cent in mathematics, 24 per cent in reading, 29 per cent in history, and 20 per cent in science. There are several networks of schools and districts working with systemic change practices and seeing results. Accelerated schools have demonstrated that children, irrespective of racial and socioeconomic background, can learn and succeed in school. The implementation of the philosophy and process in schools has resulted in outcomes such as increased mastery of basic and higher order thinking skills; more innovative and effective curriculum and instructional practices; improved attitudes towards schooling and learning; increased parental involvement; and improved school climate.

For systemic change to be effective, it is important to involve the stakeholders in the decision making and change processes and to look beyond pieces of the whole to understand the relationship between them.

The first step in the process of systemic change is to build a vision. This process should involve members of every sector of the organisation and/or community that the change will affect. Effective questions for building the vision of the future include:

i) What will the ideal look like when it's complete?
ii) What are you looking forward to most in completing that task?
iii) What specifically will be most pleasing?
iv) What has worked most effectively in similar situations in the past?

The second step is to take stock of the current situation. Collect data and opinions from throughout the community, taking care to get information from those closest to the activities and setting of a particular area. When taking stock, it is important to remain optimistic and to appreciate the success of what is already in place. Some helpful questions for preserving this frame of mind are:

i) What was particularly effective about the way that worked?
ii) What would you do differently another time?
iii) What would be the benefit of doing it differently?

The third step is to compare the shared vision with the current situation, prioritise areas for change and set goals. In making these decisions, there are several questions which will help focus your thoughts and decision making process:

i) What part of that decision are your most comfortable about? Most uncomfortable about?
ii) What specifically about that part are you most comfortable with? Most uncomfortable?
iii) If nothing mattered except what you would most like to do, which would you choose?
iv) What specifically about that is the deciding factor?
v) What would it take for your to feel comfortable in doing that?
vii) What is the biggest unanswered questions about that decision?

viii) What do you feel there is to learn from having made that decisions?

In the ever-changing world filled with new technology, our teachers and students require the right information, from the right sources, today. Having direct access to industry information gives the competitive edge needed to succeed. Student performance can be improved when the enhancement of teaching and learning using technology is adopted as the norm. We are facing a time of "information evolution". The Aspen Institute Communications and Society Programme issued the following ways new information technologies are spurring complex patterns of change:

i) Centralisation vs. fragmentation
ii) A holistic perspective vs. specialised knowledge
iii) Too much information vs. too little information
iv) Leadership vs. fellowship
v) Worker isolation/alientation vs. community connections
vi) Sharing vs. withholding access to information
vii) Information "filters" vs. disintermediation
viii) Public intervention vs. private decisionmaking

The educators must take into consideration the changes happening every day in today's businesses. It is the responsibility of our schools to provide the necessary tools for students to transition into the workplace. A report by the Information Technology Association of America warns that one out of every 10 jobs requiring information technology skills is going unfilled due to a shortage of qualified workers. The association surveyed 2,000 large and mid-sized companies and found at least 190,000 unfilled information technology jobs. The report cited a decline in college graduates with degrees in mathematics or computer science. The public is keeping abreast with the technology changes. More than ever, individuals value the importance of technology changes in education.

The learning requirements of the millennium include:

i) A greater dependence on new communication and computing technologies that support new levels of student creativity and research.

ii) A change in the role of teachers from "sages on the stage" to mentors, researchers, publishers, technology users, knowledge producers, risk takers and lifelong learners.

iv) Involvement of parents to play a major role in the education of their children and to work actively with teachers to connect formal and informal education.

v) Partnering of local businesses and other community organisations so they become actively involved in the schools.

vi) Collaborations that bring students, teachers, and researchers together to create new curriculum for learners.

Following conditions were recognised as critical elements of future schools:

i) Schools of the future must be open and flexible.

ii) New communication should promote new collaborations and a higher level of cooperation and creative problem-solving.

iii) Teachers must be supported in their use of new technologies for learning and also in their use of technology for professional development and collaboration.

iv) Learners must be able to use technology to achieve new levels of learning and to acquire new information age skills and abilities.

v) Educational managers need to use technology as a tool for managing schools and learner communities.

vi) Free from one geographic location.

vii) Supportive cf all learning styles.

viii) Teachers must be researchers and mentors.

ix) New skills required in info-society: abilities to quickly adapt to new situations and new technologies.

x) The only way a school or district will get sustained support for quality professional development in technology is when the line administrators and top administrators are active technology users.

xi) Administrators and managers need professional development as much as their staff.

xii) Principals, superintendents and school boards must provide teachers with adequate training and support to effectively use the technology in their classrooms. They need to understand how the current structure of a teacher's and learner's day impact on their effective use of the technology. In effect, managers must provide the vision of change that includes empowering teachers and learners in new ways and then must learn how to effectively manage these empowered teachers and learners

xiii) New online communities.

Boards of education need to recognise that technology integration is as much about change as it is about technology. How board members feel about change and their attitudes about people's ability to change or not change are crucial.

A broader definition of technology is used to mean a tool or instrument which helps us to organise and accomplish specific tasks and goals. Old technologies in school include: learning spaces, learning schedules, learning frameworks, learning assessments. For technology to serve the purposes of change, it must be tied to a coherent, school-wide instructional agenda. For education professionals computer networking creates a professional bond between teachers and administrators, ends isolation. For students a new system of knowledge will enhance collaborative learning; alternative assessment; and individualised learning. Rather than debating the connections between technology-based instruction and test scores, schools should focus on the most obvious and compelling reason form implementing technology-namely, that students need strong technology skills to succeed in the world of work.

The process of learning in the classroom can become significantly richer as students have access to new and different types of information, can manipulate it on the computer through graphic displays or controlled experiments in ways never before possible, and can communicate their results and conclusions in a variety of media to their teacher, students in the next classroom, or students around the world. For example, using technology, students can collect and graph real-time weather, environmental, and populations data from their community, use that data to create colour maps and graphs, and then compare these maps to others created by students in other communities. Similarly, instead of reading about the human circulatory system and seeing textbook pictures depicting bloodflow, students can use technology to see blood moving through veins and arteries, watch the process of oxygen entering the bloodstream, and experiment to understand the effects of increased pulse or cholesterol-filled arteries on blood flow.

Successful technology-rich schools generate impressive results for students, including improved achievement; higher test scores; improved student attitude, enthusiasm, and engagement; richer classroom content; and improved student retention and job placement rates.

Of the hundreds of studies that show positive benefits from the use of technology, two are worth noting for their comprehensiveness. The first, a US. Department of Education-funded study of nine technology-rich schools, concluded that the use of technology resulted in educational gains for all students regardless of age, race, parental income, or other characteristics.

The second, a 10-year study supported by Apple Computer, Inc., concluded that student provided with technology-rich learning environments 'continued to perform well on standardised tests but were also developing a variety of competencies not usually measured. Students explored and represented information dynamically and in many forms; became socially aware and more confident; communicated effectively about complex processes; became independent learners and self-starters; knew their areas of expertise and shared that expertise spontaneously.

In a 1994 Software Publisher's Association (SPA) study, research found that:

i) Educational technology has a significant positive impact on achievement in all subject areas, across all levels of school, and in regular classrooms as well as those for special-needs students.

ii) Educational technology has positive effects on student attitudes.

iii) The degree of effectiveness is influenced by the student population, the instructional design, the teacher's role, how students are grouped, and the levels of student access to technology.

iv) Technology makes instruction more student-centered, encourages cooperative learning, and stimulated increased teacher/student interaction.

v) Positive changes in the learning environment evolve over time and do not occur quickly.

A five-year report (1987-1992) by the Sacramento School District in California, found that students using multimedia and telecommunications showed improved attitudes toward reading, social studies and science, and became more active and independent in learning. Some also showed improved reading scores. A survey of 550 teachers who use telecommunications technology in the classroom reported that "inquiry-based analytical skills — like critical thinking, data analysis, problem solving, and independent thinking — develop when students use a technology that supports research, communication, and analysis. However, telecommunications does not directly help their performances on state- or city- mandated tests.

Seven or more "multiple intelligences" that are of equal importance in human beings and develop at different times and in different ways in different individuals. Multi-media can go along way to addressing these intelligences, much more than traditional teaching methods. Below is a list of the intelligences and the technology tools that can be used to teach to them:

i) *Verbal / linguistic intelligence*: The ability to think, communicate, and create through words both in speech and in writing.

   a) Computer software which allows young children to write and illustrate their own stories before their fine motor skills are developed enough to allow them to do so by hand.

   b) Word processing software stimulates learners to interact more closely with their work.

   c) Audio and video recording can give students instant feedback on their story-telling skills and can help them develop them further.

   d) Multimedia software helps students produce multimedia reports.

   e) Telecommunications programmes link students who correspond in writing.

ii) *Logical / mathematical intelligences*: Memorise and perform mathematical operations, ability to think mathematically, logically, and analytically and to apply that understanding to problem solving.

   a) Multimedia products that graphically illustrate physics concepts.

   b) Providing challenging visual/spatial tasks which develop mathematical and logical thinking .

   c) Develop higher-order mathematical thinking by making abstract ideas concrete.

iii) *Visual / spatial intelligence*: The ability to understand the world through what we see and imagine and to express ideas through the graphic arts.

a) "Paint" programmes that allow students who are unskilled with paper and brush create art on computer screens.
b) Databases of art work.
c) Desktop publishing.
d) Camcorders to create documentaries.
e) Internet links to museums and virtual tours.

iv) *Bodily/kinesthetic intelligence*: The ability to learn through physical coordination and dexterity and the ability to express oneself through physical activities.

a) Educational games which challenge fine motor coordination while developing logical thinking skills and mastery over abstractions.
b) Construction of lego robots and programme their movement through the computer.
c) Electronic fieldtrips — programmes that allow students to interact electronically with a scientist who is exploring the depths of the Mediterranean or the inside of a volcano.

v) *Musical intelligence*: The ability to understand, appreciate, perform, and create music by voice or instruments or dance.

a) Students can hum into a synthesiser and make it sound like any instrument they want.
b) Musical Instrument Digital Interface (MIDI) makes it possible to make music on an electronic keyboard, which can be made to sound like any instrument and then can be orchestrated electronically.
c) Interactive presentations of renowned classical music let students understand music on many different levels; listening to it, seeing the score as it is played, hearing individual instruments played alone, reviewing biographical material about the composer and learning about the music's historical and cultural backgrounds.

vi) *Interpersonal intelligence*: The ability to work cooperatively with other people and to apply a variety of skills to communicate with and understand others.

a) Clusters of students working together on computers learn more than individual students working alone.

b) Electronic networks linking students with their peers within the community and around the world.

c) Lumaphones allow students to see a picture of the person with whom they are speaking.

vii) *Intrapersonal intelligence*: The ability to understand, bring to consciousness, and express one's own inner world of thoughts and emotions.

a) Multimedia gives teachers the tools to turn the classroom into centres of student-directed inquiry.

b) Technology offers tools for thinking more deeply, pursuing curiosity, and exploring and expanding intelligence as students build "mental models" with which they can visualise connections between ideas on any topic.

c) Individual growth plans, developed jointly by the student, parents and teacher can encourage the development of intrapersonal intelligence. Technology supports such plans with electronic records, videotaped interviews, and multimedia portfolios of student work.

Educational technology provides significant positive effects all major subject areas, in preschool through higher education, and for both regular education and special needs students. Evidence suggests that interactive video is especially effective when the skills and concepts to be learned have a visual component and when the software incorporates a research-based instructional design. Use of online telecommunications for collaboration across classrooms in different geographic locations has also been show to improve academic skills.

Education technology has been found to have positive effects on student attitudes toward learning and on student self-concept. Students felt more successful in school, were more motivated to learn and have increased self-confidence and self-esteem when using computer-based instruction. This was particularly true when the technology allowed learners to control their own learning. The level of effectiveness of educational technology is influenced by the specific student population, the software design, the teacher's role, how the students are grouped, and the level of student access to the technology. Students trained in collaborative learning, had higher self esteem and student achievement. Introducing technology into the learning environment has been shown to make learning more student-centered, to encourage cooperative learning, and to stimulate increased teacher/ student interaction.

Positive changes in the learning environment brought about by technology are more evolutionary than revolutionary. These changes occur over a period of years, as teachers become more experienced with technology. Courses for which computer-based networks were use increased student-student and student-teacher interaction, increased student-teacher interaction with lower-performing students, and did not decrease the traditional forms of communication used. Many student who seldom participate in face-to-face class discussion become more active participants online. Greater student cooperation and sharing and helping behaviours occurred when students used computer-based learning that had students compete against the computer rather than against each other. Small group collaboration on computer is especially effective when student have received training in the collaborative process. Administrator's new responsibilities must include supporting the efforts of their staff to adopt and adapt new technologies in order to achieve new levels of productivity and achievement. In effect, managers must provide the vision of change that includes empowering teachers and learners in new ways and then must learn how to effectively manage these empowered teachers and learners.

Technology offers the opportunity to change the roles that teachers and students have traditionally played. With technology dispensing information, teachers are free to coach and facilitate students learning. With technology monitoring learning, students can become active learners, working to effectively acquire new skills as they solve problems. If the goal of creating high-performance learning organisations is to be realised, the reinvention of education has to incorporate these new tools.

The features of technology that promote engaged learning and effective instruction include:

i) *Access*: connectivity and interconnectivity, design for equitable use
ii) *Operability*: interoperability, open architecture, transparency
iii) *Resource location and direction*: distributed, user control of input, designed for collaborative projects
iv) *Capacity for engagement*: provide access to authentic and challenging tasks, interesting and useful databases or information sets and powerful relationships, take charge of learning, problem solving and exploring, provide information that is just in time and just enough, make explicit what is typically implicit, diagnose learning problems, adapt the system output and learning opportunities in light of diagnoses, customise learning for specific interests, levels of ability and learning preferences
v) *Ease of use*: effective help, user friendliness, speed of processing and operations, training and support
vi) *Functionality*: prepare learners for diversity of technology functions used in the workplace and homes in the 21st century, develop skills for programming and authoring, develop skills related to project design and implementation.

The government has an important role in promoting school reform and accelerate technology use by serving as visionary, catalyst, and publisher of pertinent information and knowledge. Specifically, the government can support change by:

i) Promulgating a broad vision of change and the use of technology to promote change.
ii) Serving as a repository of knowledge and information pertinent to learning and educational change and actively disseminating "success" stories and critical reviews of new technologies.
iii) Promoting the development of new curriculum and rich content on the networks.
iv) Bringing together critical players in real and virtual symposiums and conferences to discuss problems, solutions, and action plans.
v) Providing funds to jump start local initiatives.
vi) Ensuring equity of access.
vii) Overseeing the development of networking infrastructure.
viii) Protecting the interests of the education community.

Leading change and implementing technology often go hand in hand. The key to success in both is a thorough, inclusive planning process. A new vision of technology's place in education is required if teachers and students are to develop the skills necessary to meet the challenges of a high-tech society. Today, technology changes too rapidly to allow school leaders the luxury of planning for the future. Those involved in planning must understand the role of technology in education. Efforts need to address the uses of technology as tools that can help staff and students realise educational and managerial goals.

REFERENCES

Roberts, L., *A Transformation of Learning: Use of the NII for Education and Lifelong Learning*, In D. P. Ely & B. B. Minor (eds.), *Educational Media and Technology Yearbook 1995/1996*, pp. 50-66, Englewood, CO: Libraries Unlimited, 1996

Wentworth, N., "Educational technology: From curriculum course to the classroom", *Technology and Teacher Education Annual*, 335-358, 1996.

2

ICTs in Education

In recent years, educational access to digital information and communications technology (ICT), tools, applications, networks, and media worldwide has grown dramatically. Education is facing a significant challenge in preparing students and teachers for our future 'knowledge-based' society at a time when most teachers are not trained to use ICTs and the majority of existing school buildings, even in the most developed countries, are not equipped to integrate the new information and communication technologies. ICTs are quickly becoming more accessible, but it is important to note that earlier technologies continue to play a critical role in education worldwide. Access to films, videotapes, telephones, television or radio is still far more commonplace than access to a computer or to the internet and the World Wide Web (WWW).

The new digital ICTs are not single technologies, but combinations of hardware, software, media, and delivery systems. They differ in several important dimensions from older technologies: they can integrate multiple media into single educational applications; they are interactive and include the capacity to control, manipulate, and contribute to the information environment; they are flexible, offering freedom from rigid scheduling and from barriers of time and location; through connectivity, they provide access to every other person on the planet who has an internet account, to hundreds of thousands of information archives, and to millions of web pages. These four dimensions—integration of multiple media, interactivity, flexibility of use, and connectivity—distinguish digital ICTs from previous technologies. Because of these differences, educators are finding powerful new ways to integrate digital ICTs into the curricula.

A wide range of initiatives are taking place all over the world, at all levels of education, showing a potential for further developments which looks almost unlimited. ICT equipment and internet connectivity is much more widespread in schools around the world. For example, in the United States, the ratio of students per computer dropped from 63:1 in 1985 to 6:1 in 1997 while the number of schools with internet access has grown from 35 per cent in 1994 to 72 per cent in 1997.

In Europe, more than 80 per cent of schools in Slovenia have access to the internet — 93 per cent of secondary schools and 80 per cent of primary schools — which is similar to the percentages of developed countries. The Government of the United Kingdom plans to connect all schools, colleges, universities, libraries, and as many community centres as possible to the internet by 2002. The German Government will connect 10,000 schools to the internet by mid-1999. In Italy, plans were announced in 1998 for the installation of computer and multimedia facilities in 15,000 Italian schools to be completed by the year 2000.

In Asia, similar developments are taking place. In Japan, as of 1997, over 94 per cent of public schools were computer-equipped and 10 per cent were connected to the internet. The Government plans to achieve a pupil-to-computer ratio of 2:1 in middle schools and 1:1 in high schools by 1999. All of the public schools in Japan will be connected to the internet by 2003.

In the People's Republic of China, the central government will increase funding for basic, vocational and higher education projects over the next two years. These plans include strategies to make increasing use of internet-based educational programmes. In New Zealand, 83 per cent of primary schools and 94 per cent of secondary schools have internet access.

In Latin America, the Chilean government established the Enlaces (Links) project to connect schools and related institutions to Chile's national computer network. By 1996, over 180 primary schools and 62 secondary schools had been connected and, by the year 2000, the Chilean government plans to connect 50 per cent of the 8,250 primary schools and 100 per cent of the 1,700 secondary schools.

In. Africa, the Creating Learning Networks for African Teachers Initiative aims to contribute to educational change by encouraging educational institutions to become information and learning resource centres for their communities. It also hopes to contribute to attitudinal change among teachers with a view to stimulating ongoing professional development by creating electronic learning networks among teacher training institutions and their partners in education at local, national and international levels. These networks will allow for exchange of information, experiences and expertise, for collaborative action and for new patterns of communication.

Pilot projects were initiated in Zimbabwe by connecting five teacher training centres (TTC) and their partner institutions to the internet. Currently the project is carried out in close collaboration with the World Bank's WorldLinks for Development programme. A project in Senegal is structured in a similar way, while in Kenya and Uganda the Initiative is being introduced as part of a collaborative learning project in the area of science/mathematics teaching, linking teachers, students and researchers in Zimbabwe, Kenya and Uganda.

In the Middle East, as part of a programme sponsored by the World Bank to improve basic education, the Turkish Government will bo installing computer laboratories in over 15,000 schools and training over 200,000 teachers in computer literacy and computer-aided instruction techniques. Informal and non-formal education institutions are also increasingly being equipped with ICTs and connected to the internet. At present, about 20 per cent of libraries in the United Kingdom are connected to the internet. The government's National Grid for Learning initiative will connect all libraries and museums in the United Kingdom to the internet.

In the United States, a 1998 survey found that 73 per cent of the nation's public libraries offered basic internet access to the public. Many public and privately-funded museums are offering ICT-based learning opportunities. For example, in a joint project with the Fraunhofer Institute for Software and Systems Engineering, the German Historical Museum in Berlin and the Haus der Geschichte of the Federal Republic of Germany in Bonn are developing a virtual exhibition of German history for the internet. Community schools are also making more use of ICTs. The Lighthouse Project in Thailand is offering non-formal educational programmes at five locations in Thailand.

ICT-MEDIATED INSTRUCTION

Efforts to connect educational organisations to the internet are being driven by societal pressure. This does not eliminate, however, the need to check whether there will be positive consequences for such a move. One aspect of this question is how effective the ICTs are in education. To answer this question three aspects must be considered. The first deals with the comparison between traditional teaching techniques and those which make use of ICTs; here the term ICT-mediated instruction will be used. The second covers teaching activities which would not be possible without modern ICTs, hence the expression ICT-enabled instruction. The third concerns all the techniques, whether ICT-mediated or enabled, and raises the question as to whether they are worth their costs.

The first question to be considered about the effectiveness of ICT in education is what impact, if any, ICT-mediated instruction has on student performance. ICT-mediated instruction refers to instruction delivered through a technological channel such as television, radio, or a computer network. Evidence has consistently shown that ICT-mediated instruction using conventional teaching methods is as effective as traditional face-to-face instruction and, in the case of computer-based instruction, may in certain instances improve student learning and attitudes to learning.

However, the picture is less clear — but promising — for more sophisticated uses of ICTs in the classroom, especially for the host of applications and methods that support 'constructivist' learning, in which students are encouraged to work in rich environments of information and experience to build their own understanding of them. Research into the effectiveness of ICT-mediated instruction is continuing worldwide, and should provide a clearer picture of the effectiveness of ICTs in supporting constructivist teaching. For example, as part of the Helsinki 2000 project, Finnish researchers are conducting a five - year, multi-disciplinary study focused on analysing innovative teaching practices through intensive case studies on computer-supported collaborative learning.

A second way to assess the merit of ITC-use in education is to consider what, if anything, they enable students and teachers to do that they would not otherwise be able to do. To explore this question, five aspects of the educational use of ICTs will be considered: supporting new teaching methods, accessing remote resources, enabling collaboration, extending educational programmes and information literacy.

Modern constructivist educational theory emphasises critical thinking, problem solving, 'authentic' learning experiences, social negotiation of knowledge, and collaboration. The teaching methods concerned change the role of the teacher from a disseminator of information to a learning facilitator, helping students as they actively engage with information and materials to construct their own understanding.

ICTs have the potential to be used in support of these new educational methods, enabling students to learn by doing. ICTs can make it possible for teachers to provide students with self-paced, self-directed problem-based or constructivist learning experiences, as well as to test student learning in new, interactive, and attractive ways that may better assess the depth of their understanding of content and processes. One example may help illustrate how ICTs can support constructivist teaching methods. Computer Supported Intentional Learning Environments (CSILE), developed at the Ontario Institute for Studies in Education, is a network system that provides support for collaborative learning and inquiry within a school. CSILE promotes student interaction through referencing, connecting ideas, sharing authorship, and 'building on' the work of others to advance knowledge.

ACCESS TO RESOURCES

Connectivity is one of the main differences between older and newer ICTs. The first aspect of connectivity concerns access to material resources. Digital library initiatives that will provide collections that are electronically accessible on the internet, including printed works (e.g. textbooks, journals ,illustrations ,maps ,charts and graphs), photographs, films and videotapes, paintings, 3D models, graphics, animations, software, reference materials, audio files, and so forth are being undertaken in countries around the world.

Thousands of websites that contain collections of high quality curriculum guides, lesson plans, and instructional activities now exist. For example, the United Nations CyberSchoolBus website contains teaching units on urbanisation, health, the environment, and women and politics, as well as interactive games, maps, databases, and quizzes. In addition to efforts to digitise existing physical resources, many new information resources are being created which can only be accessed electronically. As digital representations of physical resources are created, and as more information resources are distributed in digital format only, it will be critical that students and teachers have ICT access.

ICT enables educational collaboration between individuals and groups of people. E-mail, computer-mediated conferencing, and desktop videoconferencing are all being used to support collaboration among individuals and groups. Collaboration is also taking place by means of real-time chat systems; whiteboards; newsgroups; computer-mediated conferencing (CMC); and specialised software like CaMILE (Collaborative and Multimedia Interactive Learning Environment) and The Knowledge Integration Environment. Other applications include MUDs (Multi-User Domains) MOOs (Multi-user Object Oriented domains), and MUSHs (Multi-User Shared Hallucinations). Such applications are internet-accessible, text-mediated virtual environments in which participants can both interact with others and help construct the common virtual space.

ICTs make it possible for people in widely dispersed locations to participate in 'virtual learning communities.' Virtual learning communities are learning groups based on shared purpose, rather than on distinctions of location or age. Through the ICTs, learners can be drawn together from almost anywhere in the world, and can construct their own formal or informal learning groups. Such communities may cross barriers of time, geography, age, ability, culture and social status.

Virtual education allows students to study at their own time, place and pace. In essence, a virtual education means having educational transactions accessible from the home, the workplace or anywhere that the student chooses to be. Virtual Design Studios, begun in 1993, are a form of collaboration among teams of architecture students in universities worldwide. Teachers and students, on different continents and in different time zones, work on common design projects using computer-aided design systems, e-mail, a central database, and video-conferencing.

Participants use the web to display their designs and a virtual international jury of architects and teachers judges the relative merit of the work. Virtual Design Studio techniques are also being utilised by other disciplines, such as engineering. The SIMULAB Project, supported by the European Union, involves web-based communication among language students across national boundaries.

Using specialised software, teachers can create internet-based simulations for role-playing activities in language learning. The simulations, incorporating e-mail, chat, and online creation and editing of documents, are thought to motivate oral and written communication among the participating groups, while students are guided through scenarios relevant to the country of their chosen language.

ICTs make it possible to extend the reach of educational programmes in two important ways:

i) educational programmes can be delivered anywhere in the world.

ii) ICTs can help individuals learn throughout their lifetime.

Distance education programmes, also known as 'distributed' education programmes, are those in which the teacher and students are physically separated, and teaching and learning takes place by means of single technologies or combinations of ICTs. In the past, such programmes made use of print, radio, and television.

Today, new ICTs are leading to changes in these traditional 'open' or distance education programmes. For example, the International Francophone Consortium of Distance and Open Learning Institutions (CIFFAD), a consortium of open and distance learning institutions spread over 49 countries, of which 80 per cent are in developing nations, has recently entered into a phase of re-engineering to make use of new ICTs. The group aims to provide at least one hundred access points to the internet per year in member establishments with the major part of the consortium having access to the network by the end of 1998.

In the Pacific region, the University of the South Pacific has been using Intelsat for several years. The Western Governors

University is an example of a 'virtual university', or university with no physical campus. WGU, initiated in 1996 by 18 governors in the western United States, offers more than 300 college-level distance learning courses from 30 affiliated universities and education providers. WGU has forged international alliances with the China Internet Education Center, Tokai University in Japan, the University of British Columbia in Canada, the Open University in the United Kingdom and the Virtual University of the Monterrey Institute of Technology in Mexico. The principal aim is to collaborate on the development and delivery of distance learning programmes.

In Germany, the four Baden universities, namely, Freiburg, Karlsruhe, Mannheim and Heidelberg, recently announced the establishment of that country's first virtual university. The objective is to establish individual distance learning via e-mail Integrated Services Digital Networks (ISDN) or digital television.

In Africa, the World Bank is funding the development of the African Virtual University (AVU). AVU completed a pilot phase in 1996-98 and is now moving into an operational phase when it will begin delivering full-fledged under-graduate degree programmes in science and engineering in January 1999. The AVU's programmes will be delivered by a combination of ICTs including interactive television and the internet. The programme is developing a digital library of scientific engineering as a resource for students and teachers. The Hanoi Summit entrusted the creation of a francophone virtual university to the Agence Universitaire de la Francophonie for a budget of 4 million French francs. As a beginning, six digitised campuses have been opened in Bulgaria, Cameroon, Haiti, Madagascar, Senegal and Viet Nam.

The United States Department of Education has funded the Virtual High School (VHS) project. During the 1997/98 school year, VHS offered 29 internet-based, credit-bearing courses to about 500 students in 27 schools located in 10 states. This approach is thought to be particularly useful as many of the participating schools either have no qualified teacher or insufficient enrollment to justify individually offering some of the courses which are available through this collaborative scheme.

In addition to educational institutions using ICTs to enhance or create distance learning programmes, commercial companies are offering ICT-based distance education programmes. Although alternate and distance education providers currently make up less than 2 per cent of the postsecondary education market, almost $2 billion dollars has been raised on Wall Street since 1996 to finance such new ventures.

With the help of ICTs governments and non-governmental organisations are in the process of establishing lifelong learning habits among citizens and providing lifelong learning opportunities. For example, UNESCO's Learning Without Frontiers (LWF) initiative is geared towards stimulating innovation and exploring alternative pathways/partners/technologies for the provision of lifelong and lifewide learning opportunities, particularly, to those who are currently unreached by or excluded from conventional modes of educational delivery.

In addition to this initiative, UNESCO has recently set up an Institute for Information Technologies in Education (IITE), located in Moscow and designed to act as an international clearing-house for the collection and dissemination of best practices and models in the field of application of information and communication technologies in education. It will also offer assistance in the pre- and in-service training of the teachers in the use of information technology, particularly in the developing countries, countries in transition and countries of the Commonwealth of Independent States.

The European Lifelong Learning Initiative makes use of ICTs, 'to initiate the dissemination of information, the co-ordination of projects and studies, the mobilisation of actions, people and organisations to bring Europe into the Lifelong Learning Age. It covers all sectors and all countries'. The Asia Pacific Economic Cooperation (APEC) Forum has established three mechanisms to assist countries in the region to establish lifelong learning projects: the creation of a database of scholars, researchers and practitioners in the region involved with lifelong learning issues and programming for the region; the development and publication of a book of papers on lifelong learning policies, practices and programmes in the Asia Pacific region; and a lifelong learning conference for APEC members to discuss related issues.

In the light of changing perceptions about what constitutes appropriate skills for the modern era, some organisations are promulgating educational standards that attempt to define what all students should know about ICTs. For example, the National Educational Technology Standards (NETS) project in the United States has released an initial set of national educational technology standards for pre-college students.

However, although it may be assumed that students will have to acquire new skills in order to compete and contribute in an increasingly ICT-dominated global economy, it is not clear what skills will be necessary.

Unlike the more stable content and goals we have for other areas of school study, technology continues to change and evolve; with these changes come ever-new goals for how technology should serve learning, and what students should know about technology. There does seem to be a growing consensus that all students must achieve 'information literacy.

It is the task of general education to provide every girl and boy with the versatile basic skills in acquiring, managing and communicating information which are necessary in the information society and essential for successful further study. Focusing on concepts such as information literacy, rather than on specific technologies or applications, may be essential in planning and developing new curricula.

COST-EFFECTIVENESS OF ICTs

Information is of critical importance, especially to developing countries with fewer resources to invest. However, assessing the cost-effectiveness of ICTs in education is difficult, if not impossible, for at least four reasons: lack of meaningful data, variability in the use of ICTs, difficulty of generalising from specific programmes, and difficulty of assessing the value of qualitative educational differences. In addition, traditional cost-analyses cannot take into account the societal and economic consequences of not investing in ICTs for education.

Even in the face of such obstacles, attempts to establish the relative costs of ICTs in education have been reported. In general, these studies find that the use of new ICTs is more expensive than instruction delivered by older technologies like print and radio, but less expensive than instruction delivered by television. In a World Bank report on education and ICTs in Latin America and the Caribbean, the costs of using a computer with an internet connection in a school was much less expensive per pupil than broadcast television, but substantially more expensive than radio. In 1996, M. Potashnik and D. Adkins, in spite of severe lack of data, were able to compare the per pupil costs of setting up a computer laboratory in a school for computer-assisted instruction in Belize ($78), Jamaica ($89), and Chile ($104).

A similar analysis of the costs of equipping a classroom, not a laboratory, with computers in the United States for computer-assisted instruction yielded a figure of $453. L. Osin, in a paper on ICTs in developing countries, assessed the annual per-student cost of providing computers for instruction in developing countries at $84. This finding is in close agreement with the study by Potashnik and Adkins mentioned above. On the same basis, if 30 computers were used 300 days per year, 10 hours per day, as a resource to raise the skills and education levels of all members of the community, not just students, Osin estimates the cost would decrease to $0.34 per hour of interaction. He concludes, 'There is no alternative system known that may provide the benefits possible by integrating computers in the education system, while at the same time serving the whole community'.

Another factor that must be considered when calculating the cost-effectiveness of ICT use is the question of alternatives. The costs of building sufficient campuses to handle the rising demand for education may be prohibitive. Virtual educational institutions do not require the same campus infrastructure and related costs incurred by campus-based institutions. In Taipei (Taiwan, China), the distance education-based National Open University, with its budget of NT$800 million, accommodates approximately 30,000 adult students each year. By comparison, the National Taiwan University, one of the larger universities in Taipei, has an annual budget of $NT3,500 million for its 21,000 students. Though gross numbers of this sort beg some level of refinement, the differential costs remain substantial and manifest.

When discussing cost-effectiveness, the societal costs to developing countries of not preparing their citizens to participate in an information-based global society must be considered. The World Development Report 1998/99 warns that the global explosion of knowledge may either lift hundreds of millions of the world's poor out of poverty or it may create a widening knowledge gap, in which poor countries lag further and further behind. Even in countries which do not believe in the cost-effectiveness of information technology as a tool for mass education, it is important that they begin acquiring experience using this technology for educational purposes.

In order to make use of digital ICTs, schools must be equipped with computers. In order to access the internet from a computer, schools, homes, libraries, and other educational venues must be equipped with an internet connection, either by means of the telephone or cable network and a modem or a direct connection. Many creative means of providing computers and building the necessary internet infrastructure are being explored in countries throughout the world. Collaboration, including cost sharing, between education and industry to build ICT infrastructure is becoming commonplace. For example, the Bristol Education Online Network (BEON) project and the follow-on Merseyside Education Online Network (MEON) are co-operative efforts of the commercial companies British Telecom (BT) and International Computers Limited (ICL), local schools and the University of Exeter School of Education. ICL is supplying multimedia computers and BT is providing access to remote services and to the internet to a number of schools in the area. Another promising approach to equipping schools with computers inexpensively is to transfer the technology from government organisations and businesses to schools.

Netday initiatives, which began in 1995, are characterised as 'high-tech barn-raising,' in other words, efforts by community volunteers to wire classrooms, libraries, and computer laboratories so that they may connect to the internet. Organisers of such efforts typically help schools to develop a technical plan that includes instructional goals, network and wiring architecture, network management and technical support, training, and an operating budget. On a specific day, volunteers from the local community do the physical work necessary to set up the network, greatly reducing the costs of providing internet access within the schools. Netdays now take place in many countries including Australia, New Zealand, European countries, Israel, Japan and South Africa. In Latin American and the Caribbean, UNESCO is sponsoring a netday initiative.

Many community networking initiatives have educational components and are worthy of mention. In an interesting example of how community networking can benefit educational institutions, the International Telecomputing Consortium is working with schools and universities in China to create school-based community networks. In these projects, schools establish computer centres with internet access for use by students and teachers in class. After hours, the centre remains open and training by teachers and students is made available to parents and other members of the community who may not have internet access. The school thus provides internet access for the community with some revenue returning to the school.

Beyond equipment and software, appropriate content is necessary to make use of ICTs for educational purposes. In this section, a few of the many initiatives related to the creation and standards of educational content will be considered. Although some online content is specifically designed for educational purposes, most is not. One approach to facilitating access to appropriate educational content is the creation of a 'Schoolnet'. Schoolnets, also known as 'national education grids', are local, national or regional projects that may include efforts to wire schools physically to information services, but the fundamental aim is to provide access to appropriate educational content. For example, the United Kingdom's National Grid for Learning (NGfL) is both an architecture of educationally valuable content on the internet, and a programme for developing the means to access that content in schools, libraries, colleges, universities, workplaces, homes and elsewhere. Schoolnets now exist in France, Ireland, Japan, South Africa, Thailand, and other countries.

ICTs can empower users not only to consume information, but also to produce it. With a computer, printer, and desktop publishing software, any local educational group can produce high quality printed materials. With an internet connection and a website, any educational organisation can 'publish' content derived from local knowledge and experience. For example, the Summer Institute of Linguistics (SIL) has helped set-up Literacy and Awareness Publication (LAMP) centres in each of the twenty provinces of Papua New Guinea to promote literacy in approximately 850 local languages. At these centres, literacy texts are produced that can be shared between the centres; they cover a wide variety of subjects including healthcare, hygiene and preservation of the environment. Although many tools exist to help teachers and students locate information, at present finding specific educational materials on the web can be likened to a scavenger hunt, often resulting in wasted time and unexpected results. A teacher or student may find it difficult to locate specific information or materials that might be useful within the curriculum at a particular grade level. The results of indiscriminate searches also raise the issue of the validity and reliability of the information let alone legality and harmfulness.

Because of varying technical standards, materials created with one ICT-based learning system may not be usable in a different technical environment once they have been found. Several efforts to bring order to the chaos of the internet and web are underway. To this end, the European Commission has initiated a Memorandum of Understanding: Multimedia Access to Education and Training in Europe. By December 1998, over 160 educational organisations, government agencies, and commercial companies had signed the MoU. Projects like the Dublin Core Metadata Initiative and the Instructional Management Systems (IMS) project which create technical standards, may 'help transform the end-user experience of the web from the unstructured tangle it is today into something more like a digital library or virtual learning centre'.

If international agreement can be reached on an acceptable set of technical standards, teachers and students may be able to search for educational materials with common descriptors and be assured that the materials, once found, will be compatible with local ICT applications. As noted in a Finnish government report, 'how computers are used in education depends on the pedagogical competence and technical skills of the teaching staff who must know how to exploit these modern technologies in pedagogically meaningful ways'. In some countries, for example the United Kingdom, training in ICT use is a requirement for a teaching certificate.

As educational applications of ICT continue to evolve, apart from preparatory training, refresher courses for experienced teachers will also be necessary. Furthermore, it may not be sufficient simply to provide training for teachers. ICT training for teachers must deal with at least two aspects. First, teachers need technical training to learn how to use and maintain ICT equipment and software. Such technical training is being offered to teachers in a wide variety of ways. Pre-service university-based courses, in-service workshops, commercial training programmes, and other opportunities abound, many of which make use of ICTs to deliver the training. Second, since 'integration of technologies into curricula requires changes of huge magnitude', training in how to integrate ICT use into the curriculum is necessary. Such training should include effective ICT teaching methods and the use of discipline-specific applications. In one possible framework for organising ICT training for teachers, McDougall and Squires identify five areas: skills with particular applications; integration into existing curricula; ICT-related changes in curricula; changes in teachers' roles; and underpinning theories of education.

As reported by Guernsey, 'people who fill the jobs have one thing in common: a hybrid expertise that blends academic computing with college teaching'. Staff who are both qualified academics within a discipline and who have expertise using ICTs for instruction are hired 'to provide faculty on-site, intradepartmental consulting and support in information and instructional technology for academic purposes to foster their awareness and use of technological resources, both within and without the University'. In another innovative but more costly approach, students are being enlisted to provide ICT support and training for teachers. At Wake Forest University in the United States, first-year students are hired and trained to work as Student Technology AdvisoRS (STARS). STARS are assigned to faculty members to help implement ICT-based projects.

The methodologies of training may vary, but 'training of trainers' models are common and in most instances may be more cost-effective than on-site, small group or individual ICT training. In such programmes, 'teacher-leaders' are selected using a variety of criteria such as prior experience with ICTs in education, staff development expertise, and the commitment to the programme by school and district administration. These individuals receive intensive training courses to master technical details and approaches to integrating ICTs into the curricula. Once trained, they return to their educational institutions and provide ICT training and support for their peers. Such programmes may also include ongoing, long-term support for the trainers, including site visits, computer-based conferences, and e-mail advice. In large geographical areas, the responsibility for such training and continuing support may be delegated to regional ICT consortia co-ordinated by a central administrative body.

Provision of on-site technical support is critical to the success of an ICT-based educational programme. Although standard service agreements, purchased separately or included in the purchase of ICT equipment and software, typically cover regular maintenance and repair costs, and may even include e-mail or telephone support, such arrangements may fall short of what is necessary in educational settings.

Without adequate technical support, schools have experienced 'large workloads for existing staff, maintenance backlogs, and reduced computer use because computers were out of service'. In universities, such support may take the form of technical staff assigned to a 'computer centre', 'media centre', or 'distance learning centre'. In schools, knowledgeable peers, students, volunteers and specialised computer teachers are generally providing such support; less frequently, trained technical staff, located either within the school or district office, are employed.

Use of ICTs in education is a difficult, expensive and complex undertaking and a host of issues, including infrastructure, curricula changes, teacher training, technical support, and so on must be considered. Such an undertaking, especially on a national level, requires careful planning. As noted in a World Bank report, 'Many governments stand at the threshold of the twenty-first century without clearly-defined plans and strategies about the use of educational technology — but they are making major new investments anyway'. The report identifies generic issues for planners to consider when developing national ICT education strategies. These are broadly grouped into three categories:

i) educational policy and goals setting,
ii) teaching and learning, and
iii) institutional development and capacity building.

The report also itemises several successful strategies, implemented invarying degrees, including developing a national or regional plan for country-wide deployment of technologies; implementing experimental projects to gain experience for country-wide deployment; undertaking small-scale demonstration projects; using technology to address educational equity issues; using broadcast technologies, including computer networks, to reach learners in remote areas; investing in preparing students and teachers for technology-based jobs; and creating schools using ICT as their core educational delivery system. Claeys, Lowych, and Van der Perre, in an article based on interviews with a sample of 65 experts from across Europe about introducing ICTs into education, summarise the respondents' view of the role of government as that of developing a clear vision on reforming the educational system through ICTs, enacting adequate funding measures, and establishing partnerships with education and industry for the development of educational software. In addition interviewees expect: (1) the development of a special cell in the department of education to support the introduction of ICT in education, (2) the development of incentives/projects, (3) the development of an advisory council to help the government promoting the introduction of ICT in education and, (4) the re-creation of the curriculum, in which information technology is embedded and an equivalent adaptation of the rules for examination.

The national governments have a role to play in helping to remove political and economic roadblocks that prevent the sharing of educational resources among countries. Mclsacc and Biocher, in a discussion of distance education advocate: 'Courses offered globally should encourage broad international participation and have sliding scale tuition policies. Sharing in developing educational materials and courses saves the duplication of time and effort and conserves valuable national resources'. Employers and universities are now drawing both staff members and students from all corners of the globe. Consequently, they face new challenges in evaluating course work done at, and degrees earned from, unknown institutions in other countries.

While accreditation has typically been controlled by individual countries, the globalisation of distance education has created a whole new challenge in accreditation and certification of learning. Government intervention may also help assure affordable ICT access for education. For example, telecommunications rates may be regulated to assure economical ICT access to educational institutions.

In late 1996, the United States Congress enacted the Telecommunications Act of 1996. The universal service section of the law, Section 254, will help schools and libraries obtain access to telecommunications services and technologies at discounted rates. Tax incentives, such as the 21st Century Classrooms Act for Private Technology Investment enacted by the United States Congress in 1997, are one way of encouraging corporate ICT-equipment donations to educational institutions. The Act allows companies to deduct the full price of a computer which is donated to a school within two years of purchase from their taxes. ICTs are evolving rapidly and, once established, national educational policies on ICT 'have to be regularly updated if they are to respond adequately to the challenge of effectively exploiting these constant changes to the technologies and their applications'.

ICT AS ASSISTIVE TECHNOLOGIES

The newer digital ICTs are bringing about remarkable changes in education around the world. Those changes affect both the pedagogical and the institutional aspects of education. New technologies have been remarkably effective in this assistive role; even the most disparaging critic of technology in the classroom usually praises the remarkable benefits of assistive technologies for students with disabilities. Examples providing evidence of the power of technology for individuals with disabilities are not difficult to find. For individuals with motor disabilities, the advantages of expanded keyboards, single switch devices, head-mounted infrared pointers, speech recognition software and word prediction are obvious. Similarly, refreshable Braille devices, talking word processors, screen readers, screen enlargers, and tactile graphic pads offer clear advantages for individuals who are blind.

It is not hard to envision the power of new access technologies currently being developed in laboratories all over the world: implanted sensory chips for both hearing and seeing, neural control devices for robotic arms and legs, convertible wheelchairs that adapt to both sitting and standing positions, and cognitive prostheses for memory deficits.

The assistive technologies are of tremendous value, they will not provoke fundamental changes in education for most students with disabilities. Next-stage educational technologies will go beyond providing better access to existing methods and materials; they will embody fundamentally different concepts of learning. They will change the learning goals, the teaching methods, and the means of assessment for all students. Several technologies are serving as catalysts for these new ideas and approaches.

New computer-driven technologies are revolutionising the way in which we are able to study learning as it happens in the brain. These new technologies reveal, in ways that were unimaginable ten years ago, that learning is

i) modular,

ii) distributed,

iii) parallel, and

iv) heterarchical.

These new tools and methodologies allow us to "see" the brain as it learns — by performing enormously complicated computations on subtle changes in brain activity that are then displayed as a simple "topographical" map of activity on a computer screen. The dominant impression from these computed images is how "modularised" the brain seems to be. It is immediately apparent that the brain learns, for example, about the colour of an object in a different region than it learns about the shape of the same object. Moreover, it processes the word "cat" in a different region when it is presented in print than when it is presented in speech, and it uses an entirely different area to compose the word "cat" for speaking. The brain has a large number of such distributed modules that work "in parallel," each highly specialised for learning about specific aspects of the world. The pattern of activity across different modules clearly depends on the task - different modules are active when one listens to a speech or when one listens to a symphony, for example.

In a general sense there is a "signature" of activity in the brain that corresponds to the kind of task being performed. But the distribution of activity for any task also varies across individuals. Each individual reveals a particular "map" of activity - differing both in the proportions of space devoted to each of the modules, and in the composition of different modules used to accomplish the same task. The brain of an individual with perfect pitch, for example, shows a strikingly different distribution of activity from that of an individual with "normal" pitch perception, or one who is "tone deaf."

These new techniques have also shown that the size of an individual processing module can grow with experience, even in adults. New technologies for studying the brain are yielding an increasingly more accurate articulation of the concept of learning — revealing not one generalised learning capacity, but many different "modules" and "distributed processes" for learning within the same brain. Further, it is becoming clear that individual brains differ from each other not in a general ability but in many different kinds of specific abilities.

The new media (digital text, digital images, digital audio, digital video, digital multimedia, and networked environments) provide many of the advantages of print-based media but they also bring new advantages. Notable is the malleability of the new media. While they, like print, can provide a permanent representation, they do not have the same "fixed" quality as print. Instead, they remain malleable, transformable from one thing to another, more like raw clay than fired pottery. The consequence is enormous flexibility and the capacity for transformation from one medium to another (e.g. text-to-speech, speech-to-text, text to touch (e.g.Braille), image to touch (haptic images, tactile graphics) and others).

In addition, the new media allow multiple representations of meaning that may be used redundantly for clarity, complementarily for enhanced meaning, or even discordantly for multiple meanings (e.g.using text on video (captions), video on text, multiple sound and visual tracks, graphics on video (e.g. signed captioning), sound maps, visual light organs, and others). The capacity to use multiple media in these and many other ways leads to a more diversified, flexible palette for communication - a palette that takes advantage of the varied strengths and weaknesses of each medium.

While the hegemony of printed text has already disappeared in such high-impact fields as advertising, entertainment, and communication in the culture at large, the legacy of print continues in schools. In the years ahead it is clear that text, still dominant in education, will give way to a more intentional use of varied media for instruction.

Instructional designers in the future will tailor their use of media to the task, to different kinds of learning, and different kinds of students. They will use the transformability and flexibility of digital media to reduce the barriers and inefficiencies inherent in fixed, one-size-fits all, printed textbooks. Moreover, they will develop expertise in the representational and expressive qualities of each medium, and the new blends that will develop, so that they can reach a broader set of students, with a broader range of knowledge.

Students with disabilities, for whom the transformations and multiple representations will vastly increase access and learning opportunities are the first beneficiaries of the new media. The incidental beneficiaries will include the teachers of subject matters like math, music, geography, physics, and other subjects that have never easily yielded their magic through linear text. But the ultimate beneficiaries will be all learners, each of whom has experienced in one way or another the barriers to motivation and comprehension that an over-reliance on text and other fixed media have wrought.

These new digital technologies that allow to examine the biology of learning and to discover and apply the power of new media also allow to recognise the profound and differentiated ways in which individual learners differ from each other. Continuing the pioneering work of Gardner, Sternberg, and others, this avenue of research continues to show that there is not one "typical" learner with a limited number of variants but instead a great variety of learners - as many as the interactions among modules and architectures in our brains.

In addition, the more differentiated use of media for instruction reveals that individuals who are defined as "learning disabled" within print-based learning environments are not the same individuals who are defined as "learning disabled" within video- or audio-based learning environments.

Such revelations splinter the old categorical divisions between "disability" and "ability" and create new descriptors that explicitly recognise the interaction between student and environment in the definition of strengths. As a result, educators take more notice of the "unusual" strengths of individuals with disabilities — e.g. the prodigious feats of visual memory in the autistic child, or the extraordinary capacity to recognise facial expression in aphasics. In the same context, myriad differences emerge between learners formerly classified in the category of "normal" learners.

The flexibility, malleability, and interactivity that characterise new media provide the basis for educational designs that are impossible with traditional fixed methods and materials, designs that emerge as necessary in light of changing concepts of learning and individual differences. These new designs reflect a more articulated understanding of learning and avoid "presentational" environments like books and lectures, in favour of truly instructional environments where students are consistently supported in learning how to learn.

Individualisable challenge and support are built into every element of the curriculum, every learning experience. Skill-development materials, for example, can be designed to provide built-in models of performance, opportunities for supported practice, immediate feedback, and extended "communities of practice." In that respect, these new environments more closely resemble traditional models of apprentice learning than "book-learning." Congruent with apprentice models, these new designs exploit the power of new media to individualise and customise, making it possible and imperative to meet the enormous challenge of individual differences. To do this, they do not provide one-size-fits-all presentations but highly malleable environments that provide the right level of support and challenge for every individual student.

The new learning environments provide the right level of support and challenge in three ways:

First, they provide multiple means of representation. This means that instructional designs assume that there is little value in a single canonical representation of the information in any particular task or problem. Instead, new designers will assume that to provide basic access for some students (e.g. for students who are deficient in one modality or other, like a student who is blind), and multiple routes to meaning for all students (e.g. representing a math concept both in text and graphically) it will be both necessary and preferable to provide multiple representations of meaning.

Second, they will provide for multiple means of expression. This means that instructional designers will decrease their insistence on a single mode of communication from the student as the basis for expression or evaluation. It will be routine to assume that while many students will write (or type) their essays, there will also be alternatives that involve rich mixes of writing, illustrating, speaking, video-making, and drawing. The method of evaluation will suit the task and the means. Students will be required to meet a higher standard of expressive literacy — knowing in what contexts to use text, images, sound, video, or combinations of media. Evaluation will be sensitive to purpose, audience, and the strengths of the learner. The creative expression of students with motor difficulties will not be evaluated via handwritten assignments.

Third, the new designs will provide multiple means of engagement. Most students are often unengaged or bored in school. There is no single solution to this problem because of the range of individual differences- there are many different reasons for their lack of engagement, not one. Students with disabilities, as usual, highlight the issues. The same design which would likely engage a student with a high degree of novelty and surprise, would be absolutely terrifying and thus disengaging to a student with Asberger's Syndrome or autism.

New designs will be cognizant of the centrality of motivation in learning, and of the individual differences that underlie motivation and engagement. As a result, and given the flexibility of new media, they will provide alternative means of engagement — more novelty and surprise in the learning environment for some students, less for others, for example.

In traditional assessment, the outcomes of learning are measured — the number of science facts recalled, the percentage of words spelled correctly. The interactive capacity of new technologies allows us to create dynamic assessments that measure not just the outcomes but the processes of learning. In so doing we will be able to understand what kinds of strategies a student is following, what kinds of strategies or approaches are lacking, what aspects of the task environment bias the student toward successful or unsuccessful approaches, and what kinds of additional strategies might best match their learning style.

The new technologies allow two-way interactive assessments. With these technologies we will be able to create learning environments that not only teach but also learn. By distributing the intelligence better between student and environment, the curriculum is able to learn about the student and keep track of the successes and failures of its own methods. The result is a curriculum that becomes smarter, not more outdated, over time.

REFERENCES

Bauer, J. W., and Rezabek, L. L., 1993, *Effects of Two-way Visual Contact on Verbal Interaction during Face-to-Face and Teleconferenced Instruction*, In *Art, Science, and Visual Literacy: Selected Readings from the Annual Conference of the International Visual Literacy Association*, 24th, Pittsburgh, PA, September 30-October 4, 1992.

Bengu G. and W. Swart, A., 1996, "Computer-Aided Total Quality Approach to Manufacturing Education in Engineering", *IEEE Transactions on Education*, 39:3, pp. 415-427, 1996.

Berge Z. L., 1999, "Interaction in Post-secondary Web-based Learning", *Educational Technology*, 39(1), pp. 5-11.

Betts, M., 1994, "States Bypassing Feds on Information Highways," *Computerworld*, June 20, 1994.

Bichelmeyer, B. A., Kiggins, E.A., 1998, "Using Web-based Conferencing in Post-secondary Instruction", *Proceedings of the Annual Conference on Distance Teaching and Learning*, Madison, WI, August 5-7, 1998.

Clayes, L., Vander Perre, "Innovative Education through the Use of New Technologies: Reflections from the Field", *Educational Media International,* Vol. 34, No. 3, pp. 144–52, 1997.

Duhaney, D., 2000, Technology and the Educational Process: Transforming Classroom Activities, *International Journal of Instructional Media*, 27(1), pp.67-72.

Duffy, T., Jonassen, D., (eds.), 1992, *Constructivism and the Technology of Instruction: A Conversation*, Hillsdale, N., Lawrence Erlbaum Associates.

Foa, L., Schwab, R., Johnson, M., "Introducing Technologies into the Schools: Triumph or Train Wreck?", *NEA Technology Brief,* No. 13, 1998.

Forsyth, I., 1998, *Teaching and Learning Materials and the Internet* (2nd ed.), London: Kogan Page.

Galbreath, J., 1995, "Compressed Digital Videoconferencing", *Educational Technology*, 35(1), pp. 31-38.

Kerr, E. Hiltz, S., *Computer-Based Instruction*, 17(1), 1982.

Paterson K. G. "Student Perceptions of Internet-Based Learning Tools in Environment Engineering Education", *Journal of Engineering Education*, 88:3, pp. 295-304, 1999.

Phye, G., 2000, "Engaging Technology and Learning Opportunities: Technology Assessment Tools", *Paper presented at the Annual Meeting of the American Educational Research Association*, New Orleans.

Pisapia, J., Coukos, E., Knutson, K., 2000, "The Impact of Computer on Teacher Capacity, Attitudes, and Behaviours in Elementary Schools", *Paper presented at the Annual Meeting of the American Educational Research Association*, New Orleans.

3

Web-based Educational Environment

For centuries, education has withstood the test of time, rising above the landscape like a mystic castle on the plain of human knowledge. Slow to change with technology, education has endured wars, disease and time by remaining steadfast to many of its ideals. In spite of the advancements of computer technology that have occurred over the past few decades, education has resisted much of this change, fortifying its walls against the onslaught of technology. Yet inside the monolithic towers clad in ancient ivory, some of the inhabitants of the castle, forward thinking educators, have begun to experiment with these new tools and have begun a crusade to open the castle gates to new concepts and methodologies.

Certainly few improvements in technology have fired the imaginations of educators as much as the internet. The internet can provide access to top instructors, the latest research and much more. This access is only limited by access to the internet itself, something that is becoming less of an issue in many areas of the world, giving both remote and urban students equal opportunities to learn. The potential for the internet in education is enormous and is only limited by the imagination.

The potential for the internet in improving the quality of education hinges on two principle components, the ability to communicate by private e-mail and bulletin board systems, and the ability to deliver text, graphics, audio and video over communication lines to almost any point in the world. As a communication medium, the internet can provide a closer contact than traditional distance learning communication media, giving the student a sense of belonging and reducing the feeling of isolation.

For students in metropolitan areas, the internet will provide a means of involving rural understanding into their learning. For all students the internet will provide an international communication advantage, allowing the sharing of diverse cultural and ethnic enrichments that will help to bring education into a more global understanding. The transfer of audio, video, text and graphic files offers great opportunity for improved access to knowledge. Compressed video can be delivered over the internet along with hypertext documents that link pictures and words in a myriad of ways that will allow students to explore a subject rather than simply be taught it.

Web browsers, such as Netscape, provide a simple interface for even the rank beginner to explore the power and wonder of the internet, and through the World Wide Web students will be able to not only read about items, but see and hear them as well. These multimedia lessons can involve students more thoroughly in the educational process than the written word.

Online universities and colleges will continue to grow and evolve, providing access to the best teachers in subjects and a more personalised approach to learning. New technologies that now allow students and instructors to project their images onto the screens of each other as video inserts will further reduce the sense of isolation that so often accompanies distance learning.

The future of the internet in education is full of bold new opportunities and may well represent a new frontier, with excitement and value unparalleled in the history of education. The use of the internet in education means change, and many people resist change. For the most part, people appear to be more content with their current situation rather than moving into a situation which is not well understood. This fear is quite understandable and because of the tremendous advances in technology, educators will likely view the integration of the internet into the educational system with suspicion and trepidation.

The extreme lack of understanding of technology by many educators fuels the resistance to the adoption of the internet as a tool. Additionally, the considerable misinformation that has been spread through the mass media about the darker side of the internet has created an entrenchment of these people, creating an armed camp of social defenders with intractable points of view developed from an ignorance of the realities of the internet. Resistance to the internet as an educational tool will likely come not only from educators but society in general. Again, one of the principle reasons for this resistance is due to the lack of understanding of new technology and the subsequent technophobia that develops out of this lack of understanding.

Humans are ostensibly social animals and any effort to isolate them will, and should be, met by resistance, for through the loss of belonging there is a greater risk of complacency in the face of atrocities. The isolation brought about with the invention of the bomb led to a very callous outlook on it use in warfare. Because the bombardier no longer had to face the enemy it was possible to drop bombs with greater destructive power on a wider variety of targets, both military and civilian. In recent conflicts there has been a concerted effort to restrict the selection of targets to more militarily significant ones. This sense of avoidance of collateral damage is a driving factor in the resistance to using the internet.

If by using the internet society becomes more isolationist, there is a fear that society will become less tolerant and more egocentric. This is a fear that cannot be discounted as baseless and will have to be adequately addressed if the internet is to take its place as a valuable tool for promoting education. Implementing the internet into an educational structure requires an investment in technological infrastructure, hardware, software and specialists. The price tag of such an endeavour is not small and can easily be out of the reach of many educational institutions.

Depending on the extent to which the internet is to be involved, the infrastructure can include the installation of Local Area Networks, upgrading of communication lines, the establishment of links to the internet and the subsequent investment in connectivity, the acquisition of software and upgrading of hardware to accommodate the increased demands in computing power. Many smaller institutions and districts will view these costs as prohibitive and will consider these barriers insurmountable. Such fears are realistic and innovative approaches to solutions will need to be considered. Politicians are very similar to grass in that they like to bend with the wind. Public opinion becomes political willpower which can both help and hinder the opportunities of using the internet in the educational system. When public opinion is pushed toward a negative view, the internet will be seen as a great black dragon that is attempting to breach the castle walls and every effort must be made to repel its hideous attacks. On the other hand, if the public views the internet as a positive change, it will be seen as a white knight on a beautiful black stallion racing to lift the siege on the castle and save the inhabitants. Presently, both views can be found, leading to a sense of confusion amongst the castle's inhabitants.

Many barriers exist to prevent the integration of the internet into the educational process, ranging from personal prejudices to social moods, and the lack of adequate funding further complicates the issue. For the internet to take its place in education these barriers will need to be dealt with to the satisfaction of the majority of stakeholders in the educational system. While such a proposal may appear to have no solution to many, the enlightened educators who understand technology and the potential of the internet will need to carry the torch high through the darkened halls and proclaim their faith if a solution is to be found.

Change is resisted much like an immovable object resists forces applied to it, however once change is seen as providing a positive, leadership role in the quest for educational perfection it can be converted from potential energy into kinetic energy. It is this kinetic energy in education that can provide students and educators with the means to accomplish the very difficult task of retraining a workforce for the information age.

With funding shortages, projected teacher shortages, growing pressure for distance learning and a shift in the demographics of the student population requiring more services and flexibility than in the past, the educational system of the future will need to find new ways of performing the important task of educating. Much of the resistance to change in the educational arena is due to these factors in addition to the very human tendency to resist entering the dimly lit caverns that have developed under the foundations of the castle itself.

By providing beacons of light that show these caverns to contain opportunities often unimagined until now and by using the resistance as a tool for change, change can occur. Education needs to adopt some of the principles of business, especially in the area of listening to its customers. The opportunity for such change has never been so great, thus it is time to strike while the iron is hot.

Interviews were conducted with lay persons, students, teachers and administrators from around the world in an effort to determine where the focus of a new direction for learning should be and what role the internet should play in this direction. Responses were consistent on several points, one of the most notable of which was a consensus that computers should be more fully integrated into classes at all levels. The cost of building and maintaining classroom facilities are escalating rapidly and the human resource costs have driven the affordability of traditional education literally through the roof. By addressing these issues and showing how technology, and the internet in particular, can release more funds to the development of quality programmes, it may be possible to convert more educators to rally around the circuit board in the crusade for excellence.

By using the internet as a key component in the delivery of courses, it may be possible to permit the best teachers to concentrate on reaching larger audiences while allowing the researchers to pursue their interests with fewer distractions. This combination of talents can benefit both student and teacher alike and the potential benefits are great. Convincing educators of this will not be easy however by promoting this positive aspect of the scenario, greater support for the concept will be easier to attain.

New electronic classrooms capable of serving the varied needs of students at a time with all students over a wide area having access to a central instructor of the highest credentials can form the backbone of a new dynamic educational system. Multimedia delivered over the internet can provide students with invaluable experience, but the costs associated with such an endeavour are likely to dash any hope of implementation long before it reaches any significant discussion.

By showing educators that the cost of standing aside and watching the technology pass into the hills, instead of being admitted into the castle to help man the ramparts, is far more devastating it may be possible to provide the positive leadership required to bring this technology into the system and the internet can provide access to new markets and new sources of funds. In showing how these funds can benefit the lord of the keep, it is much more likely that these new technologies will have the opportunity to man the gates and bolster a demoralised contingent.

Distance education has relied heavily on the use of print and pictures to provide a learning environment for the at-a-distance learner. This environment is primarily static in nature resulting in lengthy and expensive processes when the materials require changing or updating. When a learner's senses are engaged more fully, the learning that occurs will more deep. It has long been a goal of educators to reach this deep level of learning because it has long been recognised that deep learning is more enduring than surface learning.

In recent years many inroads have been made in the use of video and audio as an effort to involve the learner through the engagement of more senses. However, these efforts have yielded limited results and have in turn been limited in their scope due to production costs and the difficulty of updating the material. With the introduction of the personal computer, electronic interactivity has opened new doors for the distance learner. Interactive video, electronic messaging (e.g., Bulletin Board Systems, E-mail, and NewsGroups), and teleconferencing have brought the classroom to the student and provided many opportunities for students to interact with each other and the instructor.

However, these innovations fall short of a full interactive learning environment because they do not directly involve the learner in the learning situation itself. One method that has been used by educators to involve the learner in the learning situation has been the use of paper case studies. Case studies present situations and opportunities and involve the students and facilitator in discussions of the various options available. While case studies are a step in the right direction, they also suffer from the static nature of print because they are not organic in nature, changing with the reactions and choices of the students.

The advancements made in computer technology have led to the introduction of many new tools, including web technologies and the internet. The addition of computerised learning, such as computer-based instruction, computer-mediated learning and computer-based training, has augmented the educator's repertoire of learning tools with exciting new ways of involving the learner. However, the key to successful implementation of these tools into the educational realm involves fitting the right application to the right technology rather than the implementation of technology for technology's sake.

One application that may benefit from the use of web technologies is the case study. This is the basis for the interactive contextual learning environment (ICLE). The concepts of ICLE focus on learner-centered instruction and interactions between the learner and the learning medium. It inherits a sense of contextual learning from the use of virtual reality (VR) to simulate the learning environment, and uses a combination of hypertext markup language (HTML) and a web programming language, Java, to create an organic learning situation capable of reacting to student choices. It can be delivered over the internet as part of a web site or on a hard drive as a stand-alone system.

ICLE was tested on a learning module for introductory systems analysis and design using few steps. First, the development team selected a learning module and gathered information about the subject area. This included the goals, objectives and assessment strategies that were considered suitable for the module. The module selected for this study was the preliminary investigation and analysis of an existing system. A review of existing theories and materials formed the basis of knowledge upon which the ICLE was built. A contextual environment suitable for presenting the concepts and practice that the learner was set as a not-for-profit society in a fictitious town. Next, the learning strategies of the target audience, which were determined to be andragogical, were assessed using current literature.

The second step is the site design. This began with the storyboarding of the scenario, including 2D physical site drawings, flow control diagrams, and background detailing to create a sense of reality. For the HTML pages it was necessary to design the images that would be used and to choose background and text-based colour coordination schema. An important consideration was the effect of different screen displays on these objects because it was important that the resulting product be compatible with a large variety of equipment. Java applets were planned to provide real time assessment, interactive components, and live action sequencing. A suitable tool for the generation of virtual reality modeling language (VRML) code for the VR portion of the site was selected and VR components designed.

Site construction began with the conversion of existing materials electronically and the creation of new images and textures. Next, the Java applets were written and the web pages built. The VRML worlds were built last as they required linking with all other components. Once the site was built it was tested on the local drive before exporting it to the internet. The live version of the site was then tested over the internet and any errors and omissions were corrected before submitting the site to the test panel. ICLE provides a sense of an improved learning environment for learners. The challenges encountered in the creation of this environment provided considerable insight into the creation of additional sites.

EDUCATIONAL POTENTIALS OF WWW

Tools such as Inetrnet, Gopher and WWW have been developed largely to facilitate sharing of technical and corporate information at colleges, universities and research institutions. Potential educational applications of these technologies became apparent, especially for open and distance learning. In this regard, WWW has more appeal, because of its hypermedia foundation. Its use is growing very rapidly, and it can now be used to access an immense volume of rapidly evolving information. Thus, another strength of WWW is its access to the latest version of a document. Because of all these characteristics, pedagogical uses of the web can evolve along two major axes:

i) use of the technology on a closed corpus of educational material, for the hypermedia and distance delivery capabilities of the web, on one hand, and

ii) use of this technology on an organised structure of links for an open corpus of material that was not necessarily meant initially for pedagogical use, but which can be "redirected" and exploited in guided educational explorations.

In spite of its tremendous growth, WWW is still only marginally used for teaching and learning activities, probably even more so in Europe, where very few primary or secondary schools have access to the internet. In this regard, WWW is acting as a driving force, since its ease of use makes the internet trivially accessible to pupils with no prior knowledge of computers, programming or even networking, making it more tempting for teachers to take advantage of it.

The educationally attractive WWW features are:

i) the ability to have multimedia documents
ii) the hypertext/hypermedia capability
iii) WWW networked basis, allowing for distance learning,

The availability of public-domain client and server software for many different platforms, the relative simplicity of the HTML syntax and the availability of free editing tools are also essential elements to the interest that school teachers find in the WWW. A new feature that has been added recently to HTML is the possibility to include, in a document, input fields that the reader can fill out and the contents of which will be transmitted to the server when the reader pushes a "submit" button. This fill-out form capability has been essential in allowing new uses of the web, where the user can be more active than just clicking on sensitive areas of a document.

Just browsing through the web is already an educational experience in itself. Many people have lived this phenomenon by which they start browsing through the web with something specific in mind and end up diverted from their initial goal for a while because they found something interesting on the way, that they were not explicitly looking for. This is what one could call "accidental learning", that is, learning that happens at an unexpected moment, about an unexpected subject. There are however structured ways in which WWW can be used for education. Two main approaches are:

i) using the technology on a closed corpus of educational material, mostly for the hypermedia and distance delivery capabilities of WWW and,
ii) using the technology to access, in a structured way, an *open corpus* of material that was not necessarily meant initially to be used for specific educational purposes.

Closed corpus: In the first category, one can often find "hyper-courses" that take advantage of WWW's hypertext capabilities. This, combined with the fill-out form capability, can allow courseware designers to create educational material that has most of the characteristics of regular courseware that runs on a stand-alone machine, with the additional advantage of being easily accessible from remote locations. One characteristic of WWW that can appear as a limitation is the fact that the HTTP protocol is stateless, that is, there is no direct relationship of any kind between two consecutive requests to the same server, even if the queries come from the same user.

The server treats every request it receives independently from any other request it received in the past or that it will receive in the future. This statelessness allows the HTTP server software to impose very little overhead on the server machine, and keeps the protocol between the client and server very simple. However, good educational material should take into account the background of each learner to tailor its behaviour to the learner's capabilities and past history, and to provide appropriate remediation to learners who experience difficulties with some concepts. To achieve this, the educational software has to keep track of the users' states and actions, which seems to contradict the statelessness of WWW. The solution we developed to overcome this difficulty has been to combine the fill-out form capability with the possibility for the HTTP server to execute external programmes or shell scripts in response to a request.

Normally, when the HTTP server executes an external programme or shell script, it waits until the programme is finished to send the programme's output as a virtual HTML document. Among the advantages we find the portability achieved by using HTML for the spawned process output. Whatever the machine the user is working on, the viewer should be able to handle HTML documents and thus be able to display the output of the educational process, regardless of the hardware of the machine. There is therefore only one executable version of the courseware, that resides on the server machine. As a consequence, anybody can engage very simply in the educational process, from anywhere in the (internet) world, at any time, without any bootstrapping procedure. One drawback is that this server machine can become overloaded and thus unable to serve new users. Another drawback is that the user interactions and the programme output are limited by the HTML syntax.

Another approach to the closed corpus option is to define a new document type and have a special dedicated viewer handle the "document" sent by the HTTP server. This viewer can be an interpreter for some special purpose language and it will use the document sent by the server as a programme to interpret/execute on the client machine, thus removing the load from the server. This external viewer can send a specific system signal to the main WWW viewer to tell it to display a new document, the URL of which has been put in a temporary file. When used in combination with fill-out forms, this allows bidirectional communication (via the WWW server) between the main WWW viewer and the external viewer that are both running on the same client machine. A more effective scheme is currently being proposed as a Client Communication Interface (CCI) protocol, that should allow bidirectional communication between a WWW viewer and an external application, without necessarily transiting through a WWW server.

The main advantage of this approach is that it can potentially use all the graphical and computational capabilities of the client machine, thus resulting in more powerful user interfaces and faster response times. The drawbacks are that one needs to have a dedicated viewer on the client machine, and that a different executable version of the interpreter has to be produced for every different kind of hardware that the learners can potentially use. Another possible drawback could be related to security issues if the interpreter can potentially execute instructions that would harm the local computer environment (software viruses).

Open corpus: The other approach to educational use of the web is to exploit the enormous amount of information that is accessible via the internet, whether it has been put there for educational purposes or not. It is the authors' belief that nobody yet has been able to evaluate, even very approximately, the volume of information that is now available to every internet user. From the statistics of the NSFNet backbone traffic, one could conjecture that this volume is likely to be in the order of magnitude of thousands of billions of characters. Given its gigantic size, this ocean of information has to be harnessed to make it manageable and useful to users and learners. In this regard, WWW appears to be very useful in that its network-based hypertextual capabilities make it very appropriate to organise into a hierarchy this huge volume. CERN has started a very interesting project called the WWW Virtual Library. Its purpose is to create a distributed catalogue of all the internet resources accessible via WWW. It is maintained on a voluntary basis by people who are specialists in a specific domain and who are willing to share and maintain a document, or a hierarchy of documents, that reflect a certain structure of their domain, giving access to all the major internet-accessible resources that they are aware of. The subjects of the WWW Virtual Library range over a very wide spectrum, covering most regular subjects of study, as well as recreational subjects or more esoteric ones like "Paranormal Phenomena" or UFOs.

Electronic journals and online magazines also constitute interesting sources of information that are probably going to develop and grow as people get more accustomed to the electronic media. As useful as they may be for researchers or post-graduate students, these structuring resources are probably not directly usable as is for more basic educational purposes. They are nevertheless a good example of what can be done to present a subject to people who want to learn about it. One can easily imagine developing more elaborate structural documents that will guide learners in their exploration of a subject domain. The educational material would thus consist of a combination of explanatory text, pointers to more in-depth material publicly available on the internet and, possibly, some features of the closed corpus approach by which the learner could be evaluated and proposed complementary or remedial material.

An interesting pedagogical strategy one can use in the *open corpus* approach is to have pupils use WWW in their process of knowledge appropriation by giving them the task to create their own documents that will tie together the information they have collected in a more constructive way than just enumerate pointers to existing documents. These *synthetic* documents created by pupils can also help the teacher have a better grasp of the pupils' mental structures. Even more important, the pupils' documents can help the teacher offer appropriate remediation to those pupils who have not been able to go far enough in their discovery of a subject.

Distance education and virtual classroom can be considered useful tools for delivering knowledge remotely, since they allow users to create their own instructional paths by using different technological alternatives and by deeply involving users themselves within the informative contents. Psycho-pedagogical studies on the education field have shown that students can better learning by managing, manipulating, and organising the information by their own. The possibility for the users to perform a search of informative contents through hierarchical and referential links is a function allowed by WWW. This characteristic of the WWW system makes it feasible to build a particular learning environment. The potential for the actual technology and in this case for the WWW system is to create a distance education environment which can exist beyond the traditional boundaries of a particular location to a broad range of students involving them in a high interactive partecipation. Such environment must be in accordance with the new theories of communication systems; consistent with the instructor's philosophy and style of teaching; convenient, accessible, and relevant to the students.

DESIGNING EDUCATIONAL ENVIRONMENT

This section describes the architecture, design of a Mosaic application developed at the Centro Interdipartimentale della Comunicazione (CIC) at the University of Calabria. The educational environment is accessible via the Home Page of the web informative system of the Center. The basic idea of the model is to build an environment where users can investigate through the links to other documents, different fields of knowledge and to wide the functionalities of the actual virtual classroom. Students need all tools to build their own educational paths. The simulation of a real classroom through the distribution of electronic lectures (remotely or online), providing exercises, dialogue (via e-mail or private chat) with teachers or other students, creation of workgroups for cooperative work, and the attendance conferences with experts of various fields are just a part of the whole student training. In fact, traditionally, education programmes include instructional tours for visiting libraries, museums and research/cultural centres in order to allow students to get in touch with the subject they are learning.

Similarly the educational environment the authors have built, offers users the possibility to navigate in a hypermedia way through the wide range of servers which store the information such as museums, laboratories, cultural agencies, universities , digital libraries and more.

The Educational Environment Home Page provides users with an opening screen containing four links to different kinds of information:

i) general informations about the Educational Environment: how it works and which technological tools are used;

ii) informations about the activated electronic lectures;

iii) courseware registration for the new students;

iv) link to the topics on which to focus on.

Initially, the students could put their name down for a specific lecture. Then they are able to go into the "topics" HTML document containing a sensitive map, by which it is possible to start the navigation choosing one option. These topics are organised into three areas and are accessible by a simple selection in the map. Once students have choosen one topic they will be "taken to" another HTML document where the following set of instructional tools is visualised:

i) virtual classroom;

ii) museums;

iii) digital library;

iv) cooperative work;

v) seminaries and conferences.

The virtual classroom option contains pages for the lectures, informations on courseware students and on teachers. Each lecture consists of explanations on the subject with links to study in depth related arguments and related bibliography. The informations on students and teachers consist of their curricula and how they can be reached via telephone, fax , e-mail to ask for clearing up some points and for collaboration with each other. Teachers put their meeting time-table for private-chat and conference online. Moreover, they send explanations via e-mail which can contain textual data but also software applications, bibliography, WWW sites and more. The teachers, in order to temp students both to take part to the lectures and to use tools for the cooperative work, create groups of work who develop exercises on the particular subject of the lecture. The exercises are equally subdivided, in terms of tasks, among the students in order to improve the quality of the results and to temp students to collaborate with each other. This collaboration is carried out via network by exchanging files; the teachers hold periodically a conference with the students with the intention of valuating the state of art of the job. This area is also dedicated to hold exams for groups of students or for single students. The basic aim of the educational environment is actually to offer a student-centered learning environment which is satisfying in terms of subject explanation; the exams are needed just to check the learning skills of the students and to provide them with useful and effective suggestions.

The museums option allows students to access home pages of electronic museums all around the world. The collection of the museums depends on the choosen topic and it is made by the human tutors according to their teaching philosophy.

The digital library option is a set of informations and resources about the topic, organised by the tutors. It is similar to a hypermedia path or to a recommended bibliography. In this area it is also possible for the students to use special retrieval information tools such as 'Lycos' and then to start the hypermedia navigation among the internet servers.

The cooperative work option will take users to an environment for sharing data and resources with others researchers that are working on the same topic.

The last option is the for the seminaries and conferences; here students can access investigations on specific contents through the distribution of seminaries via network. In this area conferences are activated in order to allow students to formulate relevant questions which are discussed by the experts of the field.

A MODEL VIRTUAL CLASSROOM

The web is revolutionising the areas of education through increased opportunities for learning and alternative formats for information. The internet, with its ability to connect people and information around the world, is already having a significant impact on education at all levels. The lofty goal of an interconnected global schoolhouse across remote corners of the world is getting closer. Virtual classrooms are being created today for educating scientists, engineers and mathematicians, both researchers and faculty, and will provide needed experience and basic knowledge for use with other student populations in the near future. In this section we are discussing about the model of a virtual classroom provided by The Cornell Theory Center (CTC) located in Ithaca, New York.

The Center provides educational opportunities for researchers, faculty, and students in the effective use of high performance computing for the exploration of scientific problems. Workshops for new and experienced users of the Center's resources are offered on a regular basis. Workshops include lectures on system features, optimisation, introductory and advanced topics in scalable parallel computing, and visualisation. Lectures are supplemented by guided hands-on laboratory sessions to ensure that participants gain needed experience.

CTC continues to investigate use of online information systems for providing effective distance learning opportunities for students and scientists in the areas of computational science and high performance computing. Recent efforts to move lecture materials into HTML and to incorporate images, animations, and user interaction forms into the documents provided improvements to the system. Integration of training materials with hardware and software documentation, reports on algorithm design and related research projects further enhanced educational materials on the web.

The transition from providing materials over the network to a virtual classroom expanded the ability to train and educate in the areas of expertise. Online educational materials, which include lecture notes and lab exercises, are available through the web. These materials are used by the staff during workshops and by others on the internet who wish to provide instruction on these topics. In addition, the materials provide a handy access point for researchers and students to review concepts that were presented in workshops. Educational materials also include a set of tutorials especially designed for online learning. These tutorials are the recommended starting point for researchers and students desiring to become familiar with the use of the Theory Center's systems and scalable parallel computing. In addition to direct education of users they use a "train-the-trainer" model to leverage the support effort. This is accomplished through the academic affiliates activities, known as the Smart Node Programme.

Each of the more than 90 participating universities sends a consultant to the Theory Center for a one week workshop each year. At this workshop, the consultants are updated on the latest technologies. They then return to their own campus to provide support to local researchers often by re-using the training materials in courses that they offer. The online documents and training materials provide continuous access to materials for Smart Node consultants to use in training users at their local campuses. Extensive feedback from the Smart Node consultants over the past seven years has provided ample evidence that the materials are heavily re-used as is and frequently modified and incorporated into local materials to meet specialised needs. With the availability of the web, this re-use has increased dramatically.

Because of the rapidly changing technology in high performance computing, researchers who use the facility need to continually update their knowledge of state-of-the-art computational science techniques. As these users are spread across the United States, it is not feasible for frequent visits to the Theory Center to attend workshops. The centre have found that educating researchers in concepts and approaches to parallel processing is a staff-intensive effort.

While the hardware and software vendors sometimes supply user documentation in electronic format, it is often "command" oriented, but the users often require "task" oriented materials and each vendor uses a different interface for access to online materials. Even now that computing vendors are creating web servers, they are slow to include user documentation, but instead concentrate on marketing information. For all of these reasons the centre have made use of an electronic user documentation system since the founding of the center in 1985.

The Theory Center online information system contains educational materials in a variety of formats. The centre have developed more than 140 items specifically designed to be instructional tools that are referenced thousands of times each month. This electronic education system not only serves the CTC researchers, but also the international research audience, and provides materials that other educators can incorporate into their courses. Other supercomputing centers, such as the Maui High Performance Computing Center, Argonne National Laboratory, the Leibniz Computing Center and the Queensland Parallel Supercomputing Facility, maintain links to the materials.

What follows is a brief description of the types of educational materials in the online information system.

Tutorials: Electronic tutorials have been available for more than nine years. Tutorials are intended to be short, self-contained instructions on a specific topic. Each tutorial contains a short description, step-by-step instructions in using the utility, and an example code that can be executed. Researchers can read the tutorial and try the example, possibly taking the example code to use as a template for their own problem. These tutorials are task-oriented, not command-oriented.

Lab exercises: Lab exercises have been provided in electronic format for the past two years. These exercises are intended to supplement lectures given at a workshop. The solutions to lab exercises are provided in a separate file to encourage the student to solve the problem instead of following the cookbook instructions found in a tutorial. Placing the lab exercises online has allowed workshop participants to more easily continue to work on the problems after returning home.

Lecture notes: During the fall of 1994 the centre began to maintain a complete set of lecture notes online. Formatted as a traditional "overhead foils", lecture notes are frequently a list of bullets which provide a guideline for the lecturer to use in presenting the materials. Lecture notes may not contain full details of the topic, but usually contain many references to other electronic materials for more information. In addition to providing continuous access to these materials for workshop attendees and other trainers, the centre have been experimenting with using NCSA Mosaic and Netscape as the mechanism for presenting the lecture. The students can follow the lecture on a terminal in front of them or can see the instructor's monitor displayed with a large screen projection system.

Distance education, in the form of a course offered across the internet, was a logical step for the Theory Center. This course is distinct from user-initiated, independent accesses to the online materials because it have an instructor and a registered group of participants. This brought together a community of learners into a virtual classroom where they can interact with each other. The goal was to create a virtual classroom, using methods that fully engage the students in the learning process through an interactive, dynamic environment involving the student, online materials and an instructor.

There are many topics that need to be explored before being able to offer complete workshops over the internet. These range from technical considerations to sociological aspects of learning without the existence of a physical classroom. Much study has already been done in distance education. While distance education can provide efficient utilisation of scarce resources, more fair distribution of knowledge, and timely dissemination of new knowledge, limitations in its effective use exist. Student motivation is critical. Online instructors may need to take more time for the electronic course. Limits to the number of students may be required to maintain quality interaction. While generalisations in the effectiveness of distance education are dangerous, a common set of advantages and disadvantages are emerging .

The web solves some problems of traditional distance education and brings new issues to the forefront. A leading effort in exploring this emerging world is the Global Network Academy. The Theory Center faced a number of similar issues, but also have some unique situations related to the field of instruction and the network-sophistication of the intended audience. Some of the issues addressed for the pilot course follow.

Target audience: With traditional workshops, attendance is limited by the physical size of the training facility. Normally this means that attendees are users and potential users of the facilities—researchers whose backgrounds, computing experiences, and expectations are somewhat similar. With an electronic course, the size of the class is limited by other non-physical factors such as staffing requirements for account administration, limited consulting support, and CPU resources required for the class laboratory exercises. While the centre may now be able to directly impact a broader group of people, this group is likely be much more diverse in its background and computing experience. Certainly there is a number of security issues and the necessity for fire walls to protect the production computing environments if the centre wish to accommodate this larger audience.

Prerequisites: As the centre do for participation in the traditional workshops, it requires a basic knowledge of UNIX. With workshops held in the training facility the centre know what type of computer hardware, software and network connection the students is having. Even with a graphical browser, some students may find limited network bandwidth does not provide a satisfactory learning environment.

Learning environment: Extensive feedback from attendees at the traditional workshops indicates there are two benefits to learning in a classroom setting which are independent of the material covered in the course. First, students find that the ability to get away from their other responsibilities and concentrate on learning the course materials greatly increases the amount that they learn and retain. Second, the interaction with other students and Theory Center staff, whether it is side discussions during the lab periods or simply listening to questions asked by others, often results in people rethinking their own computing techniques and suggest new solutions to their problems. An electronic course need to have some of these same attributes in order to ensure that students find the experience worthwhile so that they complete the course. There needs to be some sense of an "instructor" for the students to interact with and the ability for the entire class to participate in questions and answers.

Audio-visual equipments: In a physical classroom there is a standard set of audiovisual equipment and tools available to the instructor. These might include a chalkboard, overhead projector, video cassette player, possibly a sound system, and even the textbook. Professional instructors know how to make best use of these tools. The virtual classroom need equivalent equipment and tools in the form of network-based software applications. Some of these virtual tools have a relatively long history on the internet and provide obvious applications. Other are still emerging and their potential use in a virtual classroom is not yet understood. With the appropriate design, the student should be able to take advantage of these tools without leaving the comfort of their favourite web browser interface. Some of those considered for the classroom are;

The textbook: Many courses have a textbook used to guide the direction of the course or for background material. While the online materials provide some of this function, these may sometimes not provide all of the details that a users needs. In the area of high performance computing an example of a useful electronic textbook is the Computational Science Education Project sponsored by the US Department of Energy. The growth of electronic publishing on the internet should ensure a good supply of electronic textbooks over the coming years.

The chalkboard: Even when the lecture materials are prepared in advance and made available to the student, most instructors make use of a chalkboard for further clarification of a point. In an electronic course, the instructor might make use of the shared whiteboard offered by a tool like NCSA Collage to answer a question from a student. Such tools allow images to be displayed, manipulated, annotated, and shared between two people or among a whole group.

Video cassette recorder: Use of movies and audio clips can be effective additions to textual materials. For the course on scalable parallel computing the centre might create a "cartoon" to illustrate how messages are passed between processors in a distributed system or record the animated output of a parallel trace tool. Audio clips of the instructor might be helpful in some instances to describe a particularly difficult point. Either can add some needed relief for what might otherwise be rather dry material — just as an instructor in a traditional classroom might use video tape to keep the students' attention.

The sound system: An important part of any physical class setting is the personal interaction as questions are asked by the students. Allowing all students to "hear" the questions and answers helps everyone learn and encourages additional questions to clarify a point. Use of a listserv to redistribute e-mail questions or a usenet newsgroup are simple methods for sharing this interaction. A more dynamic question and answer period could be created using a chat session. For some types of courses a multi-user, text-based virtual reality, also known as a MUD (Multi-User Domain) or MOO (Multi-user domain Object Oriented), might be effective. An example of an experiment in this area is the Diversity University.

Video teleconferencing: If you were watching a chemist describe the intricacies of a folded protein molecule and its interaction with a drug, chances are much information would be transferred through the hand motions and vocal inflections of the chemist. Body language is one component of physical contact that is difficult to convert to pre-packaged text and still images. Incorporation of these might be accomplished in the future through video teleconferencing technologies over the internet. The ability to use video teleconferencing could enhance electronic courses not only by transferring these more subtle forms of communication, but also by providing additional visual and audio cues which help the instructor and students to form an informal rapport. Work on the MBONE and with CUSeeMe have much potential in this area.

The pencil: One of the most basic visualisation tools used in a classroom is the simple pencil. The student uses the pencil to take notes on what is spoken. The instructor is using the pencil to jot down suggestions for future presentations. In the early experiences with providing only electronic copies of the "overhead foils" during a lecture, many students have been frustrated by the inability to take effective notes. Even the annotation capability with the NCSA Mosaic browser is limited by the limitation of annotation only at the full page level, and by the user interface to annotations. The centre investigated the CoNote annotation system.

The creation and use of audiovisual tools is still problematic. The same functionality or at least interoperability must be available across all popular graphical user interfaces. Bandwidth limitations to the students desk also makes many of these tool unusable. It is not acceptable to have to limit participation in the virtual classroom to only those with the best internet access and interface. Just as html has provided a standard which allows participation by users with diverse implementations of both low-end and high-end browsers, audiovisual tools are requiring similar standardisation.

The initial pilot course offered in the electronic classroom was scheduled in May, 1995. The audience were interested members of the academic affiliates programme which allow them to get feedback and refine the methods and materials. The Centre made use of existing online lecture notes, labs, and tutorials by using these in the electronic course. This course provided educational opportunities to those who cannot attend the traditional workshops held in Ithaca. The materials developed could be re-used by others, especially the Smart Node Programme participants. Enhancements made to current materials served as a useful reference guide for staff and researchers.

REFERENCES

Ackermann, E., *Tools for Teaching: The World Wide Web and a Web Browser*, 1996.

Cohen, J. A., Castner, M. H., 2000, *Technology and Classroom Design: A Faculty Perspective*, in L. Lloyd (ed.), *Teaching with Technology, Rethinking Tradition*, Medford, NJ: Information Today, Inc.

Ho, M. S., *Learning and Teaching in Cyberspace*: *An Empirical Investigation of Computer-assisted Instruction for Geography*, Academic exercise, Dept. of Geography, Faculty of Arts and Social Sciences, National University of Singapore, 1996.

Hiltz, R. S., *The Virtual Classroom*, Norwood, NJ: Ablex, 1995.

Huges, K., *Entering the World-Wide Web: A Guide to Cyberspace*, Enterprise Integration Technologies, 1994.

Maddox, C. C., *The World Wide Web and School Culture: Are they Compatible*?, in D. L. Johnson, C. D. Maddux, and L. Lieu, (eds.), *Using Technology in the Classroom*, New York: The Haworth Press, 1997.

Madhu Parhar, "Surfing Through Web—Exploring a New Educational Resource", *University News*, November, 20, 2000.

Stuart, R. and Thomas, J. C., "The Implications of Education in Cyberspace", *Multimedia Review*, 1991.

Rossman, P., *The Emerging Worldwide Electronic University*, Greenwood Press, Westport Conn, 1992.

4

Virtual Technology vs. Virtual Teachers

New information and communication technologies (ICTs) are becoming standard tools in schools of developed countries. Recognising the growing role of technology in the workplace and in everyday life, school reform panels have stressed the need to provide students with skills to succeed in an information-based economy. State and local curriculum frameworks have begun to incorporate standards for teaching students with and about technology. School districts are scrambling to keep up with ever more powerful hardware and software and are finding ways to integrate technology more effectively into instruction.

For students to become comfortable and effective users of various technologies, teachers must be able to make wise, informed decisions about technology. However, technology is not a cure—all, nor is there one single technology tool or application that must be used by every teacher. As one group of researchers suggested, "If we abandon the idea that technology is a panacea—a magic cure for all that ails our educational system we would expcct that sometimes technology will make a difference and sometimes it will not." All teachers, however, should bc confident in applying technology when and where appropriate.

Despite the central role of the teacher in educational applications of technology, there has been relatively little research on how and why teachers use technology. Most research about educational technology has focused on the impact of technology on students; little attention has been given to its impact on teachers.

Furthermore, although teachers' experience and expertise with technology varies, the data that do exist about teachers typically focus on a special subset—the enthusiastic, pioneering teachers who are "accomplished" technology users. Specifically, two major surveys assessed the goals, attitudes, and activities of accomplished teacher users of technology. While these data do not discuss technology use by the average teacher, or by teachers in general, they do offer a vision of how technology can help teachers.

For teachers to realise the potential of technology, certain basic conditions must be present, including adequate hardware, software, guidance, time, and a school climate that encourages teachers to use these resources in innovative ways. The existence of the conditions is far from commonplace. Teachers must carry out many tasks to make the learning experience a rich one. They must guide and encourage students, provide varied learning experiences, keep track of student progress, and evaluate student learning. In reality, this means they must regularly find and organise information, create lesson plans, grade papers, maintain extensive records, and deal with a range of administrative duties.

Technology can be a powerful tool for helping teachers with all the different parts of their job: enhancing instruction, simplifying administrative tasks, and fostering professional growth activities. The experience of some teachers further suggests that technology can help redefine the role of the teachers, in and out of the classroom. Although teachers have long accomplished the manifold tasks required in teaching without technology, some teachers who have learned to integrate technology tools into their teaching have found them to be useful in ways they had not imagined. These teachers describe how technology makes it possible to meet current instructional goals or pursue altogether new goals. Some find that using various technologies allows them to teach in entirely different ways. In addition, some teachers find that technology can enhance their personal productivity.

Today a wide range of technologies are available in schools with a number of applications to teaching and learning. There is no single best technological medium that suits all teachers equally well. Some teachers have focused on exploring applications of the computer; others a video camera or video cassette recorder. An in growing numbers, some teachers have become enthusiastic about the instructional and professional applications of telecommunications technologies to reach out to others and to a wide range of resources. Similarly, there does not appear to be one best way for teachers to implement technology. Different teachers and schools find different reasons and methods for using technologies

TECHNOLOGY ENHANCED INSTRUCTION

Evidence from an array of studies indicates that technology in the classroom can have a positive impact on student learning, in terms of achievement in certain subject areas, development of skills, and attitudes toward school. Although early research tended to focus on "the computer" as an independent variable that some how affected the learning process, it is becoming increasingly clear that technology, in and of itself, does not directly change teaching or learning.

The critical element is how technology is incorporated into instruction. In a review of research on computers and basic writing instruction, for example, the researchers concluded:"... the most effective utilisation of computer software in the basic writing classroom combines the best of writing instruction theory with a creative use of computer technology. Only well-informed, trained and caring composition instructors will help to bridge the gap between technology and humanity." Certain applications, such as the approach taken in the video-based problem-solving materials in "The Adventures of Jasper Woodbury," look particularly promising. Although Jasper is just one example of how new ideas about teaching and learning can be implemented with technology, it also illustrates the difficulty of sorting out the "effects" of the technology itself. In this particular example, many design and implementation features-a theory of learning and cognition, particular mathematical goals and skills, varying methods and approaches for using the materials in the classroom with students-all combine with the technology to affect student learning.

Additional research is needed to develop a deeper understanding of which instructional uses of technology are most effective and under what circumstances, and how teacher interaction with technology plays into this effectiveness. While improving student learning is a central goal, technology-using teachers express enthusiasm for additional instructional benefits of technology that may or may not be reflected immediately in measures of student learning: bringing a wider range of resources to the classroom, motivating learners, providing new teaching tools, accommodating individual learning styles, and even redefining the role of the teacher.

Technologies have made it increasingly easy for teachers to access a broader range of materials they can use in the classroom. At the most basic level the copying machine has allowed teachers to make copies of articles, charts, or instructional materials from outside sources and share them directly with students.

Supplementary computer tools-such as scanners or digitising cameras-allow teachers to bring in outside sources, enter them into a computer, and customise assignments for students. For example, a teacher can bring a timely article from the morning newspaper into class, scan it into the computer in minutes, and have her students work on rewriting, editing, or adding research to the story on the same day. Students can browse interactively or conduct electronic research searches in CDROM databases, encyclopedias, or other reference works. Thus, not only do technologies allow access to a broader range of instructional resources, but they also offer students the opportunity to learn to use electronic tools to access information and develop research skills using the technologies they will face in the future. Telecommunications creates even broader possibilities for transcending school walls and accessing a wide range of learning opportunities and resources.

Today, computers with modems, telephone lines, and local or wide area networks enable teachers and students to explore worlds beyond their immediate reach, such as perusing the card catalogue at the local library for a list of books on a research topic, sharing weather data with scientists on a network, or previewing software to see if it is appropriate for a particular grade level. Many of the teachers who access telecommunications networks do so after school or at night, on their own time and very often on their own dime-but they say it is worth it. For instance, a teacher in Arlington, Virginia, said that she pays for her subscription to America Online because communicating with a scientist at a national research lab is a great way to get ideas for student projects or to encourage students in their work.

Telecommunications connect students and teachers instantaneously and simultaneously to poets or politicians, musicians or religious leaders, university professors or researchers on a national supercomputer, or other students down the block or on the other side of the world. The number of these telecommunications-based activities is growing rapidly, in part because of teacher and student enthusiasm for the opportunity to collect, share, and evaluate their ideas, data, and writing with classes in other schools and states or even in foreign countries. Some of these links are initiated by individual teachers on a class-by-class basis.

Increasingly, telecommunications-using teachers are finding that connecting to a "listserv" gives them immediate access to classes sharing a common interest in a particular topic. For example, "GLBL-HS" is a listserv created by two New York teachers for teachers and their students interested in discussing world cultures. Another listserv, called the "Noon project," involves classes at different latitudes where students measure the shadow of a meter stick at noontime. Based on these measurements and the latitude of each site, the classes calculate the diameter of the earth. There are also a number of more extensive curriculum- based telecommunications projects using electronic networks. While many teachers have long used project-based teaching and continue to do so without technology, many teachers are enthusiastic about what technology can add by extending the project beyond the classroom. These projects have typically been created with federal or private support to cover the costs of curriculum development, organisation, and teacher support.

Teachers can create new teaching tools with technology that facilitate new forms of instruction. For instance, in US, a teacher who wished to give her students abetter understanding of music created a multimedia set of musical instruments the students could "play." Using Hypercard software on her computer equipped with a CDROM to play sound, she designed her own instructional software around a set of musical instruments and the sounds they make. Each picture of art instrument has a "button" the students can click on to hear the instrument's sound. The students can play the "game" of recognising the instrument by its sound only. It is not the same as having the real instruments in the classroom-a luxury most schools cannot afford-but the students can "play" the instruments on their own, and it is a lot more quiet. According to the teacher, the software has been extremely successful with her students. "I am already able to see how the children's increased familiarity with instruments carries over to the music appreciation class," she said. "They are beginning to understand why a composer might choose a certain instrument to convey a particular image or emotion."

Teachers can give both their own lessons and student assignments more content and depth, by encouraging students to use computers, video, and telecommunications in tandem with traditional materials, such as textbooks and other print or library resources. Teachers also require that their students use these resources to create multi-media reports. Instead of the traditional approach to written reports, a teacher can suggest that students include clippings scanned in from a newspaper, maps, pieces taken from primary sources or family journals, photographs, references from the CDROM encyclopedia, or text with highlighted words that correspond to a student-created glossary, in addition to the other traditional research materials.

Students must extend their research to include a variety of information sources; draw upon multiple ways of representing events, perspectives and interpretations; evaluate which materials work best for the presentation required; and then synthesise this material into a cogent multimedia message. For example, for a report on Martin Luther King, Jr., a teacher in Kentucky has her high school students view a full-motion videodisc segment of the civil rights leader delivering his "I Have a Dream" speech. Powerful as the speech is, it takes on additional impact when the student searches other video materials and discovers pictures of segregated lunch counters or water fountains with "Whites Only" signs, views film segments of speeches by other civil rights leaders and segregationists, reviews documents that support Dr. King's statements, and examines evidence in contemporary news articles that suggest whether or not his dream has been met. The process is as important as the product, as students develop valuable skills in finding, evaluating, organising, and communicating many types of information using new technologies as well as traditional research materials. Although students could go to a library, read books, watch videos, and interview people, technology has the means to bring together all those original source materials in an easily accessible place-such as a videodisc or CDROM. Students may not otherwise have access to these kinds of sources.

Many technology-based classroom activities can be motivating to students. Some teachers report that many students become so involved in what they are doing with technology that they arrive before the firstbell and leave after the last bus. These teachers suggest that technology can be a key vehicle for stimulating learning, primarily because it creates environments and presents content in ways that are more engaging and involve students more directly than do textbooks and more traditional teaching tools.

The interactive capacity of new technologies-wherein children can actively interact with information and receive feedback on their questions or answers-contributes to its motivating effects. For example, asocial studies teacher in Montgomery County, Maryland, uses a multimedia station in class; where teacher questions were previously greeted with silence, high school students now participate actively in class discussions. The multimedia lesson converts her lecture into more of a demonstration or slide show wherein she can easily show maps, charts, graphs, primary source documents, and video clips of news or historical footage. The computer technology allows the teacher to stop, backup, go forward, or skip to another "file" of images as students ask questions. This teacher was particularly impressed with the level of involvement and interest this approach generated in students; she reported that they ask more questions, seem less afraid to speak out in class, and were even talking about it with their parents at home. Another example of the motivating effects of technology is described by a teacher in an alternative high school who reported that he used a software simulation programme as both learning tool and behaviour motivator for his class of ten 16- to 18-year-old boys. These students, referred from their regular schools and placed in the alternative school as a last chance before placement in a more restrictive educational setting, were often unruly and needed to develop social skills as much as they needed the academic skills they had missed in their earlier schooling experiences. Engaging this group was a challenge; yet, almost all were enthusiastic when presented with a science activity using simulation software. According to this teacher, his students loved working with "The Great Solar System Rescue"; working in teams-as "experts" meteorologists, astronomers, geologists, and space historians-they were challenged to find lost probes in the solar system. Working with the packet of expert material provided in the software and analysing visual clues from the videodisc engaged their interest and focused their attention, and they learned about the solar system in the process.

Technology can be used to help teachers to individualise instruction. This has been one of the greatest appeals of integrated learning systems, computer and software systems that correspond to curricula and can be presented to each student in a class based on his or her abilities. The student can work on the material-often called 'drill and practice' 'until reaching a level of mastery, at his or her own pace. Reports produced by these systems give the teacher a record of what areas were most difficult for each student, so that extra assistance can be given in those particular areas where the student needs help. Technology has been extremely helpful in revolutionising individualised instruction for special education students, many of whom are now being served in regular classrooms. Hardware, software, and assistive devices can help special education students progress in their learning and communicate their knowledge to others in new- and accessible-ways. For example, scanning devices convert text into speech so visually impaired students, in particular, can hear the content and respond to questions. An expanded keyboard with extra large keys or a touch-sensitive screen attached to a computer monitor are alternative input devices that help students with motor control difficulties use the computer without struggling with a mouse. Even a word-processing programme with a spell-checking feature can ease the frustration for students who have difficulty with handwriting or spelling so they can progress to deeper levels of understanding the subject matter.

As even more devices are developed to enable special education students to learn in innovative ways, it is hoped that teachers will be better equipped to provide appropriate instruction. Some technology tools, like the Algebra Tutor, enable a teacher to track the paths a student takes to reach a solution to a problem, helping the teacher understand where the student is confused and needs help. Other applications such as Text-Browser, word processing, and databases, can provide a "window into the student's thinking, inquiry, and problem-solving processes teachers access to students' misconceptions, the ways in which they sort and categorise information, the relationships they form among ideas, and the conjectures they make." While this look into the mind of the individual student is enlightening, it remains a nearly insurmountable challenge to find ways to draw upon this insight and work with each individual student in a class of 20 to 30 students, all needing the teacher's attention.

Using technology can allow teachres to structure their classroom activities so that students work more independently, sometimes in small groups. This may allow the teacher more flexibility to organise time to better meet individual student needs. While there are examples of how some teachers work with limited availability of technologies, clearly a more systematic understanding is needed of the factors that lead to success in such situations. For example, in some cases, teachers have used technology as a tool for setting up activities in which students work in teams where their roles as members of the team are designed to draw upon their personal strengths and interests, to help them find areas where they can succeed and develop self-confidence.

CHANGING ROLE OF TEACHERS

When teachers feel comfortable and confident about using technologies in classroom, myriad changes occur that may ultimately redefine the roles of teachers. The change to a coaching, facilitator role can be daunting, especially when it requires them to venture beyond the teacher-centered lecturing or presentation model they experienced as students themselves or in their teacher preparation. Nevertheless, many who take on these "new" roles find the change is welcome, profound, and often necessary. Teachers at the Open Charter School in Los Angeles found that their roles were shifting as technology integration took over the school. The Open Charter School received enough technology to make available one computer for every two students. Teachers at the school also said that by becoming learners themselves, they had developed greater empathy for their students.

One new role for the teacher is as a learner alongside the students. In fact, an unexpected side effect of technology use is that students, who are often more comfortable with using technology than their teachers, end up helping the teachers. According to a US journalism teacher, initially intimidated by computers, found that her students had a totally different view of technology than she did. She described her "turnaround" this way: "Teachers tend to read the manual and say, 'This is what the computer can do.' Students tend to say, 'It's a computer, it can do anything'. This is one thing I've learned, and I learned it from my students." This teacher gained a new way of thinking about the technology (it could be manipulated), the students (they could teach the teacher), and herself (she didn't know everything after all, and that was free). Could this change have occurred without technology? Perhaps. But she maintained that, as a journalism teacher, she would be remiss in her teaching if she failed to expose students to technologies now commonplace in her field. So she has let the students help her with the technology, while she teaches them the techniques and craft of journalism. In the Olympia Washington School District, USA students are equal partners with teachers in learning about technology applications. The director of technology described the district's approach:

> Students often introduce technological innovations into the classroom and work with teachers in developing course content and goals. The result is that often initial

> [technology] use by teachers does not mimic current teaching practices. We have found that using students as technical resources pays better dividends than teachers depending on colleagues. Kids take to technology faster than teachers, are more readily available, and the children's self-esteem is enhanced by being a mentor to a teacher. The Olympia School District does not give any technology workshops to teachers. Most workshops are given to students and they are taught how to pass this knowledge on to administrators, teachers, and other students. When teachers are involved in a technology workshop, they must bring a student in their class, and together they learn the skills. The pair pool their strengths, and exciting things are happening in the district's schools.

Technological Support to Teachers

Teachers have to spend a major part of their working time inside the school building then they spend additional hours at home working on school-related projects and materials. According to data from the US Department of Education, teachers spend 35 hours a week on average performing their required duties in the school building. Beyond these required school hours, teachers report spending an average of three additional hours with students-for example, coaching, tutoring, and supervising extracurricular activities-and eight more hours a week doing work activities without students, such as preparing lessons, grading assignments, and attending meetings. In 1990-91, teachers in public secondary schools were responsible for an average of five class periods a day, each with an average of 23 students. Public school teachers who were responsible for a class for a whole day, such as elementary teachers, were responsible for an average of 25 students. Technology offers alternative approaches to many day-to-day functions that eat up teachers' valuable time and energy. Teachers who are comfortable using technology indicate that it can help with many important daily tasks, such as keeping records, assessing student learning, preparing and evaluating curricular materials, and increasing communication with students, colleagues, and parents.

Teachers, like all professionals, tend to use technology when they can see how it will help them become more productive or do their jobs more professionally. Teachers use technologies in ways that are most valuable for them, whether to record grades or videotape the performance of a school play. Evidence for how computers can support and enhance the job of the teacher emerged from a four-school pilot project in Indiana in which every teacher was given a computer and training to use it. Two years into the programme, teachers reported that use of the computer had allowed them to be more efficient with the time they spent on administrative tasks, to produce work that was more professional, and to be more confident about exploring the many potential educational uses of computers.

Technology can help teachers also in keeping their records. Gradebook or other recordkeeping software can provide a "hook" that gets otherwise reluctant teachers interested in using technology tools. Most teachers spend large chunks of their time maintaining records, often detailed ones, of student scores on tests and quizzes, daily participation, homework, behaviour, and other factors. Computerised gradebook programmes are set up as spreadsheets; each time a new grade is entered and weighted, the software can automatically recalculate each student's grade averages. The teacher can print out the student's grading history and use it as a vehicle for discussing with the student or parents what that student needs to do to improve. Electronic gradebooks can therefore become a teaching tool as well as a personal time saver, an additional benefit teachers find useful.

In USA, schools in which the central office and teachers are linked by a local area network with access to databases of student records and management software, these programmes can make it simpler for teachers to work together or with their department head or principal to analyse student work, re-examine course goals, and adjust the curriculum or instructional approach when needed. For example, at Piscataquis Community High School in Guilford, Maine, a teacher who sees that a student is having trouble in class can call up a central grade record file from the computer on his or her desk to see whether that student is doing poorly in other classes. If so, the teacher will send an e-mail message to the student's other teachers to discuss the student's difficulties and decide what actions are necessary, such as notifying the counsellor and setting up a team meeting with the student's parents. Because every teacher in the school has a computer with access to the instructional management software, they use the technology as an early warning system, allowing for intervention before student problems become too entrenched.

A transformation is occurring in education as researchers and practitioners rethink basic beliefs about teaching and learning. These research findings and the instructional theories they have spawned raise serious challenges to traditional classroom organisational models, to conventional curricula, and, in turn, to existing forms of testing. One of the greatest challenges of alternative forms of assessment, such as performance-based assessment, is keeping track of rich but extensive histories of student performance. Some teachers are using technology to meet this challenge — maintaining electronic portfolios of student work on disk, saving hardcopies of work that students create on the computer, or requiring students to demonstrate competence and understanding through multimedia or other technology-based presentations.

Performance assessment methods, especially when supported by technology, help teachers diagnose student strengths and weaknesses and adapt instruction accordingly, provide students with immediate feedback on their performance, let teachers record and score multiple aspects of competence, and maintain an efficient, detailed, and continuous history of the student's progress. For example, some teachers use video to help make objective records of student performance and growth. A teacher can videotape a student presentation, speech, demonstration, or performance and review it later, several times if necessary, to analyse and evaluate the student's performance. The teacher and student can view the-tape together and discuss progress or areas of concern. The tape can also be stored and revisited later in the year to see how far the student has progressed or to sham the demonstration with parents. In developed countries, many schools are calling for students to maintain portfolios of student activity, throughout a year or over several years. These can be extensive documents. Storage of these materials on CDROM makes them more convenient to maintain, access, and update, and saves scarce storage space in classrooms and school offices.

Preparing materials for daily lessons is one of the largest parts of the teacher's day. Some teachers are using new technologies to help them preview, access, create, and incorporate new materials into their lesson plans. Word-processing software, combined with printers, for example, have proved valuable tools for teachers when preparing work-sheets, creating tests, and updating lesson plans. Teachers take pride in being able to use programmes like spreadsheets and word processors to produce professional-looking documents. As one high school journalism teacher says, with "the right computers and software, the school newspaper actually looks like a newspaper, not a student publication." Often it is the school media centre where videodisc players, VCRs, computers with CDROM capabilities, and other hardware are available, along with collections of software and programming for preview or classroom use.

New telecommunications technologies enable teachers to access information from a variety of sources—universities, schools, government agencies, or any organisation that has a publicly available database. From the electronic files in the database, teachers may access documents, such as written reports, lesson plans, or research papers; graphic images such as weather maps and satellite or still camera photographs; or other kinds of information. In fact, information retrieval is one of the most common purposes for which teachers use telecommunications. Teachers who use telecommunications emphasise several advantages of electronic information retrieval. They can find sources of information that are far more current than materials in standard textbooks, such as satellite photos that may be only hours old. In addition, once teachers are comfortable using the technology, searching for relevant materials electronically may be quicker or more convenient; for example, perusing a library card catalogue online is usually faster than going to the library to look.

Teachers can access materials that may not be available otherwise, such as those created by colleagues, or information not published in traditional ways. Also, teachers who retrieve information electronically can easily store and use the materials when and how they want, such as adapting lesson plans for their own class.

Via telecommunications networks, teachers are now being encouraged to participate as contributors to as well as users of electronic resources. For example, the Eisenhower Clearing house for Mathematics and Science Education is creating an electronic catalogue of instructional plans written by teachers in the broad areas of mathematics and science. Other network service providers have created places for teachers to distribute their own instructional plans over a network. Virginia's Public Education Network (PEN) has areas —called Academical Villages, in the Jeffersonian parlance — where teachers place materials that other teachers may download and use in their classrooms. In fact, the state's most recent technology plan, designed to replace the existing Virginia's PEN system, was influenced in part by the idea of making teacher-created documents easier to post and more accessible to network users.

Teachers are "classroom bound" most of the day with limited access to the outside world; yet, an essential and vital part of the job of teaching is maintaining open communications with parents, other teachers, the school office, and other professionals. Teachers spend a great deal of their time worrying about, helping, counselling, and sharing information with students and parents, yet they are expected to do so in most cases without the aid of technology.

Telephones, perhaps the most ubiquitous and necessary technology available to other professionals, are rare in most classrooms. In USA, an estimated 12 percent of teachers have a telephone in their classrooms. There are other duties required of teachers that would be far simpler if they had easy access to telephones. For example, educators in New York undertook a review of what it takes to convene a meeting of the school personnel required by law to meet with the parents of each special education child to review the child's Individual Education Plan. They found that often six people, in many cases coming from three different buildings, were required to attend these meetings. For the teacher to go to the school office or faculty lounge and stand in line to make all the phone calls necessary to set up each meeting literally took hours of playing telephone tag with busy psychologists, counsellors, resource personnel, and parents. Without easy access to phones, much less voice mail or e-mail accounts where messages can be left, the task of corralling all the required players is a scheduling nightmare. It doesn't have to be that way.

Telephone system connects teachers and students to each other, to parents, and to resources outside the school. The phone lines allow for voice mail, use of modems or fax machines from the classroom, and access to parents as the need arises. Each teacher at the Lockwood Schools also has a "broadcast" mail-box to send and receive messages to groups. For instance, if a member of the school's technology committee wants to leave a message telling other members about a meeting time, the broadcast mailbox can handle it. Voice mail lets teachers leave or retrieve messages for each other and for outside callers, such as parents, calling in to check on a homework assignment. Telecommunications use by teachers, especially fore-mail, has expanded in the last few years, and with good reason: teachers with classroom access to local or external telecommunications networks can contact other educators, experts, scientists, and practitioners to discuss issues related to their teaching practice, developments in their field, and classroom experiences. Furthermore, a growing number of teacher-based networks offer teachers a chance to connect with other people in a variety of forms.

Many schools in developed countries are exploring the use of internal networks as vehicles for enhancing schoolwide communication. For example, when the principal of Webster Elementary School in St. Augustine, Florida, received a model school technology grant from the state, he chose to use it first to improve communication in his school by building a "teamwork infrastructure" that would connect the teachers in his building. Each of the school's 53 teachers, who were scattered across three building wings and several mobile trailers, was given a computer connected to a local area network that links all the classrooms and the principal. Teachers share lesson plans and files of teaching ideas with one another and have ready access to the principal throughout the day as questions or problems arise. The principal maintains that e-mail is "the most important technology" in his school; in addition to checking it constantly throughout the day, he issues a daily e-mail bulletin to update teachers and staff on the day's activities: Principal at Webster Elementary has also used the technology to streamline the paperwork within the building, creating school forms (e.g., letters to parents and field trip requests) and put them on the network so that teachers can fill them out and send them back easily. Weekly newsletters to parents, a parent-school voice messaging system, and a daily video newscast (where students, not the principal, make the day's announcements) are also important parts of this principal's approach to using technology in his school to create a "team environment" centered around open communication.

In USA, Local Area Networks (LANs) are the mode of connection planned for the Edison Project School Design. The current plan outlines a goal to provide every student with a computer at home to access "the Common," a LAN linking all local Edison teachers, administrators, students, and families. Each local school's LAN will be connected to a wide area network of all the Edison schools nationwide, enabling them to communicate with one another. Computers housed in each school's media centre will provide internet access so media specialists can tap into vast resources and gather information for their schools. Edison staff suggest that at the present time the internet is too complex for individual teachers or students to navigate. Edison leaders hope that the Common will become the centre of a geographical community and social centre for teachers and families.

Teachers need opportunities to expand their knowledge, keep pace with developments in their field, try out new methods, exchange ideas with peers and experts, and refine their skills. They are also required, in most districts, to take a certain number of continuing education credits for recertification or promotions. Some of this training comes through courses or one-day workshops offered by the district, generally referred to as "inservice training."

Most countries require teachers to attend one or more days a year of this inservice training, usually on a limited list of topics selected by the district. While this may be an efficient delivery system for the district, it is not always the training that a teacher needs or would choose on his or her own. In fact, research suggests that professional development is more likely to be effective when it encourages teachers to participate in their own renewal rather than supplying teachers with prepackaged information or training.

Yet many teachers are far from colleges, universities, or central training resources in a state or district that might offer courses or topics of interest in their teaching field. Technology is one means of filling this gap. Increasingly, technology can provide teachers access to new ideas, master teachers and other professionals outside the school setting, and courses and enrichment activities both formal and informal.

Technology-based resources can greatly enhance opportunities for convenient, flexible, continuing education courses and workshops—whether required for recertification or taken for personal growth. Educational programmes and courses offered over cable or public television, distance-learning networks, packaged video, and telecommunications networks can extend the range of options for a teacher's study. Distance-learning technologies enable learners in locations distant from one another and/or the instructor to participate in courses via video, audio, and computer technologies.

The technologies are increasingly being used to provide instruction not just for students, but also for teachers and other school staff. Teachers looking for ways to improve their own teaching may also engage in what researchers refer to as "reflective practice." Technology can provide valuable resources for extending this concept. Reflective practice involves asking focused questions, sharing concerns, seeking common meanings in teaching practice, or constructing ideas in collaboration with other teachers. Video has a long, successful tradition as a means to support this form of collaborative learning among teachers. Moreover, research supports the notion that shared observation, discussion, and planning of teaching in peer groups can lead to improved practice. Typically, to learn from other teachers, a teacher has to find time to watch and observe in classrooms-a difficult scheduling feat for most teachers. Video allows classroom interactions or master teachers to be taped for convenient viewing. Or teachers can tape themselves teaching, then ask a colleague, principal, or coach to offer a critique or perspective. One group of researchers has been organising teachers into video "clubs" on a school or district basis. Teachers make videotapes of their own teaching and teacher-student interactions. The clubs watch and discuss one another's videos as well as videos of exemplary practice. The groups have a facilitator who helps them focus on relating standards of exemplary teaching to their own practice. Telecommunications-based electronic communities are another vehicle for teachers to engage in reflective practice.

An electronic community can be a non-judgmental forum for teachers to ask questions, solicit opinions, and explore personal philosophies with the aim of improving their teaching.

Schools in developed countries are tend to be structured in ways that do not encourage collegial work among teachers. Unlike schools in some other countries, time is not set aside in the teacher's day for working with colleagues on a regular basis. Teaching, more than many other occupations, is practised in isolation, an isolation that is at times crushing in its separateness. Collegiality is non-existent for many teachers, unless hurried lunches over plastic trays in unkempt lunchrooms are viewed as exercises in colleagueship, rather than the complaint sessions they are more likely to be. Knowledge is the currency in which a teacher deals, and yet the teacher's own knowledge is allowed to become stale and devalued, as though ideas were not the life-blood of the occupation.

The organisational structure of schools, so far as the professional staff is concerned, is built on a series of one-on-one relationships. Since there is little incentive for teachers to integrate their behaviour with that of other teachers, they tend to go their own ways. Teachers are so accustomed to working on their own that they are surprised when someone tries to act as a colleague and collaborate. Most teachers' days allow them little time or specific opportunities to share ideas and communicate with colleagues, and there is little incentive for them to work together. Some teachers who have had regular opportunities to interact with other teachers-in person or electronically-report that the collegial support they receive far exceeds their expectations. Some teachers have found online resources, such as listservs, bulletin boards, or e-mail, to be a convenient and time-saving way to connect with colleagues and other professionals or resources outside the school. Some networks, such as TENET in Texas, Virginia's PEN, and the Scholastic Network, are designed specifically for teacher inquiry and growth. Teachers also use commercial networks like America Online and Prodigy for this purpose; many of these networks have educational forums. Teachers who use these services say that the exposure to new colleagues, ideas, and resources can invigorate their enthusiasm for their own learning.

A recent survey of accomplished educators' use of telecommunications found that the opportunity to communicate with other educators and share ideas is one of the major benefits of this technology. Obtaining rapid feedback on curricular issues and other topics of professional interest, and keeping current on subject matter, pedagogy, and technology trends are also important incentives. A teacher in Kentucky who subscribes to the service Prodigy and regularly uses it at home, noted that she has forged an online relationship with people in her state department of education.

Some learning opportunities allow teachers to contribute to the resource base of expertise, not just take from it. For example, the Bellevue Washington School District network—called Belnet—has been used to further the district's philosophy of peers learning from peers. Teachers use the network for planning and joint teaching efforts. New ideas about instructional practice, materials, and strategies pass through the network, as do discussions about using technology to promote learning. The system, which is connected to the internet, also provides a followup to staff development; when teachers complete a class, they can gain additional help, or advice from their peers on Belnet.

Collegial support is an added benefit of a student-centered project, as shown by the Georgia ClassConnect project, a trial project that connects four high schools and four colleges. Teachers at any of the eight sites have a chance to teach a group of students at any or all of the other seven sites. Classrooms are equipped with technologies to facilitate full interaction: monitors, cameras, instructor and ceiling-suspended microphones, a fax machine, a document camera, and a personal computer that controls the equipment at each location. Although the primary focus of this pilot project is distance

Although research on educational technology has consistently focused on how it mayor may not benefit students, students are not on their own in schools. It maybe time to rewrite the question and direct more research efforts to explore some answers for teachers. Helping teachers may, in fact, be the most important step to helping students.

TRAINING OF TEACHERS

One of the most important tasks of society is to ensure that each successive generation acquires the knowledge, technologies, skills, and customs essential to maintain that society. The history of teacher preparation has been one of changing expectations. In the 17th and 18th century teachers had no formal educational requirements as prerequisites for practice. Those who taught elementary subjects were expected to know how to read, write, and do basic arithmetic so they could teach these skills to their charges. The most highly educated were those who taught in the private secondary schools, a group made up predominantly of clergy.

During colonial times, teacher quality was variable; some teachers were barely literate while others possessed a college degree. The importance of religious orthodoxy was one noteworthy constant. Few considered teaching their primary career or goal in life. In the first decades of the 19th century, the "common school" was established in New England. Common schools created a tradition of education that was free, supported by taxes, and universally available to all students. With the surge in students attending common schools, it became clear that a formal, institutionalised approach to preparing teachers was necessary. Although the first documented school for the training of teachers in the United States opened under private auspices in Concord, Vermont, in 1823, it was the development of "normal schools" by Horace Mann in 1839 that promised to fill the glaring shortage of qualified teachers and to define teacher competence. Mann's vision aimed for "a new kind of school, a new kind of profession, the principle of taxpayer support and a new vocation for women." With these innovations, the Lexington Normal School opened in July 1839.

Although growing numbers of 19th century teachers attended normal schools, others took part-time or short courses, and some continued to have little or no formal preparation for teaching.

In the Midwest and West, the line between normal schools and post-elementary schooling blurred, as the normal school became a place where parents sent their children for a higher education, a sort of academy or high school rather than an institution for training teachers. As normal schools evolved into the model for general secondary schooling in the Midwest and West, their contributions to teacher training grew uneven. Later, when normal schools evolved into teachers colleges and then into colleges of education within larger institutions of higher education, differences of opinion emerged about whether the colleges main goal should be the preparation of teachers or education theory and research. It might be said that normal schools evolved from single-goal institutions to lower-level institutions within the higher educational hierarchy. Even after normal schools, and then teachers' colleges, had become widespread, a sizable proportion of teachers still lacked much formal training well into the 20th century; as recently as 1940, less than 50 percent of the teachers in the United States held a bachelor's degree.

Education of educators has obviously reached higher ground in recent decades; today, almost all teachers have at least a bachelor's degree, and almost half have a master's degree or higher. Nevertheless, other factors bedevil teacher preparation programmes, including misconceptions about teaching as a profession; misinformed perceptions of the intellectual capabilities of teachers; and negative stereotypes of women and minorities, who traditionally make up a large part of the teaching force. Teacher education programmes today must address countless areas-usually within a time frame of three to four years, at best. Teacher education graduates not only need to be skilled in content, methods, cognitive development, assessment practices, pedagogical theory, education history, technology, and classroom management, but they may also need to know about drug education, AIDS, environmental issues, social and family issues, and whatever else the public decides schools should handle.

Although, ideally, "the mission for teacher education should arise out of the mission for schooling," the problem is that the mission of schooling is itself unclear, indeed, schools in general operate under "fragmented goals." The way that new teachers are prepared is often under public scrutiny-in the media and press, as well as by educators themselves.

Many colleges of education have tried to implement reforms that address public concerns, yet the skepticism persists: some think undergraduate programmes produce classroom teachers with limited expertise in the subjects they are expected to teach, while graduate schools prepare specialists who spend little time in classrooms; others find the form and format of teaching in colleges of education antithetical to "real" learning, with those who prepare classroom teachers modelling the "chalk and talk" lecture teaching style. Many observe that there is never enough time for students to be exposed to good teaching or for student teaching under the watchful eye of a competent supervising teacher, nor enough topnotch teachers in model classrooms close enough to the college of education to provide enough successful student teaching placements.

The education systems being challenged by current reforms are based on a legacy begun in the 19th century, when many states took over the functions of examining and credentialing new teachers. Typically, the state departments of education controlled public normal schools and certification became a question of completing the course of instruction offered by these institutions. Today, state requirements for teachers are created by state legislatures. However, because public school teachers are employed by local boards of education, and these boards are made up of lay people, it might be said that the public is involved in employing teachers.

Thus there is a divided responsibility-among the public sector, universities and colleges, and public schools-for what should be the basis of teaching. In other professions-medicine, law, engineering, architecture-states have delegated the responsibility for licensing to autonomous standards boards composed of practitioners who establish the standards and processes of the profession for the nation. Teaching does not follow this model. Instead, each state sets its own licensure or certification process for educators and issues different types of certificates. In some cases, state departments of education determine qualifications to teach based on a requisite number of courses. State approval generally comes from reviewing specific teacher education programmes on a programme-by-programme basis, resulting in hundreds of sets of standards for teacher preparation with varying levels of quality.

One of the major issues in the professionalisation of teaching and teacher education is the accreditation of schools and colleges of education. Unlike those who practice law, medicine, social work, engineering, architecture, or other professions, teachers do not have to graduate from an institution accredited by the profession. In fact, today less than half the schools of education are professionally accredited.

Among the many demands on schools and colleges of education today, preparing teachers to use technology may seem like an additional burden. However, states and professional organisations are increasingly recommending or requiring that all new teachers be competent in the uses of technology. Moreover, emerging evidence suggests that technology can make several positive contributions to the overall preservice experience.

Technology can capture the reality of the classroom: a video-tape of a teacher conducting an actual class can "anchor" preservice students to the complex and real-life interactions of students and teachers. Technology can facilitate access to and communication with additional resources, such as experts in the field or informational databases on CDROM available to teacher education students and faculty on the same network. Technology can also support and enhance traditional approaches to teacher-developed curriculum materials and instructional practices.

Since most teacher education students receive much of their content instruction in the colleges of arts and sciences, it is important that effective teaching—including teaching with technology—is modeled in the other parts of the university preparation of prospective teachers. This is particularly important as states cut back the number of education courses a prospective teacher can take, and as they move to abolish the undergraduate degree in education. A recent survey at the University of Southern California indicates that across all areas only a small percentage of college courses and classes use technology to enhance or supplement instruction. According to the study, roughly one collage course in six uses computer labs, and only one in 10 uses computer-based simulations and software. The survey also reports that research universities are more likely than other types of institutions of higher education to consider resources such as the internet to be important for access to content that otherwise might not be available for classroom instruction.

Even if the courses prospective teachers take in the general studies programmes do not necessarily model technology use, it is appropriate that schools and colleges of education do so. However, surveys conducted for US Office of Technology Assessment (OTA) and a number of other sources suggest that this is not so. OTA finds that overall teacher education programmes in the United States do not prepare graduates to use technology as a teaching tool.

Coverage of technology in teacher education can be divided roughly into three types:

i) discussion/ demonstration,

ii) technology practice, and

iii) professional practice.

A faculty member conducting a science teaching methods course might, for example, discuss how computer-based simulations could be used in a high school science class. The instructor might even demonstrate a few simulations for the class using a large monitor or projection panel. This occasionally occurs in teacher education, but it is rare.

The next level of engagement with technology involves hands on technology practice. In the science methods course, for example, the instructor might take the students to a teacher education computer lab and have them install science simulations into the computer and examine how they work.

At the third and most critical level of engagement, professional practice, students in the science methods class might see simulations being used in a high school chemistry or physics class. They might visit a classroom, view a classroom via a television connection, or watch it from a videodisc or videotape. At the level of professional practice, these students would also practice teaching with technology. In the methods course, they might create lesson plans that include technology and practice in teaching exercises.

A typical college of education is more likely to be a "have not" than a "have" when it comes to many types of educational technology. This is a serious barrier, since access to resources is an essential element of any effort to increase both teaching with and teaching about information technology.

Factors Influencing Technology Use by Teachres

Most schools and teachers today have at least some access to multiple kinds of video and computer-based technologies. Yet much of this technology is not being used to its potential and most classroom environments are still not significantly influenced by technologies. Many of these technologies are not necessarily easy for teachers to access and use as part of their daily routines. In addition, a substantial portion of the school computer inventory is made up of older, less-powerful machines. Access to telecommunications technologies is especially limited.

Beyond these problems of access to machines, however, lie a number of other important barriers to more widespread use of educational technologies by teachers. First, it is important to recognise that technology tools require time to master. Hardware and software, no matter how "user-friendly," are complicated and constantly changing. In any profession, time must be invested in learning how to use a particular piece of software to accomplish work-related goals; furthermore, keeping up with upgrades or new software requires ongoing investments of time. But teachers, in particular, are "prisoners of time" as a national study recently underscored.

In developed countries schools require teachers to spend the vast majority of the school day engaged in actual instruction, which leaves little official time for planning, preparation, or learning new things. Even accomplished technology-using teachers, who are highly motivated, rated the lack of time as among the most problematic barriers to technology use in schools. Furthermore, teachers are an incredibly diverse group. Some teachers express eagerness to experiment with new ideas, even at the risk of failure, while others say they have little interest, energy, or time for experimentation. The great majority of teachers probably lie somewhere in between these two poles.

Even the most energetic and innovative teachers experience many competing demands to learn new things-new curriculum standards, teaching methods, behaviour management techniques, assessment methods, techniques for working with special needs children, and so on. This is also true when it comes to technology. Teachers, like others who use technology, fall along a bell curve in which there is a small percentage of innovators and visionaries eager to try new things, a larger number of those who follow the lead of others, and a small group who are skeptical of change. Teachers vary widely in their experience with and knowledge of technology. Some teachers already have computers at home, for example, while others have never been shown how to "boot one up."

Some teachers may be unclear about what technology can offer them because they have had very limited experience with technologies or little exposure to models that use technology to enrich the curriculum, deliver instruction in different ways, or improve personal productivity. Furthermore, there probably are some teachers who will actively resist or avoid learning about technology for reasons that may not be well articulated. The kinds of pedagogical beliefs and practices a teacher holds may also influence whether he or she uses technology. For example, one interview study found that "high-tech" teachers tended to hold a student-centered approach to learning and had used the technologies to implement this philosophy. The "low-tech" teachers were more diverse in their teaching approaches. Some held student-centered educational beliefs but were reluctant to use technologies because of personal fears or inhibitions or because of problems with accessibility and scheduling of equipment. No systematic data exist to tell us what constitutes the normative "technology experience" of teachers in schools today, nor whether technology is more readily used by certain kinds of teachers. However, talking to teachers-hearing their concerns and stories-can help in finding what is required to encourage more widespread use of technology. When asked what would help them use technology better, many teachers mention the need for more knowledge about how to use various technologies.

In US, giving interview to a survey, majority of teachers said that they felt they needed training in order to adequately use a personal computer (56 per cent), standard computer software (61 per cent), multimedia software (62 per cent), instructional videodiscs (67 per cent), and online databases (72 per cent). Far fewer felt the need for training in using video resources; only 7 per cent of teachers said they needed training to adequately use a videocassette recorder (VCR), 9 per cent for a television monitor, and 14 percent for instructional videotapes. Some teachers worry that their lack of knowledge might result in embarrassment or "feeling like a fool" in front of their students. For some teachers, this situation may be intolerable.

Many teachers have not had the opportunity to observe and learn about the wide range of educational uses to which technology can be put—particularly various ways it can be incorporated into different curricular areas. In US, some non-technology using teachers, while they endorse the importance of student access to computers and other technologies, don't see why technology should be used in their classrooms or what resources technology can offer them as they try to meet their instructional goals.

Teachers who want to use technology also may find that educating themselves enough to be able to use a particular piece of hardware or software can require considerable amounts of cxtra time and effort. Teachers may also need more knowledge about how to organise and effectively manage their students in technology-based environments. Some teachers have just one or two computers in a classroom, and are not sure how to use them well when only few students at a time can work on the computer. One teacher described the problem of managing a classroom of students with limited technology this way: "It is hard enough to figure out how you are going to allow 25 students access to the computer and equal time.. .That's a huge task, and if you don't really know the benefits and the advantages and the disadvantages and all the things that whatever system you have and whatever software you have can offer, the management is just such a nightmare that you turn-off the whole thing." Even when teachers have more equipment orchestrating its use often requires knowledge about how to really teach with it or how to organise learning activities to make optimal use of the technology.

In one survey, less than half of the American schools reported that an introductory computer course is available for their teachers. This pattern was particularly pronounced among teachers in middle schools, where only 27 percent of schools reported the availability of such a course compared with 51 percent of high schools and 43 percent of elementary schools. As regards video, a different set of data found that fewer than one-fourth of teachers reported having had training in the instructional uses of video or television. Fewer than one teacher in 20 reported having received formal training over the past three years in such topics as evaluating video programming or curriculum coordination using instructional television (ITV) materials.

However, this is an area where teachers feel more comfortable, and less in need of training. Data on expenditures for educational technology indicate that far more resources have been allocated to hardware and software than to training or technical support. For example, in 1992-93, a US national survey asked district technology coordinators to estimate how much of their total district computer budgets fell into each of these three categories. This survey found that approximately 55 per cent of all technology spending goes to hardware, while software spending accounts for another 30 per cent. Training accounted for only 15 per cent.

In an evaluation study of a major Educational Technology Initiative in Utah that provided schools across the state with money for technology. In the third year of the initiative, the average Utah elementary school received $15,365 and spent 68 percent on hardware, 20 percent on software, 6 percent on repairs, and 6 percent on training. With its budget of $31,369, the average Utah secondary school allocated 75 percent to hardware, 15 percent to software, 6 percent to repairs, and 4 percent to training. Data from the evaluation indicated that inservice training, though limited, had an important effect-teachers who received inservice training were more likely to use computer technology than teachers who did not receive training. Furthermore, teachers receiving training were more likely to use computers to stimulate higher-order thinking and creativity.

Overall, however, the evaluators of the Utah project concluded that the current allocation of funding to in-service training was not sufficient to realise the potential of the state's considerable investment in hardware. As states such as Utah gain more experience with technology implementation, more are be coming convinced of the importance of investing substantially in technology training, especially in the early years of the technology adoption process. For example, Florida has revised its policy toward technology training. For the 1993-94 school year, the Florida legislature allocated $55 million for educational technology and $8.65 million for educational software. The appropriation required that schools applying for these technology funds set aside at least 30 percent of the money for training. The Texas Education Agency recently recommended that districts allocate a substantial portion of their technology funds for staff development, suggesting that districts just getting started allocate 30 percent of their technology funds to hardware, 30 percent to software, 30 per cent to staff development, and 10 percent to maintenance. While Washington State does not require inservice training in technology, the state spends about 40 percent of its $4.5 million technology budget on teacher training activities.

One of the barriers to increasing technology training for teachers is the many competing priorities for limited staff development time. This makes scheduling technology training difficult. States have multiple instructional goals, approaches, and philosophies they want teachers to learn about and use. The kind of technology training provided is as important to teachers as the availability of training. Some teachers observe that the content of training they receive is inadequate; there seems to be a focus on basic training in the mechanics of operating the machines, with little training about integrating technology into various subjects or learning to use it as a pedagogical tool.

One observational study of computer use in high school found that one of the characteristics of the training teachers were most likely to complain about was its restricted technical focus. Specifically, teachers tended to be critical of the fact that the training often focused primarily on issues such as how to operate the computer without giving them much advice or assistance with two fundamental issues what software was available to assist in accomplishing their educational objectives and how to organise the class to make efficient and effective use of students' time when there were a small number of computers in the classroom. Poorly timed or piecemeal training can also be a problem. Sometimes training is provided before the hardware or software arrives or before teachers know what equipment they will be using.

Formal training sessions in the uses and mechanics of educational technologies provide only the basic knowledge that gives teachers an impetus to further experiment. Beyond this, teachers consistently report that having a person at the school site who can help them makes all the difference in the likelihood of their going further with technology-someone who is knowledgeable about technology and can help them with questions or problems. The inevitable technical and logistical problems that arise with technology are one reason many teachers feel the need for onsite assistance. These include such problems as machines that won't work as promised, restricted access to locked closets filled with equipment, media carts that must be scheduled and shared among many classrooms, equipment that remains broken for weeks or even months because no one knows how to fix it and repair requests take weeks or months to process. Problems with scheduling shared resources such as computers in a lab can also create frustration. Even experienced technology-using teachers can find themselves preoccupied with trouble-shooting hardware and software problems, rather than assisting students in their learning activities.

A great deal of what teachers need to know about technology cannot wait for a scheduled training session. As do most individuals dealing with new technologies, teachers also need informal assistance-often with a kind of immediacy that does not lend itself to afterschool telephone calls. This kind of assistance might include help setting up equipment or trouble-shooting hardware and software problems in the classroom-the more "nuts and bolts" kind of technical support. However, teachers also need pedagogical support such as advice on choosing relevant software and integrating it into a specific lesson, suggestions for ways the technology can be used to meet particular curricular goals, or ideas about how to organise the whole class to use four computer workstations or a single computer with a modem.

A study conducted in US found that onsite technology support personnel for assisting teachers are limited in most schools of the country. The percentage of schools that assign a full-time nonteaching position to coordinate teachers' and students' computer use did not change at all between 1989 and 1992 and remains very small. In 1992, as in 1989, only 6 percent of elementary schools and 3 percent of secondary schools employed a full-time school-level computer coordinator who did not also have teaching responsibilities. In nearly three-fifths of all schools, there was no one in the school who had any portion of their workweek officially allocated to coordinating or supervising the computer programme. In about one-fifth of these schools, one person, usually a regular teacher or the school media specialist, has at least half of the job officially defined in terms of computer coordination responsibilities. In those schools where there is a "major" computer coordinator, how do they report spending their time. As a group, the "major" computer coordinators report spending an average of 38 hours per week on tasks associated with computer coordination. But working with teachers to use computers is a very small part of their job, taking up an average of only 3.6 hours per week, or less than 10 percent of their total computer coordination time. Most of their coordination time is spent teaching or supervising students who are using computers in computer education classes or in other subjects. Hardware and software maintenance occupies a larger percentage of time for this group, on average, than working with teachers.

The study reported that, although two-thirds of schools id US have a person designated as a coordinator of instructional television or video, it is very rare for this to be a full-time position. In all but 3 percent of schools surveyed in 1990-91, that person had other duties; most often he or she was the school librarian, or else was a teacher, computer coordinator, or administrator. Whatever their other responsibilities, ITV coordinators performed a variety of support functions. As reported by the school principals, these included recording programmes for teachers' later use (in 81 per cent of all schools), distributing teacher guides to programmes (82 per cent), assisting with equipment (90 per cent), training teachers to use video in their teaching (56 per cent), coordinating previews and screenings (53 per cent), and helping to produce instructional TV and video materials (35 per cent).

Effective implementation of new practices or innovations in schools is influenced by many factors; these determine the extent to which new educational practices are adopted and maintained over time. Schools are organisations with many different players and constituencies. Some school cultures promote and encourage innovation, others do not. Teachers are only one part of this complex system that includes administrators, principals, parents, students, local communities, and governmental agencies.

Training and onsite assistance are the primary ingredients necessary to facilitate widespread technology use among teachers. These ingredients are not sufficient to assure that technology will be explored and used by the majority of teachers in a school. Other factors that affect whether teachers use technology resources include policies that encourage teacher experimentation and collaboration, the presence of incentives for teacher use of technology, administrative leadership about technology, and public understanding and endorsement of the importance of technology as a learning and teaching tool. Two of the most critical among these are:

i) having a vision and plan for using technology to meet instructional and professional goals, and

ii) evaluation and assessment policies that encourage technology use.

Teachers who are experienced technology users can cite many reasons for using technology in their classrooms. Less experienced users, however, sometimes give rather vague rationales for adopting technology-for example, "because students need to be exposed to technology; it's the future"-reasons that do not offer a vision of how technology might be used or a clear directive as to what a teacher might need to do differently. It is not only teachers that may lack a clear understanding of what technology can offer them, however.

Many school systems have not begun to explore the ways that technology can help them function better or differently as institutions and workplaces. Few teachers have been encouraged to view new technologies as professional tools that can help them do their jobs better, more efficiently, or in new ways.

For many teachers, the technology that has most revolutionised their working life has been the copying machine; not only has the drudgery of the ditto machine and preparing masters been eliminated, but copying substantially broadens the range of materials a teacher can easily make available to students. Yet, access to and use of copying machines is restricted or cumbersome in their school buildings—for example, there may be long lines at machines during precious times when teachers are not in charge of their students or budgetary restrictions on the amount of paper teachers are allowed to use.

Teachers will evaluate themselves and be evaluated by others based on the performance of their students. Teachers may be reluctant to experiment with new ways of teaching or new technological tools unless they are reasonably sure results will be reflected in improved student test scores. Seldom can such an assurance be made, because traditional standardised tests may not be particularly good measures of the kinds of learning fostered by innovative uses of some technologies.

This problem was illustrated by the experience of a California school that purchased computers for all its students and teachers, as well as videodisc players and television production equipment. These technologies were used for challenging projects, such as producing a television news show, that required students to work together and engage in planning and solving problems. When test scores on the Iowa Test of Basic Skills for the first year of this project failed to show any increases, disillusionment set in.

The computers were removed from students' desks or even sold and a new school board, stressing a "back-to-basics" approach, was selected. All this happened in spite of the fact that the new approach had hardly been in place long enough to reasonably be expected to show a strong impact and that the Iowa tests are not an appropriate measure of the ability to work cooperatively or to plan complex projects. The evaluation and assessment system by which teachers are judged can be either an incentive or disincentive for technology use by teachers. When decisions regarding promotions or tenure take technology use and expertise into account, teachers are encouraged to experiment and work in this area. Furthermore, if teachers are expected to use technology as a tool in their own development, this sends strong signals to the profession.

However, evaluating teachers on how often or how well they use technology in their teaching can have drawbacks, especially if, for example, the principal is not well versed in the various ways teachers can use technology effectively. Moreover, teachers may feel it is unfair to evaluate them if they have not received training and support in technology use. For example, one teacher who shared a computer among three classrooms admitted to her principal during her end-of-the-year evaluation that she did not use the computer much. She cited the logistical struggles associated with sharing the computer and the problems stemming from a lack of any computer experience or training. This teacher was marked down on her evaluation form for not using the computer, and her overall rating was lowered from "outstanding" to "good."

There are many schools that have thriving technology efforts, and many teachers who are using technology adeptly. The experiences of these places and people offer examples of strategies, pitfalls, and lessons for others that are beginning the process of integrating technology into teaching and learning. Schools have undertaken different strategies to get technologies used more widely in their educational programmes. These approaches share certain characteristics and they are not mutually exclusive; most schools combine more than one approach. The choice of approach will vary depending on the educational goals a site hopes to achieve with its technology and existing technological and human resources at the site. There are not a great deal of independent data on the effectiveness of these different strategies or which ones work best for different goals or in various kinds of schools.

There are a number of examples of approaches that schools say have worked for them. Behind each technology implementation strategy lies a set of decisions about how best to allocate scarce technology resources. Each place has made decisions about how to invest in and distribute hardware and software-not only which technology to buy, but whether to concentrate re sources to make some sites "technology rich" or spread the technology more thinly across many more sites. For example, some states have created model technology schools, described · more fully below, choosing to invest heavily in a limited number of "technology-rich" sites. Even within a building, there can be different models of implementation: distributing technology resources evenly among classes, as opposed to placing all the technology in a lab or other central location or targeting placement in certain classrooms, grades, or curricular departments.

Schools must also determine how to allocate human resource investments to assure that the technology will be used effectively in school buildings. Most of the strategies described below make significant investments in three elements of teacher support: appropriate and timely training; expertise to support and help teachers; and time for teachers to learn, "mess around" with technology, and work with colleagues. Some sites have chosen to develop a few "master teachers" at a site who are then responsible for teaching and training their colleagues, referred to as the "train-the- trainers" strategy. Other sites choose to invest more in providing an onsite expert, such as technology coordinator, who can support teachers and keep the school moving forward on incorporating new technologies. Still others choose to distribute the expertise by providing a critical mass of teachers at one site with technology tools and opportunities to learn, experiment, and adapt the technology to their own instructional needs. Additionally, giving every teacher a computer, training school administrators and establishing technology resource centres are implementation strategies, often used in combination with these other approaches.

A common strategy used to train teachers in many different topic areas is the "train-the-trainers" approach. In this model, selected teachers-those who are most enthusiastic and motivated to learn about a particular topic-are given intensive training. These teachers return to their buildings where they demonstrate and provide onsite training in the new techniques to other teachers. Teacher- trainers can share new knowledge with other teachers in any number of ways, including one-on-one peer tutoring or school-sponsored workshops on release days or in the summer.

An advantage of this model is that teacher-trainers can continue to be available to other staff after the formal training has ended. This train-the-trainers model has been used to support school improvement and change for a variety of curricular and pedagogical goals in the past, and has also been adopted in some places to facilitate the integration of technology into classrooms. The idea of training more than one person from a site seemed to be a key ingredient for the project's success. The change process follows an old notion, that two people in a building can support each other and encourage the change to take hold. However, training teachers in groups is not the only factor required for success. Another factor critical to the success of many train-the-trainers projects is the availability of support and resources for the teacher-trainers once they return to their buildings. If these trained teachers are expected to share their knowledge with colleagues, they must be given time and administrative support. There are personal characteristics that affect success; effective onsite technology leaders need interpersonal and organisational skills, as well as technical knowledge, in order to interest and motivate colleagues less inclined toward using new technology. An extension of the basic train-the-trainers model is being used at Webster Elementary School, a model technology school in St. Augustine, Florida. When their technology programme began in 1989, the school held training sessions for all staff two afternoons a week, from 2:45 p.m. to 3:30 p.m., as part of the normal workday.

As teachers began to feel comfortable with the technology and show enthusiasm, planners offered them the opportunity to become an expert in a particular piece of hardware or software. Those who were interested were given extra time to learn about the technology, more one-on-one training, and opportunities to attend technology conferences. A central list identifying these "experts" was posted in the building, and when other teachers had problems with a particular piece of hardware or software, they could consult the resident expert. According to the principal, teachers have developed pride in their new skills and have become quite self-sufficient. Technology use within the building no longer depends on outside facilitators or a single onsite expert.

A number of models have been used to supply the continuing specialised technology support that teachers find so valuable. These include providing temporary onsite support from commercial vendors or the school, or continuing support provided onsite by the school. At the beginning of a technology initiative, when a school is implementing a new technology plan or making a significant investment in hardware, bringing in a facilitator or resource person from outside of the school may be an important component of that plan. Research on implementation of innovations in schools has consistently shown that onsite assistance contributes to effective implementation of new ideas.

For example, if a commercial vendor is supplying a large amount of software and hardware to a site, its package will often include a resource person, employed by the vendor, who spends a designated amount of time at the site training teachers and helping to "work out the glitches" with the technology. Alternatively the school may commit funds for a teacher at the school to facilitate the technology implementation for an initial year or two. Often this strategy assumes that the facilitators will "work themselves out of a job" after the initial implementation phase. Some evidence suggests, however, that it may be difficult for onsite technology facilitators to phase themselves out completely.

In US a number of states have set up model technology schools, that is, regular schools in which a special emphasis is placed on developing student skills with and through the use of technology. By creating technology-rich environments and enlisting the involvement of those teachers and administrators who are most enthusiastic, model technology sites can "pave the way" for other schools to follow and can yield lessons to guide later technology investments. These sites can also serve as living laboratories that others can visit and learn from. Monterey Model Technology Schools (MMTS) Project is one such example-a partnership between the Monterey Peninsula Unified School District and the California Department of Education. The MMTS project represents one of six projects funded by the California Department of Education "to develop and validate a wide range of technology-based instructional and administrative programmes, practices and planning procedures to be disseminated to other schools throughout California."

Although there are 24 schools in the Monterey Peninsula Unified School District, only four (two elementary, one middle, and one high school) are Model Technology Schools. The four schools were selected not on the basis of their readiness to adopt technology, but on two other criteria-schools had to be located in a community where the demographics of the student body mirrored the state as a whole, and the schools participating had to provide a continuum. The project was funded by the state, and all teachers in the participating schools-whose interest in and familiarity with technology varied greatly-were asked to commit themselves to the project. It was recognised that teachers embrace instructional technology use at different rates.

By bringing together the technologically naive and fearful with the proficient and adventurous, it is possible to build a climate of mutual support and a culture of school technology use. It was anticipated that this process was more likely to be exportable to other schools than selecting a school where all teachers are "ready" to use technology. Originally funded in 1987, the first five years were focused on developing technology implementation projects and training, with dissemination activities targeted for year six onward. First-year training centered on "Technology Awareness Days" focused around the subject areas of language arts, mathematics, and science, to provide a general overview of what could be accomplished with educational technology. Gradually, what began as a technology training programme evolved into instructional mentoring, changing the focus from broad curriculum areas and operating skills to an emphasis on targeted student outcomes and behaviours.

At this point, MMTS developed the Classroom Intervention Plan (CIP), which became the centerpiece of the MMTS technology infusion model. Each teacher or teacher team develops a CIP outlining the curriculum emphasis, the desired and measurable end results; the necessary hardware, materials, and staff development; the evaluation plan; products and procedures for dissemination; and a budget. In addition to hosting scheduled visits by interested teachers and administrators, the Model Technology Schools provide three types of training and dissemination activities to teachers from Monterey and other districts in California:

i) *Technology demonstration centers*. Teachers who are well-trained veterans of the MMTS programme hold a day-long session in which they demonstrate their knowledge for a group of 2 to 12 teachers. Topics include such things as Info-Trek and Telecommunications, Logo in Mathematics courses, Using Laptops for Process Writting and Using Video and Camcorders across curriculum.

ii) *Technology training seminars*: More extensive two-day hands-on training workshops are offered to teachers on six different technology configurations: Telecommunications, One-Computer Classroom, Laptops and Process Writing, Multimedia, Video, Instructional Television. Teams of at least two teachers from the same school must attend together to facilitate support when they return. In addition to spending considerable time on hands-on exploration of hardware and courseware, participating teachers develop an individual project to use in their own classrooms.

iii) *Teacher productions*: The MMTS teachers have produced several documents, discs, and videos showcasing the projects they have implemented in their classrooms.

Some schools have chosen to start with model technology classrooms instead of schools, on a smaller scale. The Integrated Technology Classrooms (ITC), begun in 1987 in Bellevue, Washington, are one such example. Under a pilot programme in two elementary classrooms, teachers who had demonstrated enthusiasm for using computers were given a range of instructional technologies. The theory was that concentrating technology expenditures in a single classroom would demonstrate the value of technologies. The programme has been very popular and successful in drawing in other teachers. The number of ITC classrooms has grown from two in 1988 to more than 60 today. The ITC teachers, each in a different school, have worked with colleagues in their buildings to model technology use and help teach others about it.

Computers can help teachers carry out many aspects of their job, such as keeping records, updating lesson plans, and constructing tests. The rationale is that as teachers begin to see direct benefits from technology, in terms of saving time or expediting routine tasks, they will become more motivated to learn about computers. And as teachers gain confidence with and understanding of computers and related technologies in their own work, they may begin to experiment with using technologies with their students.

While some training is still important in this strategy, the real learning is believed to come from giving teachers unlimited access to the technology, new motivation for learning to use it, and a community of peers who are trying to master the same tools. Because teachers do much of their planning and paper work at home, some sites allow teachers to take their computers home routinely or keep them there; others provide laptop computers they can carry back and forth. One innovative programme that uses this strategy, and is sponsored by the Indiana Department of Education, is called A Computer for Every Teacher (CET).

Begun in 1990, CET made competitive grants to four small schools on the basis of proposals. Participating schools had to assure that all teachers and other professional staff in the school would participate. Every teacher in the funded schools received a computer and printer for use at home or in school, as they saw fit. This formal, public commitment also gave leverage to the coordinators when it was time to train the school staff. While there was some reluctance—and training did not turn around every teacher—almost all teachers and administrators learned how to accomplish some basic functions on the computer.

An outside evaluation of the project two years after it had been implemented in the four sites concluded that the programme was highly successful in meeting its goals and helped teachers improve their productivity, enhance their sense of professionalism, and increase individual and institutional esteem. Results of another experiment in Utah, the "Lifestyle Change" Project, indicated that teachers are highly motivated by the opportunity to have a computer of their own. Recognising the drawbacks of training teachers to use technology that is only sporadically available to them, this project put a computer in the hands of all teachers and administrators in Utah's Morgan School District. To qualify for a computer, which could be used at school or at home, teachers had to complete a comprehensive programme of training, including a course introducing Macintosh hardware, a gradebook package, word processing, graphics manipulation, a programme for developing classroom tests, Hypercard for software authoring, and a course on videodisc/CDROM. Teachers were also required to complete a portfolio of computer-generated materials such as grade-sheets, worksheets, Hypercard stacks, videodisc lessons, and word-processed documents.

When administrators are informed about and comfortable with technology, they become key players in leading and supporting technology integration activities in their schools. Some technology implementation efforts are building on these lessons by including principals or other key administrative staff in training opportunities offered to teachers. One approaches to include principals in school-based teams chosen to receive intensive training in technology use. For example, the Apple Classroom of Tomorrow Teacher Development Centre Project looks at the commitment of the principal when selecting teacher teams for training. Not only are principals encouraged to attend portions of the training programme with the teacher team, but they also must commit to the following conditions: release time for teachers to attend project training sessions, time for teachers to meet and plan each day, time for teachers to reflect on practise, and acknowledgment of the importance of their teachers' efforts to the rest of the staff.

Since 1990, Indiana has sponsored a statewide training programme specifically for principals. In its first two years, the Principals' Technology Leadership Training Programme served almost 400 Indiana principals. Over the course of a year, each principal takes four days of professional training with other principals at a central site. By scheduling sessions at different points in the year, the programme built in time for principals to go back to their schools, practice what they learned, and talk to staff and better define what they needed and wanted. In the workshops, principals learned about a broad range of technology and software available for classroom and office use and had a chance for hands-on exploration of a large collection of equipment. Participating principals have been very enthusiastic about the Technology Leadership Programme. In addition to reporting that they felt more confident and credible in dealing with technology, and better able to use technology for administrative tasks, participating principals said they were more capable of creatively using capital project funds, writing grants, or justifying expenditures to school boards.

After the training, many principals conducted training for their teachers; others reported that they were better equipped to think comprehensively about the technology in their schools and how best to use it. Principals rated an update session, held the following year, as very valuable, and most principals endorsed the need for some kind of ongoing "refresher programmes." Although there are no systematic data on the effects of training principals, the Apple Classroom of Tomorrow (ACOT) and Indiana examples demonstrate the feasibility and importance of enlisting principals in the diffusion of technology in schools.

Several factors seem to be essential for making the best use of hardware and software in schools. The first condition is ready access to hardware and software. Access cannot be assessed simply by looking at the numbers—how much hardware and software a school owns tells you little about its accessibility. Access also requires keeping hardware and software in up-to-date working order. For schools to incorporate technology into their programme in a meaningful, long-term way, they must recognise that there will be considerable costs. Technology must be repaired, upgraded, and replaced. In addition, seemingly small but ongoing costs-paper, printer ribbons, discs-have been known to cripple some technology initiatives. Schools must not view technology as a one-time investment but must budget for maintenance, upgrading, and replacement costs.

Available technology must be suited to the educational goals for which it is intended. Investments should not be made in technology for its own sake, but because it facilitates or extends instruction. This requires that a well-defined instructional vision should precede the technological one; teacher involvement in defining this vision is essential. Most successful schools have spent considerable time and effort planning for technology infusion before purchasing and distributing equipment. Often states require individual schools or classrooms to develop a technology plan.

The planning process requires people to think through the reasons for the technology before they buy it. It also helps to assure that sound educational reasons guide the technology decisions, instead of technology driving the educational process. Furthermore, the planning process brings people together and requires them to consider technological and instructional priorities. Although the resulting written plan affords a useful guide, it should be seen as a starting point, subject to revision over time. Nonetheless, it is the process itself that animates individuals, focuses their attention on instructional goals and technology's role in meeting them, and supports cultural changes in technology use. Plans should not be ironclad; they should make it possible to revise or adapt as the implementation process proceeds.

It is extremely important to think about continuation of the technology programme from the beginning. Although seed money can get things started, a successful programme will need to think about how technology use can be built into the continuing culture of the school. Research on organisational change has suggested that for innovations to be built into the organisation on a regular and permanent basis, adjustments must be made in at least five ways:

i) new practices must be codified as rules;

ii) curriculum must be revised to accommodate the innovation;

iii) training programmes must be established for newcomers;
iv) evaluation procedures have to reflect the new practice; and
v) project-related activities must be supported as line items.

The most central lesson from successful implementation sites is that those who wish to invest in technology should also plan to invest substantially in human resources. For every investment in hardware or software made, there should be a substantial investment in human resources, through expenditures for training, technical support, maintenance, and time to learn to use the technology. Life cycle cost models from business and industry support the critical role of training and support. These models suggest that hardware and software reflect approximately 30 percent of the total system cost over the technology's life cycle. Too often funding initiatives ignore the entire set of funding components and focus on hardware and software. And yet, experience has shown that only by addressing the other components, as well as the hardware and software, will the technology expenditures be successful. This is most particularly true of the staff development cost component. Teachers need extensive and ongoing training not only in how to use technology, but how to fully integrate it into their curriculum, instruction and assessment practices.

Some of what teachers can do with technology can be learned on their own through experimentation and self-instruction. But there are other things that teachers can learn best by attending a workshop or watching an experienced teacher. A good staff development programme will have opportunities for both types of learning. "Hands-on" training with technology is more than a gimmick or motivator; it is a necessity. Teachers must have the chance to make the computer work and gain confidence in their own competence before trying the same thing with their class. Moreover, the different types and applications of technology will require different amounts and kinds of training, support, and mentoring. For example, learning to use a telephone voice-mail system for communicating with parents and teachers is likely to require less training than learning to create multimedia. In workshops, teachers have opportunities to explore different technologies in ways that can be transferred to the classroom lessons using Hypercard and a videodisc player. There is no one generic course or workshop that can effectively teach teachers all that they need to know about technology. There is abundant evidence that "one-shot" or short duration training programmes have little impact. Teachers need time to learn, plan, try things out, reflect on their successes and failures, revise, and try again. This takes time-months, if not years.

Incentives like providing release time for teachers or paying them for staff development can increase the participation of teachers in good staff development programmes. But release time can be problematic. Many teachers want to minimise the amount of time they spend outside their classrooms. Some sites have tried to find creative and low-cost approaches to release time, such as conducting inservice activities onsite and having a teacher from the building as instructor.

Staff development is most effective when it is individualised. This means matching learning opportunities to the needs of specific teachers so they can choose what they need to know, how they wish to learn it, and the time frame in which they will learn it. This matches the "just-in-time" training models increasingly adopted by business and industry. Followup support and coaching after the initial learning experience are essential to effective staff development. Teachers cannot "learn all" they tried at a training session, even if it extends over several weeks. When they return to the classroom, the unexpected inevitably happens. At this point, teachers need to be able to access technical assistance and support. Some sites structure courses so that they meet periodically through the year or for a month or two, rather than one or two long days. Participants can try out new skills, practice, then come back to class and discuss or refine their approaches.

During teachers' initial efforts to integrate technology into the classroom, it helps a great deal to have support immediately and continuously available. Increasingly, schools are finding that electronic networks linking participants with instructors and each other provides a resource for continuing support. Technical and Pedagogical Assistance Because schools and teachers vary widely in their "technological readiness," most successful sites have found that they need to provide a variety of resources and supports. Some kind of onsite technical support-someone to set up, trouble-shoot and fix the machines—is usually necessary. However, sites are increasingly realising that it's not just technical expertise that is required of good support resource personnel.

Some technology— using educators are arguing that a new kind of professional is needed in schools—conversant in the technical issues but also experienced and knowledgeable about teaching methods, curriculum, students, and instructional design. Although most sites have made significant progress in helping teachers learn to use generic tools such as word processing, graphics, and desktop publishing, many are struggling with how to integrate technology into the curriculum. Supporting teachers in their efforts to integrate technology throughout their teaching is central if technology is to become a truly effective educational resource, yet true integration is a difficult, time-consuming, and resource-intensive endeavour. In many places technology is treated as a content area separate from the basic curricular areas.

Students and teachers are expected to become skilled in using technological tools. Yet few resources and expertise are available to help teachers put the technology to work in delivering curriculum in traditional content areas, such as English, math, or social studies. Learning to use the hardware and master the software tools is not enough; learning how to teach with technology-harnessing the tools for instructional ends-is a much more complex and lengthy process. If the goal of using technology is to change how teachers teach and how children learn, then teachers will need support and training to learn new pedagogical methods as well. More technology or more use of technology will not be sufficient to assure other innovations or reforms.

Teachers and administrators also should have a shared educational philosophy and a shared vision of how technology can facilitate that philosophy. To get going, many technology programmes have had to rely on a few particularly eager and dedicated teachers in a school. However, burnout can also be a real problem for these teacher-innovators, who are actively exploring technology resources, trying to keep up with new developments, and helping their colleagues. If a site truly wants to encourage its expert teachers to help their colleagues, these individuals could be compensated and recognised for their efforts. Although enthusiastic individuals may help spark technology efforts, experience suggests that schools should not rely exclusively on a small cadre of "gurus."

As a long-term strategy for continued technology use, expertise should be shared among multiple individuals at a single site. It is easy for a school to fall back on a technology guru who knows how to fix computers when they don't run and can suggest new strategies for using technology. But technology gurus may move to a new school, leaving the original school without a resource. Training multiple individuals increases the chances that expertise will remain. Furthermore, students can be effectively tapped as resources to help teachers with technology. At some sites, teachers bring a student or two along to workshops or other learning experiences. They are eager, available, and "free". Some knowledgeable students become great resources for the teacher.

Programmes that seek to involve a large number of teachers should identify incentives that encourage teachers to use technology. Many teachers will not be motivated by the mere presence of more technology in their classrooms, but they can be motivated by a concrete vision of how it can help them meet their instructional goals. For example, encouraging teachers to find their own favourite uses of technology or develop specific areas of expertise can be an effective long-term strategy. Putting technology in the hands of teachers can be a good motivator for teachers. Some states have given teachers computers as a "reward" for undertaking training. The role of the principal is crucial in promoting school technology use. Research has shown that leaders perform four important tasks:

i) obtaining resources,

ii) buffering the project from outside interference,

iii) encouraging staff, and

iv) adapting standard operating procedures to the project."

An essential partner in any kind of educational regimen is the community, represented by many individuals ranging from respected elders to powerful business people and officials elected at the local and the national levels. In the United States today, probably the most important agents of change in the community are the parents, in their dual roles as advocates for their children and citizens of the society. If the community fails to support the desires and standards of school people, the educators are destined to fail.

Effective technology implementation takes more time and effort than many anticipate when first undertaking technology initiatives. Changes have been continually necessary to overcome unforeseen obstacles, such as staff reassignments, delays in equipment delivery, gaps between technology knowledge and utilisation, or budget cuts, or to capitalise on unexpected success. State, and school-technology staff have continually revised their technology implementation plans based on evaluation results or unexpected events.

TECHNOLOGY ACCESS AND INSTRUCTIONAL USE

Technologies are used by schools for many reasons and to accomplish different goals. Technologies for teaching and learning vary in key characteristics: how richly they convey information, how suitable they are for whole classroom versus individual student use, how many pieces of equipment are required for simultaneous use by an entire class, how portable they are, how interactive and adaptable they are to individual student or teacher needs, and how flexibly they can be used by teachers in a school setting. These characteristics affect which technologies schools acquire and how they use them. To some extent, therefore, the amount and type of hardware and software a given site "needs" depends on the educational goals it expects to meet using technology. As a part of this planning process, the world countries are trying to designate some basic levels of technology to which each building and classroom should have access and to estimate the costs of such an infrastructure.

Technology can be a rich resource for teachers of all kinds to use in various educational settings. With available technologies, teachers can solve a range of educational problems, meet a variety of learning goals in all curriculum areas and serve varying age levels or student populations. Technologies offer teachers tools for accomplishing a variety of administrative tasks and for enhancing their own professional development. Before teachers and students can use technology for these ends, however, they must have access to the hardware and software. Telecommunications networks allow teachers to interact with other professionals and take advantage of resources beyond the limits of their school or community.

Here we will discuss an objective statistical portrait of the presence and use of educational technologies in American schools. The technologies covered include: computers of different levels of power and sophistication; computer-based equipment such as CDROMs, printers, and LANs; video resources such as televisions, videocassette recorders, cable, satellite, and videodisc players; and telecommunications networks and other technologies for two-way communication of voice, data, and graphics. Statistical information comes principally from three major surveys of schools, teachers, and students conducted in the United States between 1989 and

1993: the US portion of the 1992 Computers in Education Study of the International Association for the Evaluation of Educational Achievement (IEA), the 1991 National Study of School Uses of Television and Video conducted by the Corporation for Public Broadcasting (CPB), and the 1993 Communications Survey of Member Teachers of the National Education Association (NEA). Available data provide a picture of which technologies schools own and how much the average school has. In examining these data, however, one must remember that the presence of hardware is only a first step. They are also lacking regarding access and use of telecommunications networks by teachers and schools—in part, because these applications have been increasing so rapidly in the past several years.

Telecommunications networks allow teachers to interact with other professionals and take advantage of resources beyond the limits of their school or community. To use hardware effectively, schools also must acquire the computer software and video programming that give it life and must orchestrate the available equipment to make it accessible to teachers and students. Teachers need to see the value of using technology, have an idea of how to use technologies effectively to accomplish their instructional goals, and must receive the training and continuing support necessary to overcome the inevitable challenges technology poses. Estimating the amount of hardware available in schools today is relatively easy compared with estimating how frequently it is used and for what purposes. Yet information about the uses of technology is necessary for understanding the status of technology in today's schools.

A survey report from US illustrates the gap that often occurs between having access to technology and actually using it. Teachers who reported having various technology resources "readily available" at their worksite were asked if they used that resource "regularly." About 70 per cent of teachers who have access to video resources use them regularly, and about 60 per cent with access to personal computers use them regularly.

Among teachers who have access to multimedia, videodiscs, online databases, and other newer technologies, an even smaller share report using them regularly.

In USA of their total expenditures to date for technology, schools have spent the most on computers. Over the past decade, schools have spent roughly $500 million on new computers. Between 1989 and 1992, for example, schools added 1.1 million computers, increasing their inventory by nearly 50 per cent, from 2.4 million to 3.5 million. The typical high school in 1992 had 54 computers, and the typical elementary or middle school had about 25.

Computers

The United States leads the world in sheer numbers of computers in schools, although many of those in current inventory are older 8-bit models. Projections based on these data indicate that as of spring 1994, the number of computers used for instruction in K-12 public and private schools totalled about 4.95 million. During the last three years, the total number of computers in schools has risen by about 18 per cent annually-about 700,000 more computers per year—compared with an annual net of about 15 per cent during the those in current inventory are older 8-bit models, 1980s. Further projections suggest that by spring 1995, instructional computers in the United States will number about 5.8 million units—or approximately one computer for every nine students.

In US most schools have acquired computers incrementally, making purchases on different occasions. Consequently schools often have machines of varying age and power. The 8-bit Apple II computer, the most popular computer marketed to K-12 schools for use in instruction in the 1980s, still comprises a large portion of school computer inventories even though it is no longer made and cannot run most newer software. As of 1992, one-half of the computers used for instruction in the United States were 8-bit computers, primarily Apple IIs. An additional 26 per cent were somewhat more powerful but still comparatively limited computers with 16-bit processors and 8-bit transmission buses.

Most new software being designed today cannot run on either of these types of machines. The number of newer 16- and 32-bit computers has grown most rapidly at the high school level, where the inventories have been shifting fairly quickly away from Apple II and toward IBM PC-compatibles.

There have been several technological advances that might be called 'order-of-magnitude' improvements—changes involving a 10-fold increase in speed, miniaturisation of components, or a 10-fold improvement in capabilities. For example, at the beginning of the 1980s, floppy disks quickly replaced audiocassettes as input-output storage devices because they enabled users to access data at least 10 times as fast. Obvious examples today are the 16- and 32-bit computers whose order-of-magnitude increases in RAM memory and speed accommodate much more complex software than older machines; slowly these newer models are displacing 8-bit computers in schools. Four other order-of-magnitude improvements in personal computers have the potential to revolutionise computer use in schools: hard disk storage, LANs that connect computers within the school building, CDROMs, and laser printers. The first three each promise 10-fold or greater increases in access to programmes and data beyond the typical floppy-disk-based computer. Laser printers- especially in conjunction with LANs- promise substantial improvements in both the speed and appearance of printed output.

With hard disks and LANs, teachers and students can store programme and data files without worrying about the mechanics of loading programmes from diskettes. As of spring 1992, hard disks and LAN-connections were each available on about 20 per cent of all K-12 school computers. Based on current purchasing trends, the US Office of Technology Assessment estimates that at least 25 per cent of school computers have both LANs and hard disks today, and perhaps one-third now have one or the other. LANs are somewhat less prevalent in elementary schools than in high schools: 16 per cent of elementary school computers were part of a LAN compared with 24 per cent of high school computers.

Similarly, hard disks are found much more often on high school computers. As of 1992, 30 per cent of high school computers had hard disks compared with only 12 per cent of elementary school computers. CDROM drives allow storage of and easy access to large amounts of data, including text combined with detailed illustrations, animation, sound effects, and spoken language. Schools are at a much earlier stage in acquiring CDROM storage than hard disks and LANs, although CDROM drives are among the fastest growing computer peripherals.

According to one survey conducted during the 1992-93 school year, 44 per cent of US public schools had at least one computer equipped with CDROM, nearly triple the percentage found two years earlier; as with other computer technologies, high schools were more likely to have CDROM than elementary schools. Unfortunately, surveys have not yet collected data on the number of school computers equipped with CDROM, nor on whether computers so equipped reside on a network, what levels of schools have them, or how much they are used. CDROM equipped computers tend to be placed in the school library or media centre, to make them accessible to a larger number of students and teachers. Since the mid-1980s, when teachers and students began using computers as word processors, schools have also invested heavily in printers.

In 1989, for example, schools had one printer for every three computers, although more than 90 per cent of these printers were the slower dot-matrix kind. Four years later, dot-matrix printers still made up nearly 90 per cent of the inventory of school computer printers. Between 1989 and 1992, high schools acquired an average of one laser printer, but they also acquired seven more dot-matrix printers per school. Even less change occurred at elementary and middle school levels. In

1992, only one-sixth of elementary schools and one-third of middle schools had a laser printer for teacher or student use, compared with about two-thirds of high schools. Some of the more promising uses of computers by teachers and students-desktop publishing, mathematics instruction using analytic graphing and calculating software, information-gathering from CDROM encyclopedias or network data-bases-can only be accomplished in a limited way, if at all, on most of today's school computers.

The speed, memory, and peripherals available on school computers affect the ways teachers use them in their teaching and professional activities. Another key factor that affects how teachers use computers is the location of the computers within the school building. Placing several computers in a common location, such as a computer lab, enables teachers to use computers with the whole class simultaneously, but also makes it more difficult for teachers to integrate computer activities with other learning activities throughout the day.

When computers are in labs, teachers lack the easy access needed to use them as an everyday tool or resource. About one-half of all computers used for instruction in 1992 were located in centralised computer labs, while about 35 per cent were located in teachers' classrooms. The rest were placed in other special instructional rooms, libraries, offices.

As schools' inventory of computers continues to grow, more computers will probably be placed in classrooms, although experience from the past decade suggests that this is likely to occur gradually. Schools with a substantial inventory of technologies are investing increasingly in laptop computers, which can be moved around the school building and taken home by teachers and students. Some schools place their laptops on carts that can be wheeled around to make any teacher's classroom into a temporary computer lab. No data are available on the number of laptops currently owned by schools.

Student-computer ratio gives some indication of how many students have to share a computer. This ratio has declined dramatically over the past 10 years; as of 1992, United States schools averaged one computer for every 13 students. Closer examination of available data suggests, however, that there is enormous variability in student-computer ratios from school to school. For example, there are vast differences between schools with the lowest "computer density" and those with high computer density. For example, elementary schools with high computer density average only seven students sharing a computer, while those with low computer density average 35 students sharing a computer.

There is also a wide range in student-computer ratios across states-varying from a low of eight students per computer in Wyoming to 22 per computer in New Hampshire. This variability may reflect the fact that some schools, districts, and states launched large-scale technology initiatives over the past several years, while others have emphasised different educational reforms, placing less emphasis on computer acquisition.

Another way of looking at whether computers are equitably distributed is to compare the student- computer ratios of schools having different demographic characteristics. Using the most representative national data available, this kind of analysis shows that the most pronounced differences in computer density among schools at the same level are between small schools and large schools. Schools with fewer students tend to have many more computers per capita.

These differences are not simply due to differences between urban and rural schools. For example, in middle schools, Placing computers together in a computer lab is common and supports some forms of instruction. Teachers also need computers and other technologies in the classroom if they are to use them regularly as teaching tools. Where the differences are most pronounced, small schools have approximately 14 students per computer, while large schools have .This pattern of more resources in smaller schools also holds for video equipment such as VCRs and televisions. This finding may reflect the tendencies of many districts to allocate technology funds on a per building basis, rather than a per student basis. It could also reflect commitment to providing every school building with what is viewed as a "critical mass" of technology.

Percentage of minority students in a school has a different relationship to student-computer ratios across the three school levels. While there are small differences among elementary schools with different proportions of minority children, there are no differences among high schools. The largest differences appear in middle schools, where schools with less than 4 per cent minority enrollments have an average of 14 students per computer, while schools with more than 24 per cent minority enrollments have 18 students per computer. Ratios of students to computers do not indicate which students within the schools have access to and experience with computers. Research done in the 1980s found that in the early years of computer adoption in schools, poor and minority students had less access to computers both at home and at school. In addition, data showed small gender differences favouring boys over girls in access to computers in school.

Recent data from the IEA study suggest that while girls are still somewhat less likely to report using computers at school or receiving instruction in computers, ethnic minority students are slightly more likely than white students to report having had these opportunities. The advantage of ethnic minority students over white students will come as a surprise to those who read the statistics from previous studies in the early to mid- 1980s. There are few reliable data about how much the 4 million-plus computers in schools are actually being used; the only estimates are rough ones. One problem is that reports of use vary greatly depending on the source.

Using reports of computer coordinators and making certain assumptions about shared use of computers yields the following estimates:

i) Computers are used about one and three-quarters hours per student per week at elementary schools.

ii) Computers are used approximately two hours per student per week at middle schools.

iii) Computers are used approximately three hours per student per week at high schools.

iv) On average, computers are used about two hours per week per student across all school levels.

Data on the number of teachers who use computers vary greatly depending on how one defines a "computer-using teacher." Two different definitions- one quite inclusive, the other much more stringent-yield very different estimates. In addition, these definitions have focused on use of computers for direct instruction with students only; no data are available on other teacher uses such as administrative tasks or professional development. In the 1992 IEA survey, a "computer-using teacher" was defined liberally as a teacher who "sometimes" used computers with students. Using this broad definition of how much teachers themselves report using computers, 75 per cent of 5th-grade teachers, and about half of 8th- and 11th-grade teachers were found to be "computer-using" teachers. A more stringent way to define "computer-using" teachers is to include only those teachers who clearly required most or all students to do work on computers. Under that definition, about one-half of 5th-grade teachers, one-third of 8th-grade English teachers, and one-fifth of 11th-grade English teachers qualify-roughly 20 to 30 percentage points fewer than under the other definition. If an even more stringent criterion is employed, one related to frequency of use, the percentage of teachers who identify themselves as "computer using" is even lower-about one-third the size of the original group.

The advice of "experts" in educational technology about what teachers should do with computers has been constantly changing-from BASIC programming, to Logo programming, to tutorials provided by integrated learning systems, to generic computer applications such as word processing, to activities integrated with existing curricula, to student-developed multimedia presentations, and now to telecommunications-based learning communities.

According to survey data, however, when teachers are using technology for instruction they do so in much more traditional ways. For example, IEA survey data indicate that the most common activities on computers for elementary students have been drills in basic skills and instructional games. Also popular at all levels are general "computer literacy" activities: use of various instructional programmes and generic computer applications such as word processing. School computer coordinators estimate, for example, that students spend the most computer time learning to type on computer keyboards and use word-processing programmes. Interestingly, the estimated share of computer time students spend on mathematics declines between elementary school and high school from 18 to 8 percent, suggesting that math teachers are using computers primarily for students to practice arithmetic skills rather than to solve higher-level mathematics problems. Between 1989 and 1992, the one significant change in the allocation of student computer time was a one-third decline in the time spent teaching students computer porgramming as a part of computer literacy education.

Available data suggest that in secondary schools, computers are used relatively infrequently for teaching and learning in traditional academic subjects, far less than in classes focused on teaching students about computers. Although most middle-school and high-school students reported using computers for at least one academic subject, for most subjects, this meant using computers only once or twice over most of the school year. If one examines only those classes for which students had used school computers on at least 10 occasions during that school year (i.e., once every three weeks since the survey 'was completed 30 weeks into the school year), more than one-third of secondary school students reported using computers this often in a computer class, but for other subjects the percentages were much lower: 9 per cent for an English class, 6 to 7 per cent for a math class, and only 2 to 3 per cent for a social studies or science class. Since word processing is a major activity in secondary school computer education classes as well as in business education classes, it seems clear that high school is still primarily a place to learn how to use word processing, rather than a place where teachers have students do word processing in order to achieve other academic goals. This is even more likely for other applications, such as spreadsheets and database programmes, which have been less integrated by teachers into subject-matter instructional practices than word processing.

At the elementary school level, the survey data suggest that students use computers overwhelmingly in an exercise mode-doing drillsand playing various kinds of games with instructional content-rather than in a productivity mode, using computers as a tool to solve problems or create products. For example, 53 per cent of 5th graders said that they used school computers to play games on 10 or more occasions during that school year, while 13 per cent said they did word processing. Similarly, about 65 per cent of 5th-grade teachers report that computers in their classes are mainly used for language arts skills practice and games, while 18 per cent say they are used primarily for writing and word processing; about 17 per cent report both categories of use.

Video Technologies

For the past few years there is a growing interest in teaching that uses video as a resource. This is due to the expansion of cable programming with educational content, the widespread availability and familiarity with videocassette recorders, developments in computer-based video, and an increase in the supply of videodiscs for schools. For the next several years, the basic projection mechanism for video will likely remain the television set or the composite monitor. According to a 1991 survey of public schools in US, the mean number of TV sets per school was 12; the median per school was seven sets. Unlike the case for computers, the availability of television sets is nearly the same among elementary, middle/junior highs, and high schools. In 1991, there were slightly more than four television sets for every 10 full-time teachers at each of those levels. In a 1993 survey, 41 per cent of teachers reported having a television set in their own classrooms.

In the United States, almost every school has at least one VCR. As of 1991, the mean number per public school was 6.3, or one for every 1.9 televisions. As with televisions, elementary, middle, and high schools have about the same number of VCRs per capita. The typical school has one for every five teachers. Teachers use VCRs for showing commercially produced videos and for recording programmes from cable or broadcast television and showing them later. Most schools maintain a library of prerecorded cassettes. Based on Corporation for Public Broadcasting (CPB) data, 67 per cent of teachers reported that they record shows at home for school use, and many others said that they ask other school personnel to make recordings for them. It is interesting to note that, unlike most surveys on computers in schools, data on video and television are given at the classroom level, or per teacher, rather than per student.

Cable connections

In US between 1991 and 1993, there was a 25 per cent increase in the proportion of schools with direct cable connections, so that now as many as three-fourths of all schools have cable somewhere in the school building. Another survey found that roughly one-third of all teachers in the sample reported having cable TV service in their own classroom. "Access to cable" can mean different things to different schools, however, depending on the channels carried by the local cable provider and the type of service to which the school subscribers. One study, for example, reported that, although 61 per cent of schools reported having access to the Public Broadcasting System (PBS), and almost as many had access to national commercial broadcast networks, far fewer had access to commercial cable channels that offer a number of educational programmes, such as the Discovery Channel (35 percent) or the Learning Channel (16 percent).

Increasing number of schools and districts are obtaining satellite dishes, giving them a wider selection of programming than that offered by their local cable distributor. According to one report, the proportion of schools directly accessing satellite broadcasts nearly doubled between 1991 and 1993. As of 1993, 50 per cent of all school districts reported having a satellite dish as did 17 per cent of all public schools. High schools are more likely to have satellite dishes than are middle or elementary schools . One contributor to the recent growth of satellite dishes in middle and high schools has been the Channel One project created by Whittle Communications, Inc.. Whittle installed satellite reception systems in schools that committed to show students "Channel One," a daily 12-minute news programme, which includes two minutes of commercials. Each participating school also received two VCRs and enough 19-inch television sets to put one in each classroom. By the spring of 1993, three years into the programme, approximately 12,000 schools were receiving Channel One, according to Whittle. A three-year evaluation report of Channel One translates this to mean an audience of over 18 million teens, or almost 40 per cent of the 12-to 18-year-olds enrolled in school.

Videodisc Players

Teachers commonly videotape programming to show in a linear format; for example, to have students watch a 10-minute instructional television segment or an hourlong programme from beginning to end. An instructional videodisc, by contrast, usually contains many thematically related but short discrete segments of action and still video. The teacher or student can access and directly control the segments of visual and audio materials. Using a remote control, barcode reader or computer equipped with hypermedia software, the teacher can browse through, access, and play different segments of video in any order-using them, for example, to illustrate and enhance a presentation or discussion. The number of public schools with at least one videodisc player doubled between 1991 and 1993, to 41 percent. During that period the variety of educationally appropriate videodisc software increased substantially, and at least two states allowed videodiscs to appear on the list of "texts" approved for adoption as options to printed textbooks.

As with many other technologies, more high schools report having a videodisc player than do middle and elementary schools. Still, in terms of access, the question is not whether a school has videodisc equipment but, rather, what proportion of teachers can use the videodisc equipment without difficulty. In a 1991 survey of teachers, only 12 per cent reported that they had videodisc players readily available to them in their schools. Furthermore, less than half of those teachers reported actually using the videodisc regularly for instruction.

Camcorders

In US most schools have at least one camcorder. As of 1991, this was true of 80 per cent of elementary schools and 90 per cent of middle and high schools. Some 8 per cent of all schools even had their own TV studio in 1991, including 22 per cent of high schools. Camcorders and other video equipment allow students and teachers to undertake new kinds of learning activities, such as making their own video reports or recording student presentations. But not every school makes this equipment available to teachers or students. According to one survey, just slightly more than half of the schools with camcorder or studio facilities used these for student instructional activities, including giving students production experience or feedback on their own performance in a classroom activity.

In the CPB survey, about 80 per cent of US teachers said they had used instructional television or video some time during the school year. About one-half of all teachers said they had used TV or video in teaching in the past month. The teachers most likely to have used video recently are elementary school teachers and secondary science and social studies teachers. Estimates derived from the CPB data suggest that across all subjects, secondary students, on average, spend one and-one-half hours per week watching video material in school. The average elementary student is estimated to watch video in school for slightly more than one hour per week.

Two-Way Communication Technologies

As schools attempt to make learning more meaningful to students and to anchor it in "real world" examples and experiences, more and more educators are looking for technological tools that help teachers and students to communicate with the outside world. Schools are acquiring and exploring a range of technologies and tools that facilitate two-way communication. These include new ways of using older technologies such as telephones, facsimile machines (fax), and modems; combinations of different technologies, such as distance-learning systems; and new kinds of telecommunications hardware, software, and services. Because many of these latter applications are so new in schools and are expanding so rapidly, up-to-date survey data about access are not available. However, some data have been collected about telephones, modems, fax machines and distance-learning technologies in schools

Telephones and Fax Machines

Telephones and fax machines are two communications resources with great potential for teaching and learning; too often, however, they usually are accessible only to school administrators. Access to telephones, in particular, is currently a major technology issue being discussed by teachers' organisations. Although one-third of all teachers in a recent survey in US felt it was "essential" to have a telephone in their classroom, only one teacher in eight had a telephone in the classroom that could be used for outside calls. Less than 1 per cent had access to voice mail. Most teachers have to make calls from the school office or a faculty lounge, where many colleagues share a phone and most conversations cannot be held in private. Sixty-three per cent of teachers surveyed felt it is "essential" for parents and teachers to be able to contact one another during the school day; almost three-quarters of teachers feel that having telephones in the classroom would improve parent-teacher communication at least "somewhat." Among the reasons for restricting teachers' access to phone services are concerns about costs and unregulated use. Installation and monthly charges tend to be prohibitive for a restricted school budget, in part because phone companies often charge schools higher-priced business rates for installation and message unit charges. Teachers seem less interested in having access to fax machines. Although approximately one-fourth of teachers had access to a fax machine in their school, most did not view it as an important instructional resource. Since fax machines are relatively rare in schools, it is likely that most teachers are not aware of their instructional or administrative potential.

Modems

Modems, which allow computers to communicate electronically across a telephone line, have been available almost from the beginning of personal computing. Although many districts have modems, they were originally dedicated primarily to administrative uses. With the advent of new educational applications of electronic networking, however, modems have become an important gateway to telecomputing. In recent years schools have begun installing more modems for teachers to use for instructional activities. For example, in the 1989 IEA survey, slightly more than one-fourth of US schools had a modem that could be used by teachers or students. By 1992, that percentage had grown to 38 per cent overall, including 60 per cent of all high schools, 35 per cent of middle schools, and 33 per cent of elementary schools. As with other technologies, the presence of a modem in a school building does not tell much about the average teacher's access to telecomputing. Many teachers may consider access to a modem anywhere in the school sufficient for the occasional special project. Over the long run, however, if telecomputing is to be used regularly, classroom access to a modem or alternative connection will be necessary.

Distance-Learning Technologies

For more than a decade, schools have used live one-way video technologies via satellite or broadcasting in conjunction with two-way audio or other two-way media such as computer networks or fax machines to expand learning opportunities. Some distance-learning projects also involve two-way video communication through microwave or fiberoptic transmission. Distance learning is most often used by schools in remote, rural, or sparsely populated areas and by other schools that lack traditional educational resources, such as a qualified teacher for a low-enrolment course.

Distance-learning technologies allow high schools, for example, to offer courses, such as advanced calculus, Japanese, and Russian, that may not be available otherwise. The prevalence of distance learning is difficult to estimate, in large part because its definition is inexact and inconsistent. In US in a 1991 survey, about 17 per cent of districts reported having some capacity for live video with interactive capabilities. Another survey found that in the 1992-93 school year, 28 per cent of districts had some distance- learning capability and that 11 per cent of all schools were involved in distance-learning-double the number from their data taken two years earlier. In this survey, high schools were much more likely to have distance-learning capabilities than either middle or schools, probably because high schools use it to offer advanced courses for which they may not have enough students to hire a qualified teacher. In about 70 per cent of the districts with distance-learning capabilities, two-way interaction is limited to voice-only interactivity through dial-up telephone lines, an arrangement that allows only a small number of the participating classrooms to communicate on-air with the studio video instructor during a given class period. About 20 per cent of districts' distance learning employs two-way video. Available surveys do not assess the number of classes or students using distance learning for a portion of their instructional time. The use of distance learning in K-12 settings has increased considerably in the last several years. While fewer than 10 states were participating in distance-learning projects in 1987, virtually every state is now involved with distance learning in some way.

Technologies for Linking to WANs

Creation of networks for microcomputers ushered in a new era in the development of computers. Computer networks use electronic pathways to connect one computer with other computers, enabling a person at one terminal to communicate with other people, to transfer information electronically, and to use computers in a distant location.

Local area networks (LANs) consist of computers connected together in the same physical area, usually within one building. LANs can be connected to other LANs, expanding the people and computers with whom users can communicate. Networks of computers able to communicate over larger distances are called wide area networks, or WANs. LANs are often a building block for a WAN. WANs may span cities, states, or even continents; most are closed systems set up for a specific group of users.

The internet is neither a LAN nor a WAN but an "lnternetwork"—a net-work of networks that share a common set of protocols. It provides access to databases and networks around the world. LANs are typically used to share resources, such as printers, and to deliver instructions; schools typically use WANs or the internet to access external resources. The modem modifies the digital information used by the initiating computer so that it can pass across telephone lines. Another modem at the other end restores the information to a digital form that can be used by the receiving computer.

A variety of information services with varying levels of sophistication are available to help people com-municate and transmit information across computer networks. To use an information service, a computer must have client software to communicate with the server software at the other computer. The most common services of computer networks are electronic mail (e-mail), transfer of computer files, and remote log-in. E-mail allows the user to send messages to another person, a group of people (a list), or an electronic forum (also called an electronic bulletin board) where many people can read them. Computer networks also let users copy and transfer electronic files from a computer where they are stored, called the server, to the user's machine. These files may be written documents, maps, graphics, images or video, or software files. Remote log-in enables a user at one location to use a computer at a distant location for such activities as searching through library catalogues or making airplane reservations. These three services are the building blocks of more sophisticated applications of networks.

Some types of connections may sup-port only one or two of these three basic uses; for example, a connection may permit sending e-mail to a distant colleague but may not support transferring files from that colleague's computer. One popular service is a chat room. In a chat room, messages entered by any user immediately show up on the screen of all users, and a written record of the conversation is maintained. Chat rooms are a form of synchronous communication; e-mail, by contrast, is an example of asynchronous communication. A small but growing number of teachers are gaining access to other kinds of information services avail-able through the internet, such as Gopher, World Wide Web, and Wide Area Information Servers (WAIS). These services enable people with internet connections to view and transfer files or to access extensive.

The basic prerequisites for access include the appropriate client software and a modem or other connection to a WAN; in addition, the WAN must support the desired service. "internet connectivity" can take place at many different levels. Some

WANs have restricted connections to the internet that allow only certain kinds of services, such as exchanging e-mail or using Gopher but not using World Wide Web or WAIS. A IAN or WAN that is fully connected to the internet will support any of the varied and growing services that follow internet protocols—procedures defining how to make new services work over the internet—and will allow users to link with any other computer that is also fully connected. As yet, there is no one organisation responsible for administering or supporting the internet, so getting support in the use of internet services has been a problem for teachers. Organisations that currently pro-vide teachers with connections have only limited support for beginners and have given little thought to helping beginners acquire the necessary client programmes. Some help is available, however, in the form of books, electronic documents, and commercial products that combine books and ready-to-use software.

For each electronic community of teachers, whether organised around a curriculum project or a topic of mutual interest, there is typically a group that provides the organisation and a support structure to help define that community. Typically, the group provides such elements as a name, a registration procedure, a framework of expectations, a timeline, print or electronic materials, and support services.

Examples of organising structures include: curriculum projects, such as AT&T Learn-ing Circles, NGS Kids Network, and TERC's Global Laboratory; discussion groups, such as the Consortium for School Networking (CoSN); and programmes, such as NASA's Spacelink. Educators can access information services through either commercial service providers, such as Amer-ica Online, CompuServe, Prodigy, Delphi, and Apple's eWorld; or through nonprofit service providers, such as state-supported networks.

Both commercial and nonprofit providers are actively soliciting participation of teachers, schools, and districts. While these organisations do not presently provide full connectivity to internet resources, they do offer extensive support to users. Some of the state networks have text-based menu systems.

There are several possible ways schools can link up with wide area networks (WANs) in general, and the internet in particular. The options for telecommunications connections are shifting, as individual modem dial-up connections give way to more sophisticated and higher speed connections to WANs and the internet; these options include connections via LANs, high-speed phone lines, dedicated connections, and so forth. Other models of connectivity include Integrated Services Digital Network (ISDN), satellites, digital cable, or other linking technologies. Several connectivity formats are described briefly below; however, no national data are currently available regarding how many schools and districts are using any of these options.

Connectivity often begins with a pioneering individual teacher making personal connection to a network through a dial-up modem-in some cases a regular telephone line and a computer outside the classroom, in the principal's office or the library. The teacher might access any of several services with different features: one aimed primarily at internet connection; one that seems easy to use, such as America Online; a state-level network, such as The Texas Education Network (TENET); or a special interest network such as EcoNet for ecology. Most dial-up services now offer some form of internet connectivity, and through that, access to other services, a factor that is gradually reducing earlier problems with unconnected networks.

To reach the internet directly, a user must go through an internet node. Nodes are allocated by regional network providers who provide networking hardware as well as the electrical connection. Some schools have established their own internet node and server at a school and connect that to the school's LAN. The server can be a point of presence on the network where resources of value within the school can be published. As of December 1994, in US, there were 189 internet sites in K-12 schools. For example, the Ralph Bunche School in Harlem has its own internet server. A single low-speed data-only line is sufficient to support multiple users, providing they do not require video or heavy use of high-bandwidth services, such as the web. Other schools avoid the costs of an internet node by using an indirect connection; that is, connecting their LAN to another one nearby that has internet connectivity. This nearby connection could be a district headquarters, a college, the high school, or a friendly business.

Sending video images over networks requires substantial bandwidth and entails higher costs than other options. Networking capacity that handles digital video will also increase the performance of all other kinds of networking. In addition, there are new kinds of network-based multimedia presentation software, such as WWW browsers like Mosaic, that can be used only over networks with video capacity, even if they do not use video. An internet connection through a "T-1"1.5 Mbps (megabits per second) line connected to a school LAN could support the entire school.

Although many network services are currently offered via single modem dial-up, dedicated access to the internet is becoming increasingly attractive because, although it entails higher costs up front, it may be more cost-effective and certainly less limiting in the long run. Furthermore, these connections can support multiple users simultaneously, offer access to many of the most innovative and high-powered telecomputing innovations, and serve as a common mode of access to a broad range of electronic communities.

Despite the advantages and growth of alternative connectivity scenarios, few schools currently have any connectivity options. In those that do, most are still using a single phone line connected to a dial-up modem and computer. A lack of telephone lines in schools and especially in classrooms is cited as the greatest barrier to teachers' participation in electronic communities. Many of the telephones that do exist in schools often serve administrative purposes and are not available to teachers for classroom use or for making outside calls to networks. For example, a recent study of TENET reports that "84,683 phone jacks were in Texas' 1,058 school districts.

Faster modems and LANs that enable multiple that only 11 per cent had access to wide area net-users to connect to outside networks at the same work services as well as a local area network; none time are not yet commonly available in schools. A of these schools used their LAN to distribute data 1990 survey of 485 California schools reported from the WAN.

Teachers' and students' access to the educational services now appearing on the internet is problematic, because few schools have information infrastructures capable of routing data to individual classrooms. Unlike higher education, K-12 institutions typically have neither host computers powerful enough to allow direct access to the internet nor a web of telephones and modems that could enable individual internet usage through dialing up a provider. Further, many schools do not have networks that transmit data around the entire building, and the networks in individual classrooms often have such low bandwidth that sending educational material from computer to computer is very slow. Interconnecting different types of networks within a school or district is also a complex technical challenge.

An increasing number of states are organising and funding state networks for teachers and students and sometimes for other public agencies and businesses. In a 1993 survey, 33 states reported supporting one or more telecomputing networks, for K-12 instruction. Six more states had a partially operational network, and nine more had one in the proposed or planning stages. Some of these networks use a design whereby teachers dial into local computers, which in turn process and store messages. These local computers are placed to maximise the number of teachers who can reach them through local rather than long-distance telephone calls. Most state networks aim to provide services at little or no charge to teachers.

For teachers who are not local-a significant proportion-"800" numbers are often provided at substantial expense to the state. State networks vary considerably in their scope, purpose, sophistication, and support services. Among the most ambitious are Virginia's PEN , which aims "to guarantee access to the internet to every public school educator at no charge," and TENET. Many states have established networks with gateways to other networks. For example, Florida's Information Resources Network (FIRN) provides free electronic (e-mail) to all educators and a menu that offers access to many internet-based services. FIRN also supports distance-learning services, an automated card catalogue, a technical assistance system, staff development teleconferences, and satellite-delivered training for teachers. Other states have established less ambitious networks, offering such services as e-mail lists, news groups, and computer conferencing. Indiana, for example, supports both a statewide fiber-optic network for education called Intelnet, and a bulletin board called IDEAnet for educator communications, conferencing, and database access.

Montana administers the Montana Educational Telecommunications Network (METNET), connecting individual schools with Distance Learning Centres, Regional Training Centres, and Compressed Video Sites. Oklahoma encourages schools to link up to SpecialNet, a network designed to facilitate special education. New Jersey Link (NJLink) served over 4,000 teachers in 1993, offering free information resources, communication with other educators, and other network services.

Other networks in which educators participate have been organised by school districts, communities, and the private sector. School districts use networks to foster districtwide educational goals and to link with local and out-of-town electronic network resources. While district networks often include only such services as exchanging e-mail within the district, posting messages on bulletin boards, and reaching the internet with e-mail, some are more ambitious. The Boulder Valley internet Project, for example, is a collaboration of the local university and the school district that aims to link as many schools as possible with high-speed connections and to encourage teachers to use these resources. Similar efforts are under way in other districts.

Community-based electronic networks link many of the functions of community life with one another. In these electronic communities, anyone in the geographic area served can participate. As of January 3, 1995, there were 130 of these local FreeNets in 42 states, according to an online survey. These networks offer bulletin boards for students sharing work, expedite inquiries to local public agencies, facilitate information sharing and research, provide local databases, and so forth. With over 35,000 registered users and over 10,000 logins per day, the Cleveland FreeNet, operating out of Case Western Reserve University, is probably the largest community network in the world and a model for community-based networks.

The network provides users with everything from e-mail services, to information about health care, education, technology, recreation, law, auto mechanics, or just about anything else the host operators would like to place on the machine. Anyone in the community with access to a home, office, or school computer can connect to the system, 24 hours a day, and use these services. All of it is free and all of it can easily be accomplished by a first-time user. Not surprisingly, community-based networks face the challenge of developing viable models of low-cost network services that are accessible to all community members. Some keep costs low by offering users access to larger networks for the cost of a local telephone call.

Current survey data provide some information concerning the school use of telecommunications hardware and software for information gathering, electronic mail, and collaborative instructional work. In the 1992 IEA survey, data collected at the school level indicated that in 10 to 15 per cent of schools at least one teacher used electronic mail/information networks; usage was higher at the high school level than in elementary schools. Approximately the same percentage of high schools reported using online databases such as Dialog. IEA also asked separately about two instructional programmes involving telecomputing — AT&T Learning Circles and the National Geographic's Kids Network. According to the survey, AT&T Learning Circles had been tried in about 4 per cent of schools nationwide at all levels, and the K-8-oriented Kids Network garnered participation in 6 per cent of elementary schools and 3 per cent of middle schools. Altogether about 20 per cent of schools reported using one or more telecommunications service. However, no information was available about the number of teachers using the service at any given site.

A year later, the 1993 NEA Communications Survey inquired of its sample how many teachers had ever participated in a "learning network at school, such as the AT&T Learning Network or the National Geographic Society's Kids' Network" (6 per cent had); whether the respondents were currently engaged with their students "in an online collaborative teaching or distance learning [activity]" (4 per cent were), and whether they "had access to" public electronic mail and information utilities such as Prodigy (19 percent), Compuserve (14 percent), America Online (7 per cent), and Dialog (9 percent). In addition, 4 per cent said they had access to the internet through their school. Altogether, nearly 25 per cent of the NEA sample of responding teachers reported having access to at least one of these telecommunications services. While the NEA sample is not representative of the US teaching population, if the same percentage were applied to all US schools, it would mean that as many as 600,000 teachers nationwide were involved in telecomputing. The extent of telecomputing activity among teachers is not well understood-especially now as potential opportunities for participation are mushrooming. Furthermore, although the number of telecomputing teachers is growing rapidly, these data indicate that the great majority of US teachers still do not have access to telecommunications services.

To meet the needs of teachers, telecommunications software should have the following features: a user-friendly interface; network connectivity among multiple computer systems; multiple options for connectivity, including the internet; the capacity to send formatted nontext enclosures, such as graphics, spreadsheets, and data video images; the ability to enable the same message or formatted data to be sent to multiple parties who use diverse software and hardware configurations; the ability to download and manipulate files at user computers without re-formatting; and be capable of being easily updated.

There are a growing number of internet-based telecommunications software tools for information searching and retrieval. NCSA Mosaic and other similar tools are among the most powerful because they provide a user-friendly means of connecting with World Wide Web and Gopher resources on the internet. The web includes online documents that consist of text, images, sounds, video, and animation on a range of topics, such as Gaelic texts, art exhibits, movie clips, and electronic magazines. Documents can include footnote like links to other files, so that by pointing and clicking, the user can move from one document to retrieve relevant information from other documents located elsewhere on the internet. In addition, the telecommunications functions in the Mosaic interface are automated so as to be nearly invisible to the user. However, Mosaic is useable only through a direct, relatively high-speed connection, and this type of connection is still rare in school settings. Telecommunications, with the access it can provide to resources beyond the classroom walls, has considerable educational potential.

POLICIES ON THE ACCESS OF TECHNOLOGY

In US, the state policies have an important influence on teacher use of technology. A telephone survey and review of state literature indicates that states have taken diverse approaches to addressing the challenge of educational technology. One way that states can influence local technology use is through state staffing and support for educational technology. Staffing policies vary considerably across states. In one state, the educational technology coordinator is an associate commissioner; in others, a part-time consultant. Some coordinators are located within a media division, others in an instructional technology unit, and some in a telecommunications office. Some state educational technology units have budgets in the many hundreds of million dollars; other states fund little more than a single staff person. All but seven states reported that they require or recommend integrating computers or information technology into the curriculum. About 25 per cent of the states actually mandate the integration of computer technology across the curriculum. In some states continue to equate technology policy with mandating courses about computers rather than assisting teachers to learn to teach with a range of technologies. Twelve states require that public schools offer computer-related courses such as keyboarding or computer literacy, while an additional 20 states recommend to districts that such courses be offered. Today 19 states mandate computer competency requirements for graduating seniors. Additionally, as states define and set new achievement standards consistent with the Goals 2000: Educate America Act, many are attempting to address skills students will need to work with technologies. M

Many states do not mandate technology competency, but recommended that districts make computer competency a graduation requirement. North Carolina recently has designed an innovative, detailed competency-based curriculum in technology including considerable emphasis upon "information skills." Beginning in 1995, students will have to pass a performance-based competency test. The state survey suggests that the amount of educational technology hardware in a state is not correlated with the state's tendency to establish requirements in either student technology competency or in teacher technology training. The relative amount of computer technology available in a state should be used with great caution as an indicator of that state's commitment to technology in instruction.

The most common uses of technologies in schools reflect educational philosophies of instruction that view students as recipients of information dispensed by the teacher and the acquisition of specific skills and knowledge. However, many technology experts feel that the real potential of technology lies in its capacity to support pedagogical approaches that encourage students to become active participants in their own learning and to acquire critical thinking skills and more complex understandings. The potential for more than an electronic blackboard is one of the most compelling reasons for pursuing educational technology. Right now, however, a gulf exists between the ambitions of technology experts and software developers and the practice of teachers in classrooms. Helping teachers use technology to facilitate different educational philosophies and teaching practices will require substantial change in curriculum, instructional methods, and teacher understanding. In addition, further study is needed about the quality and relative effectiveness of various instructional uses of technologies and their applications.

REFERENCES

Ackermann, E., *Tools for Teaching: The World Wide Web and a Web Browser*, 1996.

Jay P. Sivin and Ellen R. Bialo, "Microcomputers and Related Technologies: An Overview," a report on research covering 1986 through 1990.

Karen Sheingold and Martha Hadley, *Accomplished Teachers,* New York, NY: Bank Street College of Education, 1990

Patil, V.T., *Virtual Education: Dimensions of Educational Resources*, Authorspress, New Delhi, 2002.

Gene I. Maeroff, *The Empowerment of Teachers: Overcoming the Crisis of Confidence,* New York, NY: Teachers College Press, 1988

5

Technology for Teaching and Learning

A medium is in part a channel for conveying content; new media such as the internet allow us to readily reach wider, more diverse audiences. Just as important, however, is that a medium is a representational container enabling new types of messages. Because the process of thinking is based on representations like language and imagery, the process of learning is strongly shaped by the types of instructional messages we can exchange with students. Emerging representational containers like hypermedia enable a broader, more powerful repertoire of pedagogical strategies.

The global marketplace and the communications and entertainment industries are driving the rapid evolution of high-performance computing and communications. Regional, national, and global information infrastructures are being developed to enhance our abilities to sense, act, and learn across barriers of distance and time. The ways in which information is created, delivered, and used in business, government, and society are swiftly changing. To successfully prepare students as workers and citizens, educators must incorporate experiences creating and utilising new forms of expression, such as multimedia, in the curriculum. Information infrastructures offer channels for delivering these technology-intensive learning experiences to any place on demand.

The information superhighway metaphor now widely used to convey the implications of high-performance computing and communications is inadequate. Backward-looking metaphors focus on what we can automate—how we can use channels to send conventional forms of content more efficiently—but they miss the true innovation: redefining how we communicate and educate by using new types of messages and experiences to be more effective.

Because emerging forms of representation such as hypermedia and virtual reality are in the early stages of development, we are just beginning to understand how they shape not only their messages but their users. Many people are still reeling from the first impact of high-performance computing and communications—shifting from the challenge of not getting enough information to the challenge of surviving too much information. The core skill for today's workplace is not foraging for data but filtering a plethora of incoming information.

The emerging literacy we all must master requires diving into a sea of information and immersing ourselves in data in order to harvest patterns of knowledge, just as fish extract oxygen from water with their gills. As educators, understanding how to structure learning experiences to make such immersion possible is the core of the new rhetoric. Expanding traditional definitions of literacy and rhetoric into immersion-centered experiences of interacting with information is crucial to preparing students for full participation in 21st-century society.

Conventional distance education is similar to traditional classroom instruction except that it uses technology-based delivery systems. In contrast, emerging forms of distributed learning are leading to a reconceptualisation of education's mission, clients, process, and content. This new instructional paradigm is based on shifts in what learners need to be prepared for the future as well as on new capabilities in the pedagogical repertoire of teachers.

The following four new forms of expression are shaping the emergence of distributed learning as a new pedagogical model.

i) Knowledge webs complement teachers, texts, libraries, and archives as sources of information.
ii) Interactions in virtual communities complement face-to-face relationships in classrooms.
iii) Experiences in synthetic environments extend learning-by-doing in real-world settings.
iv) Sensory immersion helps learners grasp reality through illusion.

Using information infrastructures, educators and students can join distributed conferences that provide an instant network of contacts who have useful skills and immediate answers to questions. In time, these informal sources of expertise will utilise embedded groupware tools to enhance collaboration. On the internet, online archival resources are increasingly linked to the World Wide Web, accessible through webcrawlers like Mosaic and Netscape.

Eventually, artificial-intelligence-based guides will facilitate navigating through huge amounts of stored information. Virtual exhibits that duplicate real-world settings are emerging; these environments make a wide variety of experiences possible without the necessity of travel or scheduling. Distributed science projects enable shared experiments to be conducted across time and space, with each team member learning more about the phenomenon being studied and about scientific investigation than would be possible in isolation. Combined, all these capabilities to enhance information-gathering and creation form knowledge webs. However, access to data does not automatically expand students' knowledge; the availability of information does not intrinsically create an internal framework of ideas that learners can use to interpret reality. Although presentational approaches transmit material rapidly from source to student, this content often evaporates quickly from learners' minds. To be motivated to master concepts and skills, students need to see the connection between what they are learning and the rest of their lives and the mental models they already use.

Even when learners are drilled in a topic until facts are indefinitely retained—we all know that the sum of a triangle's internal angles is 180 degrees—this knowledge is often "inert;" most people don't know how to apply the abstract principles they memorised in school to real-world problems. To move students from assimilating inert facts into generating mental models, teachers must structure learning experiences that highlight how new ideas can provide insights in intriguing and challenging situations.

The curriculum is already overcrowded with low-level information; teachers frantically race through required material, helping students memorise factual data to be regurgitated on mandated, standardised tests. Using information infrastructures as a fire hose to spray more information into educational settings would make this situation even worse. Without skilled facilitation, many learners who access current knowledge webs will flounder in a morass of unstructured data.

A vital, emerging form of literacy that educators must communicate is how to transform archival information into personal knowledge. However, moving students from access through assimilation to appropriation requires educational experiences that empower knowledge construction by unsophisticated learners, helping them make sense of massive, incomplete, and inconsistent information sources. Weaving learner-centered, constructivist usage of linked, online materials into the curriculum and culture of traditional educational institutions is the next stage of evolution for conventional distance education.

The involvement of global media networks in higher education has been widespreaded. There is ample evidences of individual projects and gatherings focusing on the use of new media and technology in higher education by established and new higher education institutions. In some instances, major computer hardware and software companies are acting as a catalyst for change, providing expertise and resources to institutions to encourage them to adopt technology in their administrative and academic endeavours. In this respect, the companies are seeking to establish a presence as a carrier, rather than a provider, of educational content.

The use of technology and new media is in many cases still in its experimental stages. While it is facilitating expansion into distance education by many higher education providers and brokers, and the rhetoric is global, the focus is in most cases at this stage on a local or at best national market. This may well change in the future, as programmes become established and appropriate technological infrastructure becomes more widely available. There are already several examples of small-scale master of business administration (MBA) courses which enrol students internationally and which employ a variety of media and technologies.

There are new providers emerging, and that some of these have global aspirations. Many originate in North America, in contexts that differ significantly from the Australian environment. For example, the use of the word 'university' is regulated in Australia. In the United States, many organisations use the word in circumstances that differ from the Australian understanding of the term.

There is evidence of a major segmentation of the market, with new providers targeting the 'lifelong learning' cohort. This includes corporate training/education, a domain only partially catered for by traditional universities, and a profitable market—being largely self-funded and employer-funded. Continuing and professional education is a component of lifelong learning for those in the workforce. There is a widespread perception that traditional institutions are not meeting the needs of the lifelong learning cohort and that the field is open for new providers to meet market demands.

One obvious, and problematic, outcome of this segmentation is that traditional institutions may be left serving the less-profitable traditional undergraduate market, which is largely government-funded or family-funded, in a time when governments are increasingly endeavouring to cut public outlays. Looking further into the future than the medium-term prospects, this arguably represents one of the most significant challenges to, and opportunities for, established higher education providers.

Converging technologies and the potential for global reach have led some to assume the existence of one 'global market'. Conversely, this investigation would support the notion of the fragmentation of world markets and the development of numerous niche markets on an international and regional, rather than global scale. There is no 'blanket' approach to delivery of a global education programme and that the education providers who identify their niche and meet the demands of the relevant stakeholders are those that will be best placed in a global marketplace.

The development of high-performance computing and communications is creating new media, such as the World Wide Web and virtual reality. In turn, these new media enable new types of messages and experiences; for example, interpersonal interactions in immersive, synthetic environments lead to the formation of virtual communities. The innovative kinds of pedagogy empowered by these emerging media, messages, and experiences make possible a transformation of conventional distance education—which replicates traditional classroom teaching across barriers of distance and time—into an alternative instructional paradigm: distributed learning.

As life and workplace demands have changed as a result of this "technological revolution," so have conceptions of the skills and knowledge children will need to become successful adults and the relevant educational experiences they should encounter while attending school. As a result, technology, specifically in the form of computers and the internet, has become a major focus of education policy and reform in recent years. National, state, and local initiatives have provided schools with computer hardware and software, allowed schools and classrooms to connect to the internet, and supported technology-focused professional opportunities for teachers. As the numbers of computers and access to the internet in schools have grown, so have the number of questions being asked about the extent to which these technologies are being used in schools and classrooms and for what purposes.

Over the past 20 years, education technology has been a major focus of reform and policy at the state and local levels. Such initiatives have been guided by the goals of increasing the availability of computers in classrooms and schools, assisting schools with internet access, and providing resources and guidance for teacher training and the integration of technology into the curriculum. The availability of computers and the internet has increased significantly in the nation's schools and classrooms. This increase has been coupled with initiatives aimed toward understanding how best to use technology to improve teaching and learning and training educators to use technology effectively.

Existing research on education technology includes a small number of national studies that describe teachers' use of technology, as well as their training to use these tools. Specifically, this research suggests that most current and past uses of education technology have typically supported traditional notions of teaching and learning. For example, in the early 1980s, students most often used computers for drill and practice. Typically, drill-and-practice software consists of sequences of worksheet-style questions that automatically adjust their difficulty to match individual students' responses. Also, in the early 1980s, teachers typically used computers to teach students programming skills. They rarely used computers for content-related instruction; students were more likely to learn about how to use computers at school than they were to use computers to learn about mathematics or social studies.

In the early 1990s, the practice of using computers for programming had declined considerably and an emphasis on using computers as a tool for learning content had emerged. However, the primary use of computers remained drill and practice in elementary schools in the early 1990s. In high schools, it was classes on computer education, and middle schools provided a combination of drill and practice and computer education. Finally, as the decade of the 1990s progressed, school computer use had shifted to some degree to reflect a greater emphasis on problem solving and in-depth learning and less emphasis on drill and practice and basic skills.

Teachers are in fact using computers or the internet generally more frequently to complete a number of instruction-related tasks than to augment instruction itself. For example, they may use these technologies to help prepare for classroom instruction (e.g., to access research on best practices, download information to present in class) or to complete administrative tasks (e.g., to record and calculate grades). In US, two-thirds of all teachers used the internet in their effort to find information for use in their lessons, and about one-third reported doing so on at least a weekly basis. In addition, teachers may also use technology to communicate with parents or students about students' performance, assignments, or special events. They may also use technology to communicate with other members of their profession to share ideas or strategies for presenting content or helping students who are struggling with the content.

As the brief history of technology use for learning suggests, the way educators teach and students learn has not changed dramatically over the past two decades. The research on teacher change and instructional reform in general indicates that such changes in teacher practice are often slow, minimal, or even nonexistent. A number of factors contribute to the success or failure of instructional reforms.

One important factor the literature has identified is that teachers do not always have opportunities to learn about and practice instructional reforms. In the area of technology, teachers may have learned about how to use computers and adapt their teaching from a variety of sources—teacher preparation programmes (for prospective teachers), professional development activities (for practising teachers), and informal learning opportunities such as assistance from classmates, colleagues, or students. Professional development research suggests that teachers' opportunities to learn about education technology during traditional professional development activities are often lacking. Often described as an important vehicle for school reform, professional development activities in general have been widely criticised for being relatively ineffective.

Specifically, they have been described as short term, devoid of continuity due to inadequate follow-up and the lack of ongoing feedback from experts, isolated from the participants' classroom and school contexts, and characterised by too few opportunities to learn by doing and reflecting with colleagues. In fact, while a majority of teachers participate in such activities, a small percentage of teachers report feeling very well prepared to integrate technology into instruction.

Teacher preparation programmes have received similar criticisms. Traditional programmes for prospective teachers have been described as fragmented, superficial, and unconnected to real classroom experiences. With respect to education technology, some observers have claimed that prospective teachers are not getting the training they need to successfully integrate technology into classroom instruction. For example, some researchers have reported that most students training to become teachers do not routinely use technology while in the field and do not work under supervising teachers who can advise them on using technology in the classroom.

Additionally, about half of the technology training that prospective teachers get in the classroom is delivered as part of other classes (i.e., methods and curriculum classes), and the other half is provided in the form of stand-alone technology classes. Furthermore, most teacher-preparation programmes provided by schools, colleges, and departments of education do not have written, funded, regularly updated technology plans.

Informal learning opportunities, in addition to these formal learning opportunities, may also provide teachers with assistance using technology. Peer collaboration, in particular, has been heralded by many teachers, researchers, and policymakers as essential for teachers' continuous learning. Teachers may benefit when they learn about technology from one another and provide one another with motivation to continue working with this resource.

In recent years, policymakers have recognised that teachers and administrators need resources and organisational capacity to implement instructional reforms. For example, teachers' ability and willingness to use computers and the internet may depend, to some extent, on the schools and classrooms in which they work. Specifically, certain characteristics of classrooms and schools, such as equipment, time, technical assistance, and leadership, may act as either barriers to or facilitators of technology use.

On a most basic level, teachers may be more likely to integrate computers and the internet into classroom instruction if they have access to adequate equipment and connections. As the number of computers in schools has grown, so has the availability of the internet in schools and classrooms. Between 1994 and 1998, internet availability among public schools increased from 35 to 95 percent. However, availability is not the same as use.

Although the presence of computers and the internet has grown sharply in recent years, much of the technology equipment currently in schools and classrooms is from an earlier generation of technology—computers with less processing power, less storage capability, and limited capacity for being linked together electronically. Using data from 1998, Anderson and Ronnkvist have concluded that although computing capacity for instruction has improved substantially over the past several years, there are a number of "major deficiencies". For example, they found that most of the computers in schools do not have the capability to run a large variety of multimedia software and are also limited in how they can access graphical information on the internet.

The nation's schools have been increasingly challenged by policy initiatives "to do better, and to do differently", pushing teachers to change the way they teach. At the same time, teachers face many other challenges, including rapidly increasing technological changes and a greater diversity in the classroom. With regard to technology, there is often little time in teachers' schedules to become familiar with hardware and software or to learn to integrate the new technology into their lesson plans. Lack of time to become acquainted with technology and learn to use it has been identified as the greatest obstacle to the effective use of education technology.

A full-time computer coordinator, for example, may assist teachers with using computer software and hardware or adapting their teaching practice to include computer or internet use. However, according to one study, less than 5 percent of all schools have such a staff member. Furthermore, where they are present, computer coordinators typically spend a significant amount of time teaching students, and much less time assisting teachers.

Principal leadership has been described as one of the most important factors affecting the effective use of technology in classrooms. Principals who exhibit leadership are instrumental in modelling the use of technology in classrooms. They understand how it can support best practices in instruction and assessment and provide teachers with guidance for its use. Principals may also participate actively in professional development activities related to education technology and provide teachers with opportunities to learn how to use these resources. For some teachers, lack of principal leadership may prove to be a barrier to their effective use of technology.

ACADEMIC USE OF TECHNOLOGY

The increasing ease of use and improved presentational and interactive features of technologies such as the world wide web are leading many academics to use technology for teaching for the first time in a significant manner. However, although there has been widespread adoption of new technologies for teaching in the last few years, they have yet to bring about major changes in the way teaching is organised and delivered. Without such changes, though, technology-based teaching will remain a marginalised activity, while at the same time leading to increased unit costs.

Following are the number of different reasons to justify the use of technology for teaching and learning:

i) to improve access to education and training
ii) to improve the quality of learning
iii) to reduce the costs of education
iv) to improve the cost-effectiveness of education.

Different people in different positions tend to place different emphasis on each of these rationales. For instance, what has really set fire to many university professors is the possibility of improving the quality of learning through the use of multimedia. The same professor though who is a startling innovator in the use of the technology for teaching can at the same time violently oppose any suggestion that more students might be served by the institution through using technology: more means worse — or at least more work for faculty. Other professors are fired up by the idea that all the world can access their ideas, their research, their wisdom through the web — a passion to widen access to their teaching. This is not always accompanied though by a similar passion to improve the quality of their teaching, as can be witnessed very easily by surfing their web pages.

Some politicians and business people see technology simply as a replacement for labour, and therefore anticipate that technology when applied properly will reduce the costs of education. Unfortunately, this is to misunderstand the nature of the educational process. While labour costs can be reduced by applying technology, unless done sensitively and carefully it can also lead to a large decline in the quality of learning, which in turn will eventually lead to a less skilled workforce. Lastly others look to technology to improve the cost-effectiveness of education. This is not the same as reducing costs. The argument is that for the same dollar expenditure learning effectiveness can be increased, or more students can be taught to the same standard for the same level of investment.

While then technology is unlikely to reduce substantially the costs of education without a parallel loss in quality, the wise use of technology can simultaneously widen access, improve the quality of teaching, and improve the cost-effectiveness of education. Using technology for teaching can help universities serve the public more cost-effectively, and in particular can prepare students better for a technologically based society. There are also many things that are valuable in education, as in life, that technology cannot do, and we need to recognise that, but that is another topic.

Before putting forward the strategies for institutional change to exploit fully the potential of new technologies for teaching, it is important to understand the relationship between technology and the organisational structure of institutions using technology.

Most manufacturing companies producing physical goods have until recently adopted a 'Fordist' organisational model. This is characterised by the production of uniform products ('you can have any colour you like, so long as it's black'), economies of scale (initial setup costs are high, but large volume results in each extra unit having increasingly lower marginal costs), a division of labour (work is broken down into different elements conducted by different classes of worker), hierarchical management (decisions are made at the top, and passed down the line of command), and organisation of people and processes into discrete, large units which themselves are hierarchically managed (e.g. production, payroll, personnel, marketing, sales). Best examples of this kind of manufacturing organisation and structure in education are the larger, national autonomous open universities in countries such as the United Kingdom, Netherlands, Thailand, Indonesia, India, etc., many of which have over 100,000 students.

However, the rapid increase in the size and scale of 'conventional' universities in Canada, the USA, and many other industrialised countries since the 1960s has led to many elements of the industrial model being found in today's universities, such as division of labour and increasingly large classes. Nevertheless the core activity of teaching in conventional universities has been relatively untouched by the industrial process.

Information technology though has led to the growth of many knowledge-based and service industries which have a very different structure from the industrial or 'Fordist' model. These newer forms of organisation have been labelled as 'post-modern' or 'post-Fordist' in structure and are characterised by the following:

i) heavy dependence on information technologies (telecommunications, computers);
ii) customised products and services tailored and adapted to needs of individual clients;
iii) creators and developers of new knowledge/new ways of doing things, or transmitters and modifiers of existing information;
iv) directly networked to clients: rapid and immediate feedback used to modify products and services;
v) rapid development and change: organisations are dynamic and move very fast;

vi) often small-scale and specialist; dependent on partnerships and alliances with other organisations with related but different competencies;

vii) decentralised, empowered, creative workers, often working in teams;

viii) strong leadership characterised by clear but broad vision and objectives, playing an integrating, co-ordinating and facilitating management role;

ix) global operations post-modern industry sectors are often chaotic and characterised by new players, new amalgamations and unpredictable emergence of dominant technology-linked organisations.

The new technologies will be exploited best by those that establish post-modernist forms of organisation. We have not yet seen any advanced and sustainable form of such an organisation in higher education, but elements are already visible in organisations such as the University of Phoenix's online programmes, Nova South-Eastern University in Florida, the National Technological University, and the proposed Western Governors' Virtual University in the USA.

Nevertheless, there are certain features of a traditional university that lend themselves to the new post-Fordist environment. First of all, a university is an extremely decentralised organisation. It has a large and highly creative 'core' of staff, faculty, who when they apply themselves are capable of creating new applications software, developing expert systems, and adapting or even inventing new forms of teaching and learning. Furthermore they have one valuable commodity or quality that is lacking in many dedicated open universities: they have a research capability that enables them to generate new knowledge in a wide range of subject areas that can be assembled and marketed through the use of technology. Lastly, conventional universities have the advantage of what the marketing people call a strong brand image. There are signs that some conventional universities, with good leadership and a shared vision, and sometimes goaded by strong external pressure from government, are regenerating and restructuring themselves to meet the technological challenge.

TECHNOLOGY-BASED LEARNING

The ease of use or 'transparency' of technologies such as the web and video-conferencing makes it much easier than in the past for faculty to develop technology-based learning materials and course delivery. The web, for instance, allows a teacher easily to adapt materials created for lecture or classroom use and present them as attractive colour graphics and text. Once the materials are created as web pages, it is a simple matter to make them available for off-campus as well as on-campus students.

In an increasingly competitive environment, and where technology-based teaching is increasingly open to public inspection, the organisations that will survive, as with any of the other new knowledge-based industries, will be those that provide services that the public values, at a better price and quality than the competition. However, on most Canadian university campuses, amateurism rules in the design and production of educational multimedia.

There are several components of quality in technology-based educational materials. The first is the quality of the content, which is where the brand image and the research capability becomes critical. Is this unique or valuable teaching material for which there is a need or demand? This is not usually an issue in most research universities.

However, the second component of quality is the standard of media production. Are the graphics clear? Are the screens easy to read? Is the sound and video easy to hear and see? Are the unique features of each medium (video, audio, text, computing) fully exploited? Is the material well assembled? Is the screen designed in such a way that students intuitively understand the range of activities open to them and how to accomplish them (interface design)?

The third component of quality is instructional design. Are the learning objectives clear? Does the material result in the desired learning outcomes? Does it have the appropriate mix of media to achieve the learning outcomes in the most efficient manner? What is the quality of the interaction between student and learning materials? What is the role of the tutor/instructor relative to the technology-based learning? Is it well structured? Can the students easily find all the material they need and move around the teaching materials easily?

The fourth is the quality of delivery. Are the materials easy for the student to access? Can learners ask questions or discuss materials with other students? Who gives feedback? What happens if they have technical problems? At what times is help available?

New technologies are likely to remain marginal, despite high levels of capital investment, and will merely add costs to the system, if we do not at the same time deal with structural changes in our institutions, and in particular if we do not make fundamental changes to the ways we organise teaching.

Web-based Learning Tools

E-learning is the systematic use of networked multimedia computer technologies to empower learners, improve learning, connect learners to people and resources supportive of their needs, and to integrate learning with performance and individual with organisational goals. It is capturing the interest of corporate leaders in ways which previous incarnations of educational technology failed to do. Market research and the pronouncements of global opinion formers are creating a perception of a world in which e-learning will become one of the dominant applications on the internet. For academic educational technologists, this presents some interesting opportunities and challenges.

The educational system of today needs to impart to all learners three new foundational skills: to make learning a relevant and lifelong process—a process of continuous growth change and evolution and adaptation. Technology deployed in education can help remove inequities between the schools of developed and developing nations, between inner cities and suburbs, between urban and rural areas.

The true challenge is for education to freeze a model that captures quality and computer technology into an integrated communication system. The web-based learning modules promises to change how some students learn and how some faculty teach at the university. The decision to build a site involves a careful consideration of costs in terms of time and effort weighed against potential beneficial learning gains for students. Possible benefits for students using web modules include convenience for distance learning, expanded and easier access to digital materials, greater student control of learning, and enhanced online collaboration. The modules can be used as homework for face-to-face classes, as the building blocks of distance education courses, and as stand-alone instructional units for public outreach. Web-based materials incorporate the latest in web design with interactive exercises, video, audio, and communication features and often meet high standards of instructional and graphic web design. The faculty who create such modules learn quickly that designing and assessing their value can be challenging, requiring skill in instructional and graphic design, programming, and assessment of learning outcomes.

Understanding the benefits of the web can help instructors decide if producing web-based materials is worth the effort. Remote access is the primary incentive driving web-based instruction. Web-based learning materials are a convenient alternative for students who cannot or do not want to take face-to-face classes, go to the lab during open hours, or attend a recitation in person. However, the realities of users' hardware can make assigning web-based materials problematic. Web sites with complex graphics or large video or audio files can cause painfully slow downloads on computers with 56K or slower modems.

Research shows that web users are impatient, waiting ten seconds or less before they lose interest in a website. Before building a site, make sure that the end user will be able to easily access the site given your anticipated technical design. Easy access to information is an integral part of web-based technology, as users are immediately linked to up to date digital libraries, online publications, and more. Access can also mean exposure to authentic, real-world information not easily available through other sources. For example, foreign language students can view the websites of real businesses, universities, online museums, or other websites in different countries. Some links to websites are an integral part of learning, as students find specific information, analyse documents, or evaluate the credibility of sources others, like dictionary or library links, are embedded throughout the site as resources. The web can present video, audio, and animated materials as well as give programmed feedback for user-entered responses.

The web-based materials can be regularly updated or revised. Java applets can be used to create complicated interactive learning materials; easy-to-use freeware for creating interactive assessments is available on the web. For example, instructors can automate tedious or time-consuming tutorial activities such as memorisation, the correction of mathematical problems, musical ear training, or foreign language production and comprehension. For those deciding to use any of these capabilities, the cost of development, greater download times, and more complex hardware capability must weighed against the benefit for the student. The overarching concern about the use of more complicated programming is whether the outcome of using a particular type of software actually helps a student achieve the learning objective of a lesson. Some web-based lessons allow students to choose which instruction they receive, making more individualised learning possible. Student control is especially desirable for lessons that cover a wide range of difficulty so that students can enter and exit the lesson at an appropriate difficulty level, and is also important for skill building exercises so that students can repeat a lesson until it is learned. While student control is often seen as desirable, it also means he instructor must relinquish some control of how students use materials.

Bulletin boards and e-mails built into learning modules allow students to respond to each other and the instructor, giving people the opportunity to revise and reflect upon their work. E-mail can also enable collaboration among students from different schools, states, nationalities, and ethnic and socio-economic backgrounds. Many web modules are now used in hybrid contexts, as students in face-to-face classrooms work and communicate with each other online, either during or outside of class. Bulletin boards can remove discussions from classrooms or extend them, allowing students to communicate with each other at their own convenience and in a safe environment. They also make course dialogue both visible and permanent, as threaded discussions are archived and referenced by both students and faculty.

If managed well, online discussion can make possible more reflective discussion, as students have the chance to revise and think about written statements. Yet online discussions must be monitored and sustained, and students must perceive that there is good reason for participation, especially if it means extra time. For the instructor, the amount of time and effort devoted to moderating online discussion is not trivial. The decision to build a complex, web-based learning module should not be taken lightly. The costs in terms of money, time, and effort that could be better used elsewhere can be formidable. Instructors can reproduce the successful efforts of publishing companies by making conscious choices about lesson content and instructional design and by carefully assessing the value added to student learning.

Learning materials contain philosophical assumptions about how students learn. These are implemented in an instructional design. It is important that philosophical and design choices are conscious choices, yet in many cases these decisions happen by default as designers unconsciously translate and reproduce existing instructional methods used in books, other media, or in their classroom practice directly to their online lessons. If resources are available, hire an instructional designer; if not, have a designer review the plan and make suggestions. Some important considerations for designing the core of a lesson are the following:

Intended use and audience: Class-linked websites are usually either supplements to class work, or substitutes for existing class material. Supplementary materials may be optional, providing for a more comprehensive understanding of class content, or required, such as exercises that allow for extra skill development. If, on the other hand, the lesson is used as a substitute for class work and/or materials, web content should function as class material and equal or improve on the quality of existing materials and instruction. Outreach websites used by the general public face a different kind of scrutiny and planning than sites used by classes, departments, or campuses. These sites are meant to be used by a wide variety of people and are designed to motivate and entertain as well as educate. Outreach sites should have a professional appearance and should be easy and enjoyable to use. Large-scale curriculum efforts conduct surveys and interviews to learn if the planned lesson fit the needs of the projected users. For smaller scale projects, a needs assessment is a more informal effort: the instructor can talk with students, other instructors, and content experts about what they want from new lessons, how lessons fit with current class activities, and how projected lessons fit with recent trends or discoveries in a discipline.

Learning and performance objectives: web-based learning materials are built around a learning goal, which can be as straightforward as students will learn the four bones of the knee or as complicated as students will have a comprehensive understanding of the factors leading to the great depression. In self-contained materials, the learning objective should be explicitly stated so that students will have a clear idea of what they will learn by the time they finish the lesson. Students also need to understand when they have achieved the learning objectives, so some way of letting them know when they are successful should also be built into the site. Stating the learning objective explicitly will also help outline the lesson and guide the development of assessments. Performance objectives are derived from learning objectives. These are clear statements about what students should know and be able to do at the end of a lesson stated in terms of empirical assessments or observations.

Instructional method/pedagogy: Much of modern instructional design is grounded in pedagogical theories emphasising inquiry-based, active, or problem-based learning. Developing learning materials on the web that are personally meaningful and which engage students in the active analysis, synthesis, and evaluation of information is challenging. Interactive, hands-on exercises or simulations embedded in web sites are a step toward active learning. Active learning activities also include visiting websites with authentic contexts or sites that afford access to primary source documents. Electronic communication can also foster collaboration and distributed expertise by removing spatial and temporal barriers to collaboration, and by allowing access to common data sets. Some critics of the recent push for educational technology observe that many web-based lessons merely reproduce traditional instruction by emphasising the memorisation of content and its regurgitation on tests. "Gift-wrapping" is a common practice of professors who take written lecture material and post it on the web, but there is nothing about the web that forces instructors to present material in this manner.

Scaffolding: While students are learning independently, it is essential to build ways to access help with subject matter. Hypertext can link students to terms, definitions, explanations, and images. Help can be in the form of text, supplementary links, illustrations, or video/audio files and can be programmed so that they are always available, or delivered to students only after they make repeated attempts at an exercise.

Assessment online: Assessments are an excellent way to add interactivity to the site, keep students engaged and reinforce material through the movement of clicking typing, and dragging and dropping. When giving feedback, decide whether the students are told only "correct" or "try again" or if they are given more detailed responses. Feedback can include extended explanations of why specific answers are correct or incorrect, and assessment questions can also link back to the material in the lesson. Web-based assessments are an appropriate way to provide instructors with a valid picture of what their students know. The two related issues for assessing students online are item type/assessment method and communication with the instructor.

Computers are good at automating multiple-choice, matching, and short fill-in-the-blank test items, but are usually not set up to grade essays and performance assessments. There is a relationship between item type and the kind of knowledge that can be validly assessed. Multiple-choice, matching, and short answer items are more suited to recognition, memorisation, and problems with clearly defined answers, while essays, performance assessments, and portfolios better assess higher-order thinking skills such as analysis and problem solving. To use these latter types of assessment, a certain amount of personal interaction and communication are required. Essay questions can be submitted via e-mail or students may post a response to a threaded discussion question.

Clear instructions and navigation: Instructors often counter that students could stop and read the instructions, but people tend to scan,. rather than read, what they find on the web. Developers find a way to force users to read the instructions, such as presenting a page with instructions which the user cannot skip and asking that they click an "ok" or other button to continue into the lesson. Another suggestion for improving both instructional design and website design is to include a site map or "concept map", so that students always know where they are in a lesson. This allows students to move to various parts of the lesson with a click of the mouse, to visualise how different components of the lesson relate to each other, and to know when they are finished. Depending on the intended use of the lesson, time and money can be spent ensuring smooth usability.

The content and the instructional design of the site are more heavily influenced by the programmer than by the content and instructional experts. The designing begins by creating an outline or map of the site. This can be easily done in a low-tech manner on a piece of butcher paper with movable "sticky notes" used to represent separate screens or even by tearing out pieces of notebook paper. Using this type of schematic, decisions can he made about what sections follow and/or link to each other. Next, draw a rough picture of each screen that will be included, indicating text and picture layout. Finally, attach to the storyboard an "asset list," including and describing all text, image, video, or sounds and links to be included on each screen include the computer file names for all elements of the site. After the storyboarding is complete, review all the features of each page to be sure they are essential for student learning and not merely included to enhance graphic design. Working with experts will help in the development of easy-to-use, visually pleasing web-based materials with sound instructional design. When the site is ready to pilot, show it to a small group of faculty, graduate students, or others who will try it out and look for technical problems, typos, or other obvious mistakes. Be sure to test with different browsers and on different operating systems. Ask testers to go out of their way to use all of the site's features or even to try to break it. Provide a simple survey form so they can record the location of technical glitches, poorly worded instructions, download times, or other design problems. After correcting the first wave of errors, ask a small group of students who are representative of target users to try the site. This means if the web module is intended for students in the 1,000 level class, ask 1,000 level students who have not yet learned this content to try it out. Try to find students with different levels of computer proficiency and academic standing, not just students who show an interest in computers, the best students, or the students who benefit most from extra credit. Again, the computers and connections used should also be similar to those that will be used by the target users. At least two test-and-revise cycles will be needed to ready the site for use. Observe how students use the site. A directed interview or survey can occur during or after use when student impressions of specific components or features of the site are wanted. Surveys can also be administered to students who try out the site at home.

During the later phases of usability review, interviews can be used to test changes made to the site by asking students directly about specific features of the site. Now the site is ready to be piloted with real students in classes. This is necessary because students using materials which make up part of their grade may use the site differently than those who are just trying it out. Informal class discussion with students after they use the site is a good way to learn general impressions of the site, but again, better feedback is gained through an anonymous survey. Instructors using web-based materials as a substitution for existing material want to be sure that students learn at least as much with the new materials as with the old. In collaboration with faculty, we often compare groups of students who have learned the materials with different teaching methods, assigning different materials and methods to two groups of students, then giving both groups the same test and checking to see if test scores between the groups are significantly different.

While general equivalence between different types of material or teaching methods may be a desired outcome, care should be taken when drawing this kind of conclusion from a single comparison. It is possible to miss a difference due to small numbers of students in comparison groups, a shot and unreliable test, or because of a variety of other confounding influences and failings in a research design. It is also possible to make the opposite mistake and claim that there are differences when none really exist. Selection bias is a serious issue because it is usually not possible to randomly assign students to comparison groups. Testing for selection bias is possible through the use of pretests and/or surveys to determine whether existing groups of students have about the same level of knowledge, computer skill, attitude, or any other variable at the beginning of a class.

If the materials or the learning objectives are a new addition to a syllabus, an effort can be made to assess if students learned something by using the website, and if so, what exactly was learned. Pre- and post-tests are the traditional method of gauging if students have reached a pre-determined objective. Performance assessments often give a more valid understanding of what students know and can do than traditional written tests. A more subtle concern with any type of comparison involves changes to curriculum arising from the use of technology. One reason instructors choose to use a multimedia environment, such as the web or CDROM, is because they think they can achieve a learning goal not possible using traditional methods. When conducting a comparison, an instructor must be very confident that both the new and traditional methods are teaching the same material; if adaptation of the technology has changed what is taught, comparisons are complicated or rendered invalid.

Internet in schools

The internet provides students with confidence in learning. It is seen as an alternative to the teacher-directed learning environment by encouraging active learning. The internet gives simulation of real-world settings as it allows students to visit those places while in class. Use of the internet can save time for other activities in class because the instructor can post materials online so that students can have access to them, and thus time that would have been used going through those materials in class can be used for other activities. Novice users often do not have an idea of how to use the internet, even with the help of search engines and directories. In citing Oliver, Kelch and Karr-Kidwell state: the internet may pose a challenge for some students in finding information needed for a certain topic, and not knowing the key search word can be a detrimental when using the web.

Although internet use in class has been to allow students access to information, quite often they get lost in the world of the internet only to end with irrelevant information. The completion of the study found that the internet provided both positive and negative influences on the themes. The positive influences are:

Source of information: Internet provided a rich resource of materials, while it also became an alternative source of information for students. The students acquired materials and information from the internet for their projects. The internet gave students access to information on text, video, and audio, which they could not obtain from the teacher or textbook. The students also used the internet when the teacher was busy helping other students. For those who feared asking questions in class, the internet was a quiet, private replacement of the teacher. The internet also provided up to date information for students and the teacher.

Independent and individualised learning: Internet encouraged independent learning by students. It was a learning aid that made it possible for students to obtain online help for their projects by using tutorials found on the internet. As observed and pointed out both by the students and the teacher, the internet individualised students' learning. Although students in the class consisted of experienced and novice students in technology use, the teacher did not individualise instruction for the class.

In-depth understanding: The teacher and the students agreed that the internet gave students an in depth understanding of what they learned. Due to time constraints in class, students are given skeletal information requiring the students to turn to other sources of instruction and reference such as the internet for supplemental materials. Students stated that the use of the internet to supplement instruction increased student understanding.

Motivation: The teacher and the students voiced the belief that the internet motivated students in their learning. Being an extraordinary source of information, with a combination of visual, graphic, sound and movies, the students found learning with such technology interesting and fun.

The negative influences were focused around four themes:

Interference: Internet interfered with students concentration on class work. The researcher's interviews and observations found that the internet 'dilutes' the academic environment of the class, and in effect removes students from the classroom. As students read e-mails, or were caught up with news on the CNN web site, followed sports on ESPN, accessed the Napster site for the latest music albums, and saw advertisements of leisure products, they often became distracted from the class environment.

Time consuming: In the class, students wasted time surfing the internet. Searching the internet does not mean using search engines or directories and simply getting information needed. It requires skills to get the right information with the least time possible. As observed in class, students moved from search engine to search engine and between directories looking for the same piece of information. Students' time was also wasted when the internet became slow because the networked system could not cope with many students online at the same time.

Questionable resources: Students' learning involves using resources that are credible. With the internet, there is no control. It is a free-for-all information source where anyone can publish online any time. This has the danger of having inappropriate and unreliable information posted. In using the internet, students copied materials whose reliability, and credibility was questionable.

Dependency: Students developed a dependency on the internet during the class. Students turned to the internet for information rather than using the knowledge they already had, and regarded the internet as indispensable to their learning even when inappropriate.

Unlike the traditional class, where the teacher is the *de facto* head of the class as a source of knowledge, and controller of class activities, the internet had reduced the role and significance of the teacher in both perspectives mentioned. Students no longer felt that they had to rely entirely on the teacher when in class. The students and the teacher concurred that there is need to control internet use in class. The teacher indicated that the uncontrolled use of the internet would in the long run hurt the students instead of helping them. Internet use in the class conducive for the classroom environment.

Electronic books

More and more of our educational technology is wired or connected in some fashion. From computers, to video-conferencing, to CDROMs, to distance learning systems and yes, to the internet, the demands to have a connected network of educational mediums is a major drive today to fulfil traditional, non-traditional, and corporate education needs. The electronic book (e-book) provides an interesting avenue in the quest for better education and better educational technology use. The e-book, in its raw form, is nothing more than electronic text. The e-book reader is the vehicle that is garnering the lion's share of attention in the industry today. The development of HyperCard and hypertext technology provided the enabling software and tools to create electronic, interactive books. These books could be downloaded to a PC, where non-linear, random accessibility was possible. The problem was that since the electronic text was stored on the hard drive, the portability, unlike a hard or soft copy book, was very limited.

Today, a variety of e-books are available, such as the Rocket eBook, the SoftBook, the Everybook, the Classbook Reader, the

Librius Millennium Reader, the RCA eBook, and so on. These first generation e-books are gathering attention, both from consumers and the computer and publishing industries. Trade publishers estimate that within a few years, 10 percent of all books will be sold to be read as e-books. Even others, namely software providers such as Microsoft, claim within 20 years, 90 percent of all books will be sold to be read as e-books. Some go as far as to suggest that eventually e-books will do the heavy work of conveying information and entertaining us while the traditional book will retreat to the status of a collectible.

The e-book itself is a relatively small, hand-held device, that is today primarily a storage-and-display unit. The device plugs into a cradle that attaches to a computer, or in some cases, when a modem is included, to a phone jack, where access and textbook download is accomplished. Prices are as low as $ 300. It can hold about 10,000 pages of text, so the reader/student could carry multiple books, for multiple classes, without the physical strain of lugging around a heavy back-pack throughout the day. But the e-book is more than just a lightweight, portable reading device. E-books offer a variety of features and functions that turn it from newfangled electronic reader into a useful, educational technology. Whether in a traditional classroom setting or distant, independent study, the book, or some form of printed instructional material, is almost always used.

The e-book offers features and functions that not only save time or open up a "virtual" book library, but also a means of personal creativity. Many of them come with a stylus, allowing the reader to underline passages or scribble notes in the margin. This is ideal for the student who wants to capture key thoughts without having to "maim" a paper book. Furthermore, e-books offer the option of book marking pages by simply touching the page. Higher-end e-books come with full-colour, high-resolution displays. So, high-impact graphics are available in addition to the text, creating a multimedia reading and learning experience. Additionally, many magazines and newspapers are also available in electronic format.

Even today, the book is a dominant part of the educational landscape; this is not going to change anytime soon. The book has, for hundreds of years, influenced the way we reason, imagine, invent, and yes, learn. However, in a world of the 'wired', the book arguably has a big shortcoming: It is not connected to anything else. This shortcoming limits the book as an educational technology. E-books can and do have the ability to connect to networks via built-in modem ports. They can be docked to personal computers to further extend their networking capabilities. In the not-so-distant future, e-books will be able to directly connect to other e-books and will gain the ability to functional as a small digital libraries.

VISIONS FOR ONLINE TEACHING

An educational organisation should have a clear vision of the full range of possibilities for teaching and learning that technology can facilitate. It helps people working in an organisation to identify and share certain goals. Even more importantly, a shared vision is necessary as a benchmark against which to assess different strategies and actions regarding the development of technology-based teaching. In particular, an institution needs to define what balance it wants between face-to-face and technology-based teaching. An institution could for very good reasons decide not to go down the technology-based teaching route and place special emphasis on face-to-face and personalised teaching. It is likely though to be a very elite and high cost institution. Alternatively, an institution might wish to vary within its structure the degree of dependency on technology-based teaching, giving more emphasis for instance to face-to-face teaching at the graduate level, and more to technology-based teaching at the undergraduate level.

One of the main challenges of making technology-based teaching a core function is to extend its implementation from a relatively small number of enthusiasts and early adopters to the main body of the teaching force. This means introducing a strategy for inclusion, to ensure that all faculty are encouraged and supported in their use of technology for teaching. Many universities have old buildings without adequate conduits for wiring, or asbestos fillings within walls that need to be removed before modern cabling can be installed. Many faculty and staff will not have a computer or know how to use one. Servers will need to be installed within each department, and networked to other servers on campus. Internet connections with the outside world will need to be established, and ports and other communications facilities installed to enable students in residences or off-campus to access the main university campus, or satellite campuses and other institutions to be linked.

While such a technology infrastructure strategy is absolutely essential, unfortunately it is often the first strategy adopted by universities: build it and they will come. However the technology infrastructure plan should be driven by, not lead, the university's overall vision and strategy for its teaching. There are in fact three levels of support required to fully exploit technology. The most obvious is the technical support, the people who make the networks operate and service the computers and telecommunications. At the second level are media production and services, those who produce educational products or supply educational technology services, such as interface designers, graphics designers, video-conferencing managers, or graduate students who do HTML mark-up. At the third level are those that provide educational services, such as instructional design, faculty development, project management, and evaluation. The major part of physical infrastructure, such as networks and major equipment purchases, is usually funded from capital budgets, and as such is less likely to compete for funds that impact directly on teaching, such as general operating budget. The cost of the human support though does compete directly with funds for teaching and research.

The human cost of infrastructure support is recurrent, i.e. has to be found each year, whereas physical infrastructure is often seen as a once-only investment, although rapid advances in technology and hence the need continually to replace or update networks and equipment make this a dangerous assumption. As a consequence, the human support side is often underfunded. Probably the most consistent complaint across universities from those responsible for technology applications is the inadequacy of resources for technical support. Even so, the further down the chain, from technological support to educational support, the more difficult it becomes to secure adequate resources. If the network crashes, its impact is obvious; the value of an instructional designer is much harder to sell when funds are tight.

In US a recent national survey found that 60 per cent of university and college students had convenient computer access. At UBC, 70 per cent of all undergraduates already have internet accounts. However, while access continues to grow, it is strongly related to income, gender and profession. Many of those that do have computers have machines that are not suitable for multimedia or internet access. There is also a chicken and egg issue here. If students are not required to have a computer for their studies, they are less likely to purchase one. If students who are thinking of purchasing a computer are not given clear specifications as to what is needed, they are more likely to purchase a less powerful model. Nevertheless, it would be a reasonable assumption to assume that within five years, at least in North America, most university students, both on and off campus, will have convenient access to a computer and internet access.

Universities though will need to put in place strategies to help students acquire the most appropriate kind of computer for their studies, and to help those students who do not have and cannot afford to purchase their own computer and network access. There are several strategies that can be used to provide support for student access to computers. One is to provide computer labs on campus for students. Once again this is a useful start-up strategy, but in the long run it becomes unsustainable as the primary source of student support. There are several drawbacks to relying on computer labs for access. The first is that as the need to use computers for learning increases, either capital investment costs get out of control, or students' lining up for access reaches unacceptable levels. Secondly, given the rate of technological change, computers in labs quickly get out of date. More importantly, it requires students to access learning from a specific place, often at a specific time, if they have to book, thus removing one of the main advantages of using technology, its flexibility.

There will always be a need for specialist computer labs, for those subject areas requiring exceptionally high end or specialised machines and software. There will also always be a need for on-campus access through plug-in ports or drop-in labs for casual use. However, in the long run the most flexible and most cost-effective approach is to encourage students to provide their own computers and internet access. Such a policy though cannot be implemented unless it is clear that students will need a computer, and that means ensuring that there are sufficient courses designed to exploit fully the instructional benefits of using a computer. Sonoma State University, California, spent two and a half years preparing for the implementation of a policy requiring all freshmen students to have a computer. They made sure that there were sufficient courses developed in a way that exploited the use of a computer, and therefore made it essential and valuable to use one. This required a major investment in faculty development.

Sonoma State found that there was very high compliance for its policy of requiring all its freshman students to have a computer, it was well received by parents and by employers, who praised the university for making higher education more relevant, and also most students seemed to be pleased with the policy. The important point here is that it was a total strategy. Implementing only part of it — such as a technology fee when many students clearly don't need to use a computer for their studies — can lead to considerable student and faculty resistance. Other strategies to increase the accessibility of computers and networks for learners are the development of government-funded educational networks, through contract leasing or bulk buying of telecommunications services, tax breaks for students on computer purchase, and the development of local community learning centres equipped with advanced technologies.

While technology may open up access to some and deny it to others, computer ownership is not the main obstacle to university access at the University of British Columbia. Many more potential students are denied access by restrictive grade point average entrance requirements, arbitrary prerequisites, residency or attendance requirements, and barriers to credit transfer from other institutions. If a primary purpose of introducing technology-based learning is to increase access, these admission policy issues need to be addressed as well.

The newer technologies are quite flexible in that they can be used in a variety of different ways for teaching. Technologies can be used to replicate traditional forms of teaching; at the same time, they can be used in quite new and different ways, depending on the imagination, skills and resources available to the teacher or learner. Nevertheless, despite this variability, certain trends in the use of technology are evident. It appears that some technologies lend themselves more easily to certain approaches to teaching and learning, while other technologies lend themselves to others. There is no super technology that can meet all teaching and learning requirements, so technologies need to be mixed and matched to the educational purpose.

Thus we find that instructional television and video-conferencing (one- or two-way television from one site to a class in another site) and certain applications of the web (for instance, where information is posted for students to read) tend to be used primarily for information transmission in a didactic style, very close to the classroom lecture model. Other technologies, such as computer mediated communication using software such as Soft Arc's First Class, Simon Fraser University's Virtual-U, and Netscape's Hypernews, allow for more collaborative learning models. These technologies encourage or require a high level of discussion and participation by the learner, and very much resemble the seminar model of classroom teaching.

Although CDROM technology is often used merely to replicate a book (i.e. a didactic style), but with better graphics, animation, audio and video, a number of applications that more fully exploit the technology are emerging. Thus CDROMs are increasingly being used to simulate human interaction (for language teaching), for representing expert systems, such as forestry management, and for problem-solving approaches based on scientific methodology, through for example the use of virtual laboratories.

These approaches to learning enable students to apply their learning to para-realistic situations, to test their own ideas and use their own experience, and as a result to make and test decisions drawing on their previous learning, or even learning facts and principles during the process of decision-making. The web is a particularly interesting technology in the way that it is evolving. It has the ability to combine all these various approaches to learning. For instance, WebCT, designed at the University of British Columbia by Murray Goldberg, is a web authoring system that combines didactive and collaborative learning tools, as well as a student learning management system, allowing subject experts without any specialist computer skills to construct their own courses.

The limitation of the web at the moment is bandwidth and the power of desktop machines, which make it difficult or impossible to run the more powerful applications needed for expert systems, complex simulations and problem solving. However this will change quite rapidly. These technologies enable more powerful applications of such teaching methods in more flexible and accessible forms for students, with also the potential for economies of scale. Furthermore, what all these technologies have in common is that, when well designed, they enable learners, irrespective of the subject matter, to develop skills of information navigation, acquisition, and analysis, application of knowledge to new situations, new knowledge creation, and decision-making, all skills essential for survival in an information society.

In terms of change strategies, these new approaches need to be tested and developed not just in a narrow setting of a particular class or course, but in a system of teaching as a whole, where appropriate replacing, not adding to, conventional teaching methods. Thus technology-based teaching needs to be built into the mainstream teaching, and not offered as peripheral or optional learning for students.

Teaching with technology is not something that can easily be picked up along the way, as something to be done off the side of the desk while engaged in more important or time-consuming activities such as research. The most common form of training given to faculty is to show them how to use the technology. This though is starting at the wrong place. Many faculty need to understand why it is important to use technology for teaching in the first place. It has to be related to the changing environment in which universities find themselves, and in particular to the changing needs of learners.

Some basic understanding of the teaching and learning process, and in particular the different kinds of teaching approaches, and the goals they are meant to achieve, need to be understood. The faculty need to understand the different roles that technology can play in teaching, and how this alters the way that teaching needs to be organised. Only then does it make much sense to train faculty in how to use a particular piece of technology. While this sequence may be logical, it is unlikely to be the most effective way to help faculty develop skills in using technology; 'show and tell' and hands-on experience are most likely to lead to this full range of understanding. Nevertheless all four aspects need to be deliberately targeted in faculty development.

University teaching is probably the last craft- or guild-based profession. However, the changing nature and variety of learners, the growing complexity and volume of knowledge, and the impact of technology on teaching now really require that university teachers should have formal training and qualifications in instructional methods. This should eventually become a condition for tenure.

Even more fundamental than faculty training is the need to change the reward system for faculty. While many universities have statements that equate teaching with research for tenure and promotion, the reality in most research universities is quite different: the only criterion that really matters is research. Thus there is no point in pouring millions of dollars into infrastructure and computers and multimedia unless the faculty reward system is changed.

Teaching ability must become in practice at least equal to research for promotion and tenure. The good news though is that technology-based teaching is usually more public, more observable, and hence more easily evaluated than conventional classroom methods.

Furthermore, multimedia technologies provide an excellent means to convert research knowledge directly into teaching and into promotional material for the research itself. Another way to reward faculty is to ensure that revenues generated by the use of technology by a department flow back into that department, and do not get swallowed by the central bureaucracy. Innovative mechanisms need to be developed for faculty (and other creative staff) to share in rights and royalties from the development of generic educational software and learning materials.

Lastly the very sensitive issue of faculty agreements needs to be addressed. There are short-term advantages in leaving things loose, but technological innovation will become unsustainable as faculty become more experienced, suffer from increased workloads, and find that they are still unrewarded.

New technologies require new applications, a great deal is already known about the process of producing high quality, cost-effective multimedia learning materials. This knowledge has been developed both in the large autonomous distance teaching universities, and also in private sector multimedia companies in areas such as advertising and film and television making. This means establishing each course or teaching module as a project, with the following elements:

i) a fully costed proposal, which identifies,

ii) the number and type of learners to be targeted,

iii) clear definition of teaching objectives,

iv) choice of technologies,

v) a carefully estimated budget allocation,

vi) a team approach, involving any combination of subject experts/faculty, project manager, instructional designer, graphics designer, computer interface designer, text editor, internet specialist and media producer.

vi) an unambiguous definition of intellectual property rights and a clear agreement on revenue sharing,

vii) a plan for integration with or substitution for face-to-face teaching,

ix) a production schedule with clearly defined 'milestones' or deadlines, and a targeted start date,

x) an agreed process for evaluation and course revision and maintenance,

xi) a defined length of project before redesign or withdrawal of the course.

More recently universities have established large central computing organisations. Too often these central services have had little impact on the core teaching activities of an institution, partly because faculties have felt that they do not control them. Such units are often subjected to attempts by Deans to break them up and reallocate their funding back to the faculties. Although often dependent on centrally provided networks, new technologies such as the web are more decentralised. The power is often on the desktop. This provides considerable empowerment for the individual faculty member. However we have seen that high quality educational multimedia requires a range of specialist skills that go beyond the capability of any single individual. Furthermore the appearance of decentralisation in the new technologies is deceptive. They depend on agreed standards and networks for communication and inter-operation, and they depend on human and technical support infrastructures that require policy making across the university.

A major study of managing technology for teaching and administration in Australian higher universities classified universities into three different groups: old, divisional and new. The study argued that while centralisation of services is appropriate in a new institution with a major commitment to make IT a centre of its vision and strategy, this is less likely to be appropriate for large, well-established 'divisional' universities with a strong faculty structure.

New technologies are resulting in global competition for universities. The need for systematic research and evaluation into the use of new technologies should be obvious. However it is important that the right kind of research should be done. The wrong kind of research is to compare the learning effectiveness of technology-based teaching with the learning effectiveness of classroom based teaching, using the classroom based model as the baseline. Many hundreds of thousands of such comparative studies have been made in the past, and the usual result when the comparisons have been done using sound research methodology is that there is no significant difference.

As long ago as 1974, Wilbur Schramm pointed to the flaw in this kind of approach: technologies allow the achievement of new or different learning outcomes to those of the classroom lecture method, but if the classroom 'event' is the base, then the new learning outcomes that could be achieved are not usually measured. For instance, if a lecture is used primarily for transmitting information, but a CDROM is used for applying that knowledge to solving a problem, then the measure of success for the CDROM has to be different from the classroom lecture. The aim then should be to measure the success or otherwise of new technologies in extending the range of learning skills, as well as content acquisition. Even more important than research into learning outcomes is research into learners' response to using technologies, and in particular what learners and teachers believe may be lost or gained in using such approaches to learning.

These results are likely to vary considerably from individual to individual, so it is important to see whether there are groups or types of learners who benefit more than others from technology-based teaching. This kind of research should also help identify the critical aspects of face-to-face teaching, which are likely to be as much social as instructional.

REFERENCES

Anderson, A H, Newlands, A, Mullin, J, Heming, A. M., Doherty-Sneddon, G and Van der Velden, J., "Impact of Video-mediated Communication on Simulated Service Encounters", *Interacting With Computers*, 8, 2, pp.193-206, 1996.

Anderson, D. T., Garrison, D.R., "Transactional Issues in Distance Education: The Impact of Design in Audioconferencing", *American Journal of Distance Education*, 9, 2, pp. 27-45, 1995.

Auter, P. I., Hanna, M. S., "The Challenge of Developing Online Courses", *Paper presented at the Annual Meeting of the Speech Communication Association*, San Diego, CA, November 23-26, 1996.

Bauer, J. W., and Rezabek, L. L., 1993, *Effects of Two-way Visual Contact on Verbal Interaction during Face-to-Face and Teleconferenced Instruction*, In *Art, Science, and Visual Literacy: Selected Readings from the Annual Conference of the International Visual Literacy Association*, 24th, Pittsburgh, PA, September 30-October 4, 1992.

Beare, P.L., "The Comparative Effectiveness of Videotape, Audiotape, and Telelecture in Delivering Continuing Teacher Education, *American Journal of Distance Education*, 3(2), 57-66, 1989.

Bell, D., "The Social Framework of the Information Society", In Forester, I (ed.), *The Microelectronics Revolution*, Blackwell, Oxford, 1980.

Bengu G. and W. Swart, A., "Computer-Aided Total Quality Approach to Manufacturing Education in Engineering", *IEEE Transactions on Education*, 39:3, pp. 415-427, 1996.

Berge Z. L., "Interaction in Post-secondary Web-based Learning", *Educational Technology*, 39(1), pp. 5-11, 1999

Brown, J. S., Duguid, P., *Learning-in Theory and in Practice*, In J. S. Brown, P. Duguid (eds.), *The Social Life of Information*, Cambridge, MA: Harvard Business School Press, 2000.

Duffy, T., Jonassen, D., (eds.), *Constructivism and the Technology of Instruction: A Conversation*, Hillsdale, N., Lawrence Erlbaum Associates, 1992.

Entwistle, A and Entwistle, N., *Experiences of Understanding in Revising for Degree Examinations Learning and Instruction*, 2, pp.1-22, 1992.

Forsyth, I., *Teaching and Learning Materials and the Internet* (2nd ed.), London: Kogan Page, 1998.

Indira Madhukar, *Internet-based Distance Learning*, Authorspress, New Dehi, 2002.

Galusha, J. M., *Barriers to Learning in Distance Education, Interpersonal Computing and Technology*, 5(3-4), pp. 6-14, 1998.

Roberts, L., *A Transformation of Learning: Use of the NII for Education and Lifelong Learning*, In D. P. Ely & B. B. Minor (eds.), *Educational Media and Technology Yearbook 1995/1996*, pp. 50-66, Englewood, CO: Libraries Unlimited, 1996

6

User-Centred Educational Technologies

The field of educational technology, and particularly of instructional design, now has a good history of creating innovative technology-based learning resources through the application of principled development methods. Educational technology is facing a new kind of challenge, or, more positively, a new area of opportunity. If we want to develop new practices within educational technology that are compatible with a valuing of autonomous lifelong learning, then we need to recognise that an image of the compliant learner has had a strong influence on the mainstreams of educational technology.

With the rapid growth of the WWW and the internet, since 1994, and especially since we have begun to glimpse what user experiences will be made possible by the convergence of internet multimedia and virtual reality techniques in the near future, the design image has begun to fix around networked ('online' or 'virtual') learning environments, configured for use by communities of learners. Some of these communal virtual environments are taking on familiar shapes: virtual universities with campus 'buildings' housing online learner-support services like libraries and cafes, for example. It is too early to know what to make of this trend. Within two decades, this may look like a familiar, understandable but aberrant path, analogous with seeing and designing early versions of the car as a horseless carriage. Or, as some have argued, rendering cyberspace navigable and legible through capitalising on people's ability to 'read' architecture in the material world may be the bes way to move forward.

In many learning situations it is reasonable to expect learners to comply with the instructions or expectations of those who are placed in a position of responsibility for their learning. We can readily think of 'ideal cases' — such as in certain areas of military training, or in the learning of well-defined procedures for dealing with civil emergencies, or in many other areas of high-risk training. Many of the core ideas, theories and methods in the field of educational technology, and especially in areas like ISD or instructional design, have origins which were heavily shaped by reasonable assumptions about a compliant learner.

Educational technology is now called upon to find ways of supporting the learning of a great variety of people, quite a few of whom cannot be described as 'compliant'. The recent history of government-funded investment in educational technology in UK higher education shows how miscontruing students' use of learning resources can waste tens of millions of pounds worth of public money and of precious staff time. Evaluative data seems to be indicating that, however good the learning software, students will rarely use it unless they are obliged to do so. They will use it if it is part of their normal timetabled activity. They will use it if they need to do so in order to pass some assessed task. But they will not use it just because it is good for them. This is not because they are perverse, lazy or technophobic.

Most students use ICT every day — but they use it for their own purposes. They use it for emailing their boyfriends, finding interesting material on the web, writing coursework essays and so on. They don't use 'courseware' for the same reason that they don't make as much use as their teachers would like of the university library: they are too busy and it's not on the critical path for any of the significant problems they have to solve each day. Particularly where students are poor and over-assessed, supplementing their income and meeting the next coursework deadline take precedence over 'reading around the subject' or browsing through optional pieces of courseware. The same kind of arguments apply to busy managers, knowledge workers and other creative people for whom very focused 'just-in-time learning' is all their stressed schedule can afford.

It is now part of the folklore of information systems design and software engineering that technology needs to be built around a well-founded understanding of what people actually do. Just listening to the managers' accounts of how work should be done is a recipe for disaster and leads to unused and unusable software systems. Of course there is something inherently conservative in building technology around existing practices. The biggest problem we are facing is that of learners 'voting with their feet'. However beautiful our theories or our interfaces, learners are not choosing to spend their time using our products.

Now is the time for a user-centered educational technology to begin working on methods through which we can come to understand the real needs of our target users, and design technology which helps them meet the real challenges they are facing. The current paradigm is centered around embedding tasks in technological artefacts. That is, we create courseware in which tasks for the learner are embedded. The courseware drives the learner. We need to shift to building technology around learners' real world activity: to create learning environments which are properly supportive of real world activity.

There may be good reasons for allowing and perhaps encouraging learners to create their own learnplaces, configuring the physical resources available to them in ways they find most comfortable, efficient, supportive, congenial and convivial. But we can't expect them to create their learnplaces from nothing. It is the duty of the educational technologists to design appropriate learning spaces: which can become local habitations for individual learners or for learning communities. Such spaces are the embryonic physical manifestation of the learning environment, in all its nested complexity. Some parts or sub-elements of the learning environment represent familiar challenges — the design and crafting of appropriate cognitive tools for example. But others offer new and important challenges — such as the challenges of meshing micro-, meso- and macro- levels of a learning environment within a learning organisation, and working with the multidisciplinary teams responsible for managing and maintaining that learning environment. Educational technologists need to respond to the growing wave of interest and enthusiasm for the social, collaborative or communal aspects of learning.

We have the world of asynchronous text-based communication: e-mail, computer-mediated conferencing, etc. and a world of synchronous multimedia communications: live audio-conferencing, live video-conferencing. Multimedia communication, in principle, offers a number of benefits. It allows us to demonstrate and show, not just describe in an abstract way. It allows us to incorporate gesture, tonc of voice and other cues that are not readily available in text-based communication. It offers richer and more vivid information transfer. For some purposes, people find it easier and quicker to speak than to write, so it can be more time-efficient.

The use of multimedia communication in synchronous mode also has a number of benefits, such as the possibility of supporting a highly interactive discussion. But synchronicity also has some limitations. It gives little time for the communicating parties to think and reflect, to formulate thoughtful questions and answers. It demands that all the parties communicating should be available at the same time. It can be frustrating when used by large numbers: only a minority can contribute to the discussion; complicated protocols may be needed to support a smooth 'discussion' when it is distributed over a number of sites, etc. One does not have to dismiss all the advantages of text-based communication and synchronous communication to see that there may be some advantages to the use of asynchronous multimedia communication.

NETWORKED LEARNING ENVIRONMENTS

Technology changes both what we can do and what we decide is best to do; big shifts in culture cannot occur until the tools are available. Although before the invention of the printing press, people could read and write, it was the press that enabled widespread literacy, and an almost total accessibility to the written word. This spread of literacy changed both class structure and the educational system, with consequences that still shape our attitudes today. The impact of the printing press upon students of the time has been analysed and reanalysed. The press made it possible for all people to accumulate knowledge, to record it, and to preserve it. But always, as new technology enables shifts at the level of delivery, old technologies are augmented, not totally replaced.

Today, although many of us have access to inventions such as radio, television, and computers, we still use and will continue to use books, speech, and pen or pencil. Just as the printing press caused change in the system of educational delivery but did not result in a complete abolishment of either the written word or the oral/aural connection, so too the new electric and electronic technologies will find their level before settling comfortably and permanently into the education scheme. Schooling is only a part of education. Much of education takes place outside of schooling, both as planned activities and as unplanned learning. If we envision computers and telecommunications merging as a new tool for teaching and learning, now is the time to clearly articulate and promulgate our goals in order to shape future uses of instructional technology.

For communications to take place, there must be a sender, a receiver and a message. If this message is intended as instruction, then besides student, teacher, and content, we must also consider the environment in which this educational communication occurs. Environments that benefit the educational system in some ways may also constrain it in others. Part of the "new" learning environment will probably include various technologies and media. If "the medium is the message," that is, if technology changes what we can do and how we think about it, then the various media enabled by instructional technology can also change both what we can do in education and how we conceive of it.

For many years, educators have been exploring ways in which to combine theories of differing learning styles and student-constructed knowledge with the theory of practice-centered learning. Instead of being considered passive recipients of knowledge poured into them by the teacher, students are now seen as being capable of constructing their own knowledge with guidance from the teacher. We can offer part of this tutorial guidance by setting up an environment that will provide students the resources necessary for independent exploration.

Internet is a tool that will enhance the basic interactions that are at the heart of teaching and learning through offering new ways of increasing students' ability to interact with their tutor, peers, and therefore the ideas of their particular subject. It offers a new form of communication specific to its nature that is a hybrid of traditional papers and debating norms, the textualisation of asynchronous conversations that allows for a synthesis of ideas with a communal solution to problems, an inherently more collaborative and dialectical form of learning. The paper-based medium has its own driving force; it owes its form to its physical limitations. The web allows us to make a paradigm shift. The speed of information that can be transferred means that an electronic magazine can in effect become merely an overarching structure, a virtual conference, where resource material becomes the conference papers around which the participants discuss. It allows the readers to form a community and become creators/participants.

Using emerging computer-based technology as a resource, we can encourage students to explore their own interests and to become active educational workers, with opportunities to solve some authentic problems. The concept of "tutorial," however, puts focus on the question of isolation vs. socialisation, an issue in technological education delivery.

As an agent for socialisation and collaboration, the networked computer has a greater potential in education than does the stand-alone, knowledge-server computer. The active environment of social learning provided by a computer with access to local, national, and international networks actually increases interaction and communication among students, teachers, peers, parents, and other members of the world community.

Changes in our environment involve more than just adding new technology to old ways of organising teaching and learning. The paradigm shift is from a teaching environment to a learning environment. Another notion current in educational circles is the need to develop motivated, skillful, life-long learners. As knowledge in many fields increases exponentially, aspiring professionals must acknowledge that during formal schooling, they can acquire only a small segment of the knowledge base they will need in their careers. Teaching and learning in their fields that may have been static for decades are now undergoing extraordinary change.

Educators now have use of a technology that merges computers and telecommunication. Known as Computer Mediated Communication (CMC), it can be used in instruction in three ways--for conferencing, informatics, and computer-assisted instruction (CAI). Computer conferencing provides e-mail, interactive messaging, and small and large group discussion. Informatics (repositories or maintainers of organised information) include library online public access catalogs (OPACs), interactive access to remote databases, programme/data archive sites, campus-wide information systems (CWIS), wide area information systems (WAIS), and Gopher/Veronica.

A seemingly indisputable plus resulting from technology is the ability to deliver distance-education. Although there are some differences between distance education and classroom education, the significant issues concerning the use of computer networking and other emerging technologies to promote learning in both are similar. Distance educators are beginning to focus on a related set of notions:

i) that there are different learning styles,
ii) that students create their own meaning when learning new things, and
iii) that what makes a difference in content retention and transfer is not so much what is done by teachers, but what students as learners can be encouraged to do.

CMC mergers of computers and telecommunication technologies give us new tools to support teaching and learning by using computer systems and networks to transfer, store, and retrieve information between humans. The computer network in this model serves as a mediator rather than as an information processor. CMC provides electronic mail capabilities, delivers instruction, facilitates student-to-student and student-to-teacher interactions across a desk or across the world—a truly valuable tool for distance-education.

CMC promotes paradigmatic shifts in teaching and learning from distance education to distance learning to merging informal dialogues, invisible colleges, oral presentations, and scholarly publications. But our new visions of distance learning must drive our decisions about our use of technology, not vice versa. While major cultural shifts do not occur without the tools that make them possible, once those tools are at hand, the shifts are inevitable.

Emerging technologies such as interactive television and the "superhighway" for information exchange may look different depending upon who builds them, but we may be assured that they will be built by someone. How we as educators will participate in this enterprise is a vital issue. Uses of computer conferencing, informatics, and CAI include:

i) mentoring, such as advising and guiding students
ii) project-based instruction, either within the classroom or in projects involving community, national, or international problem-solving
iii) guest lecturing, which promotes interaction between students and persons in the larger community
iv) didactic teaching
v) retrieval of information from online information archives, such as OPACs, ERIC, and commercial databases
vi) course management
vii) public conferencing
viii) interactive chat, used to brainstorm with teachers or peers, and to maintain social relationships
ix) personal networking and professional growth, and such activities as finding persons with kindred spirits on a scholarly discussion list
x) facilitating collaboration
xi) individual and group presentations
xii) peer reviewing of writing or projects involving peer learning groups/peer tutorial sessions/peer counselling
xiii) practice and experience using emerging technologies deemed intrinsically useful in today's society
xiv) computer-based instruction.

The reengineering of education involves not only rethinking the organisation of site-based schools, but also finding ways to unite computers and telecommunications and bringing down the schoolhouse walls—a means to deliver instructional content when and where it is needed, whether in the home, the workplace, or the school. CMC promotes interaction that is often lacking in the traditional teacher-based classroom. It allows learners the freedom to explore alternative pathways—to find and develop their own style of learning.

Computer technologies allow professionals to share with students the tools to provide guidance to help students develop meaningful ways to construct their own knowledge. Technology enables us to implement these new visions in distance learning. Technology overcomes limits to investigations, opening them to students from any or many classrooms, schools, grades, countries, and including experts in the field of inquiry from the collaboration.

Effective learning hinges on active engagement by the student and the construction of knowledge on their own leads to understanding. This learning then becomes not a solitary process, but rather an occurrence in a larger world of people and technology. More than merely a shift within education, this movement will bring about major shifts in society and culture. As the number of students increases, and the number of persons requiring off-campus classes rises, the very existence and future of a university or college may hinge upon serving this newly defined and diverse population.

In combination with other media, computers can utilise an instructional design that teaches to the multiple intelligences —linguistic, logico-mathematical, intrapersonal, spatial, musical, bodily kinesthetic, and interpersonal—that Gardner speaks of in *Frames of Mind*. The idea behind this instructional design is to use as many methods and formats for instruction as possible, provided that instructional goals and design dictate their use. Benefits and limitations of CMC teaching and learning. There are many benefits to using CMC, but there are also some limitations that we should recognise.

One of the greatest benefits of CMC is its ability to liberate instruction from the constraints of time and distance. The convenience of access from home, school, or office permits many students and instructors to better meet travel, job, and family responsibilities. CMC promotes self-discipline and requires students to take more responsibility for their own learning. Using CMC, the course's instructional design can be varied from structured projects to open projects, where students are free to work on "messy" but authentic problem-solving. Teacher-caution is advised, however, because for some students more structure may be needed. Our goals should be to develop self-motivated learners, but also to offer help where needed. If designed well, CMC applications can be used effectively to facilitate collaboration among students, teachers and guests or experts from outside the classroom.

Writing is essential across the entire curriculum; to communicate on a computer network requires writing. Used effectively, CMC encourages and motivates students to become involved in authentic projects, to write for a real audience of their peers or persons in the larger world community, instead of merely composing assignments for the teacher. However, educators must still recognise that not all students can express themselves well in writing, and that even for those who can, the act of writing and using online text-based applications can be a time-consuming struggle.

A bonus service of CMC is highlighted by an emerging body of literature, added to by several authors in this volume. They speak from their own experiences, and deal with the empowerment of persons with disabilities or physical traits, such as disfigurements or speech impediments, that might prevent them from equal participation in face-to-face encounters. CMC promotes an equalisation of users. Because CMC is at present primarily text-only, the consequent reduction in social cues leads to a protective ignorance about whether the person is someone of greater, equal, or lesser social self-image. It is impossible to see if the writer took several hours to draft a one screen response, or several minutes. Responses are judged by the ideas and thoughts conveyed, more than by who is doing the writing.

The lack of social cues and the asynchronous nature of the medium affords those with physical limitations or personal reticence the possibility of participating fully and equally in communicative activities within a main stream environment. However, the researchers realise that the changed social context cues can encourage the opposite response, encouraging non-reticent personalities to become overly zealous in their responses, or even to become publicly inflammatory and aggressive on a personal level in ways that are generally considered offensive. It has also been noted that some students prefer the social aspects of the classroom and are unsettled by the lack of the face-to-face interaction in CMC, or the lack of a charismatic lecturer during presentation.

Another potential benefit of CMC is in promoting multicultural awareness. With the demographic makeup of many countries changing so rapidly, it is becoming increasingly important to develop communication skills for a culturally diverse community and world. On the other hand, because the bulk of CMC is conducted in English and in the written, rather than spoken word, it may perpetuate some cultural hegemonies. Technical benefits to using CMC include the ease of circulating and archiving files and documents.

The cost of buying and supporting systems, or accessing other networks is a significant "overhead" item in schools and colleges today, as is the cost and inconvenience of repairing or replacing hardware. Further, systems are not 100 per cent reliable, which adds to inconvenience and wasted time. With so many systems to learn and sources to tap, information overload has become a problem as some users struggle with the lack of criteria to help them in deciding what to keep and what to discard from the swiftly flowing stream of incoming information.

Computer-mediated conferencing has emerged as a tool for instructional communication not bound by prescribed meeting times or by geographic proximity. Successful integration of CMC into the curriculum, however, depends on our ability to design and use CMC applications which meet course goals, delivery goals. CMC should be used for what was impossible or very difficult to do without it. CMC can provide an efficient way for students to turn in and receive back their homework, reduce the cost of classroom handouts, cut travel costs for students and teachers. Some instructors have used CMC to create a virtual laboratory to allow teaching and learning to transcend time and place, while expanding access to the very best instructors. Educators have also used CMC for:

i) homeschooling
ii) to reduce barriers for persons with various physical and learning disabilities
iii) to promote and defend native cultural beliefs and values
iv) to increase information sharing and communication without geographic barriers
v) to widen student experience in other countries/cultures
vi) to reduce the isolation sometimes felt by teachers and learners
vii) to cushion the difficult transition from student to teacher in supporting first-year teacher initiatives

Most of the changes educators propose involve three types of problems and opportunities: access, quality, and productivity. One of the goals of education must be equal access to (quality) education for all persons seeking it. Educational systems, in their struggle to provide equal access, must not lose sight of the need to provide a high quality of education, despite limited resources available.

USAGE OF HYPERTEXT

The traditional classroom scenario has changed little for decades. The teacher stands in front of the room and talks, sometimes with charismatic force, informing, explaining and modeling a disciplinary mode of inquiry, perhaps engaging a few students in dialogue or provoking a general class discussion. Instructors who adopt technology in their classes use it primarily to enhance the traditional teaching paradigm, not significantly altering the way they teach. Audiovisual presentation of lecture materials can engage students more than straight lecturing, whether that presentation involves overhead projection or more stimulating colour and action of graphics and videos. Some professors also offer these presentation materials on computers outside the classroom for students to review at their own pace. Lectures can be more effective and efficient with technology, including computers. However, the computer, especially when used outside the usual classroom setting, offers powerful ways of transforming teaching into a more interactive and personalised process.

For teachers who are convinced that students learn to think better by writing and responding critically to the course materials and to each other's written responses, the computer, especially when networked through a LAN, an intranet, or the web, offers an unequaled tool for facilitating student-centered discussion. The computer now offers tools which can transform teaching by translating a discipline's modes of inquiry into an interactive and collaborative medium.

Hypertexts of literature can be prepared, by teachers and students, which allow students to study works intensely, informatively, at different levels, and in context. Online discussions and writing involve all students in the study of the work interactively and personally. Combining these two elements into a dynamic syllabus, where students and teachers create a "class hypertext," can empower students as readers and writers in unique ways which challenge traditional paradigms of teaching literature.

The networked computer system used synchronously in a computer classroom or asynchronously has provided the environment to change the teaching paradigm radically from lecture/discussion mode to the collaborative mode. A hypertext document is a text with links which activate when the reader clicks on words, passages, graphics, or icons that are marked. The programme allows the author to create definition links that pop up a box with text or pictures in it, reference links that move the reader to other materials or to other points within the text, expansions that open up new information even to several levels, and commands that launch other programmes. The help screens in many software programmes are done in a similar fashion. Perhaps the easiest way to think of it is as unlimited annotations, marginalia, and writing spaces, all a click or two away from the text.

Embedded in the study hypertext document are definitions, (key words, words with several definitions operating), the occasional irreverent remark, and open questions that highlight gaps, contradictions, and issues in the text. Reference links to larger blocks of materials, which may go to several levels of specificity, may end with a journal entry, a letter, or some other primary text. Often these are inter-textual, presenting parts of relevant works, written either by the same or related authors. Inner-textual links may trace the progression of key themes, images, or repeated patterns, or may be expansions that present more detail or possible interpretations. Hypertext documents allow the teacher to share information, insight, and questions in a much less intrusive, "authoritarian" manner, essentially "behind" the text.

Online discussion and writing is a way of creating the hypertext of the class, as students write, read, rewrite and rethink their own interpretations online. Many web-based communications tools can also serve as student-centered discussion, either public or class-based. Students are encouraged to use this writing space as an unlimited margin for responding to the hypertext document, thinking through questions, noting other gaps; these notes often become the basis for responses and papers on the text.

A "class hypertext" is made up of all the class materials—hypertext documents, plain electronic texts, electronic transcripts of discussions, student papers, teacher notes and "lectures"—linked in a dynamic syllabus that continues to develop as the course progresses. It can also include URL links to resources on the web, including discussions that originate on another site.

The web is accessible from both Windows and MAC platforms, and perhaps on most university computers; it may also be available to students at home or in their dorms. The syllabus could also reside on a campus network to which students have broad access, and/or in a programme that students can install on other computers that they have access to. Such broad access is one major advantage, because students can read them at their own pace and repeatedly.

Since the hypertext syllabus is constantly changing and growing, students need to be able to see those changes; taking some fixed computer files home is not enough. It can stretch a class beyond its boundaries of time and space, a great pedagogical advantage. Students can read, analyse and critique interpretations and papers about the class texts that were written by writers not in the class, perhaps by students who study in another institution or who have studied the same works in past classes.

Generating and critiquing multiple interpretations of a text is the ideal way to study a complex work. Students can compare their own ideas and enhance them by encountering other interpretations, in and outside of their own class, with little fear of hurting someone's feelings. Addressing their writing to a broad and responsive audience, not just the teacher, makes most students regard their writing much more seriously. They also learn a great deal from reading each others' writings; and soon figure out which ones are stronger and why. They generally fine-tune and support their arguments more carefully than they would otherwise—not for a grade, but for personal satisfaction.

INTERACTIVE DISTANCE LEARNING

In the current education systems, there are increasing pressures to diversify the forms of learning opportunity available. The pressures are quite varied and apply with different strengths in different circumstances.

i) there may be economic incentives to increase the throughput of learners. Traditional forms of teaching and learning impose increasingly unacceptable restrictions, e.g. through pressures on staff: student ratios, space, equipment and services.

ii) there are social incentives to broaden access - to raise the participation rates of ethnic and other minorities, and of groups which are under-represented in various sectors of education and training more generally.

iii) though by no means finally, there are calls for greater learner autonomy — both from learners themselves, wanting to take greater control of their learning, and from other interested groups, such as employers wanting personnel with a demonstrable capacity for on-going self-directed learning and professional development.

Within many countries, specialist distance education institutions have been created and are providing models for mass, or at least large-scale, distance education. While more flexible and more open forms of learning — including the use of distance learning — are becoming increasingly common, the connotations of these terms vary from place to place. Recognition of this diversity of interpretation is important when trying to share experience and opinions even within one linguistic community. It has proved especially crucial in European educational R&D, where collaboration across linguistic and cultural boundaries is involved. Within Europe, different sets of terms have gained ascendancy in different countries to encapsulate the movements towards greater flexibility of provision. For instance, in Spain the emphasis is upon distance teaching and modularisation of courses; in Portugal upon the encouragement of self-directed adult learning; in Denmark upon learner control of the fine-tuning of content; in France upon the use of multimedia technologies.

Distance learning is primarily concerned with breaking down certain kinds of administrative or logistical constraints and does not necessarily impact upon educational constraints or independence of mind. Some distance learning schemes are highly prescriptive and compel the learner to follow a narrowly defined educational path at a prescribed pace. It would therefore be wrong to equate distance learning with open learning. Flexibility or openness of educational provision are probably best thought of in relative rather than absolute terms.

Distance learning implies a physical separation between tutors and learners, facilitated either by communications media such as TV, telephone or radio, and/or by the use of packaged learning resources. Use of the term does not necessarily mean that no tutor is physically present with the learners. Indeed a number of distance learning schemes involve both remote and local tutors.

For it to be distance learning, a significant amount of the pedagogical work must be done, or have been done, by tutors, writers, courseware developers, etc. who are not co-present with the learner. The renewed and rapidly broadening interest in distance education methods should not distract us from two important considerations, which combine to highlight the fact that many of the features of distance learning are not new. First, distance education methods have been around for a long time. Second, learners in conventional learning environments, especially in universities, have long spent significant periods of time in forms of independent study which are virtually indistinguishable from the forms of study, that is, the learning activities, characteristic of distance learning courses. Many of the claims made for distance learning boil down to economic, or at least material, benefits that flow from relaxing "logistical" constraints. It is important to recognise that these benefits can accrue in different ways and in different amounts to the various parties involved. One needs to consider the interests of:

i) the learner
ii) the educational provider, and
iii) the body or bodies funding the education or training activity concerned.

Evaluation of such benefits also needs to recognise the crucial difference between what can be claimed for distance education in the general case and what any specific instance of distance education can hope to deliver. In the general case, the main practical consequences of distance education are:

i) Reduction in time spent away from the workplace and/or home.
ii) Reduction in travel and subsistence budgets — a major factor in driving the shift from residential to distance training in the corporate sector.
iii) Increase in course preparation costs consequent on a shift from face-to-face teaching and learning to resource-based learning.
iv) Increase in course revision costs.
v) Reduction in face-to-face teaching costs.
vi) Increased control over the use of time by learners and tutors, especially where there is a reduction in the need for synchronised tutor:learner or learner:learner interaction.

If people can have access to distance learning at appropriate times in their normal workplace, their learning can be bound much more closely to their professional needs. In the limit, this approach dissolves the boundaries between distance-learning and online help or embedded job-aids.

Systems of support for the distant learner that can help them structure their use of time, help maintain their motivation, and deal promptly and efficiently with specific learning queries, therefore become key objects of attention. Two important distinctions can be drawn with regard to such support: when it is provided, and by whom.

Synchronous support: Synchronous support is provided for the learner through interactions which are closely interleaved in time. A familiar example would be a telephone tutorial, in which tutor and learner engage in a discussion about the learner's work, or some topic on the syllabus, or some problem they have encountered. The logistical constraint of synchronisation means that the participants have to be available to interact at the same time. This has the disadvantage of reducing the participants' control over their use of time but brings with it the possibility of rapid turn-taking in a discussion. This is of great benefit when the tutor needs to refine his or her understanding of the learner's problem and can embark on a series of questions and answers to focus in on the core of the problem. It gives correspondingly less time for the participants to reflect on the interaction, to clarify their understanding of an issue or consult reference material. There is a subtle distinction between synchronicity of support and timeliness of support.

Asynchronous support: Asynchronous support does not require simultaneous interaction between participants. A familiar example would be the use of fax. The most commonly used CMC systems are essentially asynchronous, in that they neither require nor support interactions which are closely interleaved in time. The advantages and disadvantages mirror those of synchronous interaction: participants get time to reflect, think, consult resources etc., but the passage of time separating each exchange imposes a different discipline on communication/messages. There is a strong need for clarity, lack of ambiguity, coherence etc. in messages.

Except in the special case of the technical meaning of synchronous and asynchronous communication as applied within computer science, for example, the basis of the distinction between synchronous and asynchronous communication is far from obvious. One could argue that they are not discrete categories, rather that there is a continuum along which the frequency of interchange of message decreases. But this would deny the experienced nature of synchronous and asynchronous communication, as well as ignore some important differences. Two key differences are the possibility of interruption and the cost of communication failures.

Tutorial support: Tutorial support in CMC environments can be deployed in a number of ways. The two most common approaches are tutor as "helpline" and tutor as moderator. In the helpline approach the tutor fields questions and problems posted by individual learners and aims to provide a response tailored to the specific needs of the learner. If the tutor thinks the issue is likely to be of general interest, they may post it, in a suitably anonymised form, in a place where other members of the group can read it. As a moderator, the tutor's main role is to facilitate discussion, or other appropriate collaborative activity, within a conference, by provoking debate, focusing the issues, summarising, restating goals, introducing new material, etc.

Most of the descriptions of educational uses of CMC are derived from formal educational settings, especially university settings. In such settings, it is "natural" for participants to take and be given formal roles, e.g. as tutor or learner. It would be foolish to ignore these role distinctions, and the accompanying status and power differences, in any analysis of a CMC environment. Nevertheless, it is important to point out that, for a mixture of pedagogical and ethical reasons, many tutors who are actively engaged in CMC-based work are pre-disposed to break down inherited role definitions, adopt learner-empowerment strategies and in other ways work towards a greater levelling of status and power.

ICTS IN HIGHER EDUCATION

There are two main forces shaping the actual use of ICT in higher education. On the one hand, we have waves of programmatic investment in technology-based innovation. Each of these waves has its own lifecycle. Each wave gains energy from ignoring some of what has happened in the past. Few waves have the energy to succeed in disseminating their innovative work such that it can secure a sustainable place in mainstream higher education practice. On the other hand, we have a steadily accelerating investment in the ICT infrastructure for learning and teaching — an investment which is both substantial and, in general, not justified on educational grounds. Associated with this growth of ICT infrastructure, we see a burgeoning use of ICT by students and staff alike, for a variety of purposes, only some of which seem to be aligned with what educational technologists believe to be the central benefits of ICT.

We are moving closer to a common view on what higher education is for. A common language is needed for discussing educational aims and processes and for designing and managing learning environments. The new opportunities, which were largely unavailable to us in the last 30 years, for using a consensual view about higher education to articulate our beliefs about valuable educational processes and to plan the resources and infrastructure needed for their support.

The new information technologies are forcing major changes on both traditional campus-based institutions and the large autonomous open universities. In 1969, with the establishment of the Open University in Britain, the face of distance education was changed for ever, and open learning as most of us understand it finally arrived. Thirtyfive years later an equally dramatic shift is occurring in the world of open and distance learning, this time caused by rapid developments in technology, and especially the internet. While the establishment of the Open University initially made little impact on established universities and colleges, most of whom were quite happy to ignore it, this time technological change is striking at the very heart of conventional schools, colleges and universities. Distance education in particular is no longer a dirty word, but something we all do now in public.

Distance learners have far greater technological obstacles to overcome than campus-based students with access to a computer lab. Distance students need access to a computer, and not just any computer if the World Wide Web or CDROMs are to be used — we are talking several thousand dollars for this kind of workstation. They need a modem at a sufficient speed to download at least a few pages within an evening over the plain old telephone system, they need a telephone line that can be dedicated for several hours a week to being on line, they need an internet service provider capable of explaining to someone without a PhD. in computer science how to set the parameters for their machine to enable them to log on, and often they have to bear the cost of long distance calls.

There are already lessons to be learned from the campus-based institutions that have required students to have a computer. For instance, Sonoma State of US spent two and a half years preparing for the implementation. They made sure that there were sufficient courses developed in a way that exploited the use of a computer, and therefore made it essential and valuable to use one. This required a major investment in faculty development. They put in place a whole range of strategies to help students who cannot afford a computer. There is a work-on-campus scheme whereby students can get a computer then work to pay it off. Relatively few students qualify for some form of supplementary State or federal grant on an income basis to purchase a computer, as those eligible for a grant are usually already 'maxed-out, i.e. are already receiving maximum allowable benefits. For these students, there is a low-cost rental scheme and for some free loans of computers from a pool donated by IBM and Apple. There is a $40 'technology fee' imposed on all students. This is used to provide help support for students, improving the local area network, providing docking ports for portables, and making available easy access to public computers in public places on campus. Students themselves play a large role in managing this fund and in approving the level of the fee. While some of these strategies are inappropriate for distance learners, it does indicate the extent to which an institution may have to go to provide sufficient support for students.

The Sonoma State that there was very high compliance for its policy of requiring all its freshman students to have a computer, it was well received by parents and by employers, who praised the university for making higher education more relevant, and also most students seemed to be pleased with the policy. Sonoma though, in the heart of the Californian wine-growing area, is not one of the poorest parts of North America. Another development that is impacting on open and distance learners is the concept of distributed learning. A distributed learning environment is a learner-centred approach to education, which integrates a number of technologies to enable opportunities for activities and interaction in both asynchronous and real-time modes. The model is based on blending a choice of appropriate technologies with aspects of campus-based delivery, open learning systems and distance education. The approach gives instructors the flexibility to customise learning environments to meet the needs of diverse student populations, while providing both high quality and cost-effective learning. This is blurring the distinction between distance and campus-based learning, leading to what many, including myself have called the growing convergence of distance and campus-based teaching.

For example, we now have courses for fully registered, on-campus students where a substantial part is available on the web or on CDROM. Students can access this material at any time, from either terminals on the campus, or from home. It certainly makes the course more easily accessible and convenient for students than attending lectures at a set place and at a set time. However, these students have to be 'resident', i.e. available for lectures. This is certainly distributed learning, but it is not distance learning. Nor is it open learning, since students have to meet all the stringent entrance requirements to be registered as a UBC student.

Many American state universities often use technologies such as instructional television or video-conferencing transmitted from one campus to several other campuses, thus enabling students at the 'guest' campuses to access courses that would otherwise be inaccessible. This is often called distance education in North America but students still have to be at a set time and a set place. It is also a very different form of distance education from that delivered to individual learners in their home, accessible at any time over the internet. On the other hand, the community skills centres originally established by the Open Learning Agency in British Columbia, which have now multiplied to more than 20 community-run sites in medium to small towns, do provide truly open access. Building contractors such as bricklayers, joiners, plasterers and labourers who need to upgrade their basic adult education such as reading and numeracy can drop in at any time to these learning centres and study their courses through computer-managed learning.

Not only does the programme develop reading and numeracy skills, it 'remembers' the last lesson studied by the learner and automatically starts up at the next lesson, no matter how long it is since the learner was last logged on. So while this may be open learning it is not really distance learning. The point here is that we need to serve an increasingly heterogeneous student population, and that means servicing them in a wide variety of ways. Institutions that do not have a requirement to make their courses available to anyone who wants to take them can be more adventurous in their choice of technologies, targeting courses to particular groups of students who are more likely to have or be able to acquire access to the relevant technologies.

Institutions with on-campus students can be even more adventurous, and distance educators can benefit from this experience, and migrate those courses that can be supported at a distance, and adapt those that would otherwise not work at a distance.

Distance students need an online help service that covers both technical and academic issues. What works beautifully between Sun workstations over fibre optics and/or Ethernet on campus can take several hours to download over standard telephone lines, or may not run at all on a 486 computer. Teachers who are comfortable managing 20 campus-based students online find they cannot cope when this is expanded to another 50 distance learners. Many distance educators are increasingly interested in new technologies such as computer-conferencing and the web is their potential for asynchronous two-way communication, thereby allowing the student to interact directly and flexibly with a teacher or other students, even if at a distance. When this is combined with high quality asynchronous interaction with learning material, such as a CDROM or a web site, then we can provide the distance learner with a very powerful learning environment. What we are seeing with these new learning environments, particularly but not exclusively at a higher education level, is a transition from traditional models of teaching, based on a model of information transmission and comprehension through the lecture mode, through more collaborative learning models, but still with strong referents to face-to-face teaching, such as seminars and discussion groups, to completely new paradigms of learning, such as simulations, games, problem-solving and decision-making.

Furthermore, this transition is technology-related. Thus video-conferencing and the web are often strongly associated with the lecture or information transmission mode, computer conferencing and Hypertext with collaborative learning modes, and CDROM and other forms of stand-alone multimedia with problem solving and decision-making, through the development of virtual labs, simulations, games and expert systems. This is not to say that these technologies cannot be or are never used in different ways, but that they lend themselves more to one form of teaching than the others. In addition, the form of some of these newer technologies is both requiring and helping to develop new skills necessary in an information society, such as information navigation and acquisition, and analysis and application of information, and knowledge creation, i.e. when this information is transformed into something new and different.

Imaginative teachers are developing applications software such as WebCT, virtual labs and expert systems that have the potential for developing these new or higher order skills. What is lacking at the moment is any convincing or systematic research evidence to suggest that students are actually acquiring and using these skills, or that this is the best way to get to these outcomes — hence the need for more research similar to the that which we and others are carrying out in British Columbia and Canada. Nevertheless, the potential for developing higher order skills relevant to a knowledge-based society is a key driver in developing computer-based distance education courses. These new technologies require new kinds of educational organisation that can fully exploit the potential of new information technologies. Technology should not be bolted on to conventional institutions; instead they need to restructure their organisation in order to exploit new technologies in a cost-effective manner. The new technologies will be exploited most by those that establish post-modernist forms of organisation, with a high degree of decentralisation, but overall leadership and direction in terms of broad but clear goals and directions for the organisation, customised products and services, alliances with key partners that provide complementary services to the 'core' activities of the organisation, and highly networked and flexible communications systems linking them with their clients, so they can identify and respond quickly to changing market needs.

There is often a major challenge to those in specialist open learning or distance education units. For many years these have been seen as being on the periphery of the organisation, but considered a useful service to an organisation where most faculty have been uninterested in open learning or distance teaching, and where faculties have been more than welcome to leave the main burden of doing this to the specialist units. However, it is often not the open learning or distance education units, who have tended to consider themselves more advanced pedagogically than the professors, who have lead the rush to new technology, but the professors themselves. The professors are often driven by the attraction of a particular technology, they often do not recognise or accept the need for instructional design.

Distance educators and open learning specialists, trained in instructional design and media selection, may shake their heads in dismay, but the reality is that the faculty, at least in universities, control the curriculum process, and if they want to create courses in this way, there is nothing the specialists can do about it.

There are several components of quality in technology-based educational materials. The first is the quality of the content, which is where the brand image and the research capability becomes critical. Often the graphics and the interface have needed improvement to make them acceptable to students. Products when finished have limited applicability because they are not of high enough standard in terms of graphics and interface, or sufficient in volume, to become a commercial product. Instructional designers and distance educators can add value to technology-based teaching materials. While there are additional costs up front in using a project manager, an instructional designer, or even better a team approach, this can lead to substantial savings in production, a better quality product, and the opportunity for revenue generation.

In recent years it has become common for the more strident spokesmen of government and industry to chastise higher education for its conservatism, for its adherence to tradition and to outmoded and privileged practices. If one believed these spokesmen then one would carry in one's head a vision of ivory towers, of elite leisurely institutions for the rich and underemployed — of institutions which have not learned to live in the hard, competitive world of global capitalism. Universities have yet found a way to become fully aligned with the needs of an open democratic society.

However, the picture of elite, unchanging institutions populated by dusty, ineffective, unaccountable teachers simply will not do. Consider some evidence from the UK higher education sector. In the last 35 years, the full-time student population has grown from 200,000 to over 1.1 million. In 1961, less than five per cent of UK school leavers went on into higher education. In 1997, that proportion had risen to 33 per cent for the UK as a whole and to 45 per cent for Scotland and Northern Ireland. This growth has been accompanied by a fall of 40 per cent in resources per student in real terms. The increase in productivity in the UK HE sector has been three times the increase in productivity in the UK service sector. The organisation of teaching methods has also been changing profoundly. In relation to ICT, there is evidence of substantial growth in academics' use of new technologies. In 1992, over a quarter of academics were using some form of computer-based learning in their courses. By 1997 this had risen to between 50 and 60 per cent .

While the changes to be observed in UK higher education may not be uniformly found across Europe, in many European countries, the forces which have been stimulating change are very similar. Much of what has been happening is associated with global shifts from elite to mass higher education systems, increasing accountability and deteriorating per capita resources for the support of learning and teaching. This may seem an inauspicious background for innovation, yet it seems evident that energetic, ambitious and entrepreneurial staff within higher education are responding to adversity in innovative ways. A vital source of support for such innovation comes in the form of programmes of investment organised at national and institutional levels.

In the recent past in the UK, there has been a three phase national investment in the development of innovative ways of using ICT in universities: the Teaching and Learning Technology Programme (TLTP). TLTP is the largest coherent programme of investment in learning technology for higher education in the world. TLTP was launched by the then Universities Funding Council in February 1992. Phase 1 of the programme funded 43 projects at a combined cost of £22.5 million over the three year period 1992/3 to 1994/5. Phase 2 of the programme funded a further 33 projects at a combined cost of £11.25 million over the three year period 1993/4 to 1995/6. Transitional funding of £2 million was made available at the end of each Phase in order to allow some projects to move on to a self-supporting status. Investment has also been made in the establishment of a Teaching and Learning Technology Support Network (TLTSN) based around nine institutional projects. In addition to the investment made through TLTP itself, the institutions involved in the various aspects of the programme, and the staff of those institutions, have made very substantial commitments of staff time and other resources.

Phase 3 of TLTP is getting underway in the spring and summer of 1998. Some £10.5 million is expected to be available for projects, running between 1998/9 and 2000/1. The majority of these projects will be implementation-oriented and will seek to increase the use of existing TLTP materials rather than create new materials. TLTP aims 'to make teaching and learning more efficient by harnessing modern technology'. Its objectives include a commitment to widespread dissemination and take-up of TLTP products and their integration into courses and other forms of support for student learning. There is also a serious concern that all areas of the HE sector, all subject disciplines and all staff and students should reap the benefits of TLTP.

Almost all of the Phase 1 and Phase 2 projects have delivered their products and are at or very near to completion. A key question for TLTP concerns the extent of take up of its products by academics who have not been directly involved in the development projects. A major evaluation of TLTP carried out four years after the start of the programme, reported that it was premature to gather data on take up. A study of the extent of take up of Phase 1 and Phase 2 products is currently underway. We therefore have, as yet, very little systematic data on TLTP's success in dissemination. While it has directly funded the innovative activity of hundreds of staff, we simply do not know how far it has impacted on mainstream practice. A concern about the dissemination of innovations beyond the core team who are directly funded to develop new resources is, of course, a recurring preoccupation for funding bodies and other concerned commentators.

The UK National Development Programme in Computer Assisted Learning (NDPCAL), TLTP's forerunner in the 1970's, placed 'institutionalisation' at the heart of its agenda. NDPCAL was concerned that the projects it funded did not 'remain in the laboratory' but were actually rolled out into mainstream use in the institutions concerned. According to Hooper, this could be said of 27 of the 35 projects funded under the programme. Involvement of staff other than those directly funded by the projects was also significant. NDPCAL projects directly funded about 100 staff. By the end of the programme, a further 690 teaching staff were also involved in the use of NDPCAL materials. Probably about half of these were working in higher education. In the last 20 years then, the numbers of teaching staff in UK higher education making some use of computer assisted learning has risen from around 400 to between 45,000 and 55,000.

From Callender's complementary survey of students in UK higher education, we know that 48 per cent of students claim to have made some use of computer-based learning packages. Among the things we don't know from the survey is whether the use of ICT in learning accounts for 1 per cent , 10 per cent or 50 per cent of an average student's learning experience. From an educational technologists point of view, it would be nice to know what kinds of learning resource are bundled up under the headings of 'multimedia' or 'interactive coursework'. In the absence of firm quantitative evidence on these key matters, there are reasons for being cautious in assuming that programmatic investment in ICT for learning and teaching is delivering the goods.

Much of the evident growth in use of ICT in higher education has relatively little to do with the success or failure of programmes like NDPCAL or TLTP. Such programmes may colour the background against which growth in use of ICT is set - such that most knowledgeable people in UK higher education can refer to the running of TLTP materials as a legitimate means of using ICT. But this is very different from saying that

ICT is being bought primarily to run TLTP and other courseware.

What then, is the underpinning rationale for higher education's very substantial ongoing investment in ICT? This colossal sum is being found, in times of considerable financial adversity, without any clear or convincing educational rationale. As yet, only a minority of universities have an overarching ICT strategy which firmly links ICT investment to institutional goals. Few universities have adopted methods of business process analysis, let alone business process re-engineering, to see how ICT may be used to obtain significant gains in efficiency or effectiveness. Rather, it has to be said, universities are buying and using ICT because it is there and because cognate areas of activity outside academia are buying it. Academic staff are 'knowledge workers' par excellence, and if knowledge workers need a desktop PC and internet access, then so do academic staff.

The investment in ICT to date has not been driven by an unmet demand for computers on which to run the kinds of courseware being produced by TLTP. If anything, the reverse is true. When asked why they were making greater use of multimedia in their teaching, between 40 and 50 per cent of academics said that it was because the technology was available. Fewer than 30 per cent said the main reason was that it would bring benefits to students.

The main driver for increasing use of ICT in higher education is that ICT has become a ubiquitous technology in the world of work. Higher education is just another workplace. Academics and students are just plain workers. It is not that a case has been proven that ICT can make higher education more efficient or effective. Rather, for those working in higher education to be denied access to the defining technology of the information age is simply unthinkable. On this account, what is sustaining higher education's investment in ICT is not the winning of arguments about the relative efficacy of new educational technologies; rather, continuing innovation in the

ICT infrastructure will be sustained by much more powerful forces shaping the acquisition and use of ICT in the world outside academia. Those of us who are concerned about how universities can make good use of ICT in support of student learning can draw some comfort and an important lesson from this fact. Whether or not we are able to demonstrate radical improvements in student learning on the basis of students' use of ICT, it is probable that universities will continue to invest in ICT.

Let us examine that what we are trying to achieve through greater use of ICT in learning and teaching. Basically, there are three main interpretations of the purposes of higher education: the traditional academic, the vocationalist and the critical.

Traditional academic view: The traditional academic view places value on the disinterested acquisition of academic knowledge. It holds that the acquisition of knowledge and understanding is intrinsically good and justifiable, whether or not that knowledge can subsequently be used to take action in the world beyond the university. Students are asked to become competent in academic discourse, with its heavy reliance on declarative conceptual knowledge, contemplative forms of analysis and use of textual representations. Implicitly or explicitly, it acts as if the aim were to induct students into the work and world of the academic and their discipline. Though its position as the dominant model for higher education is now seriously contested, it nevertheless underpins much of what goes on in educational technology.

Diana Laurillard's influential book on *Rethinking University Teaching: A Framework for the Effective Use of Educational Technology*, for example, pays no sustained attention to other conceptions of what university education might be for. The main kind of learning outcome associated with this conception is the ability to recall declarative conceptual knowledge and deploy it in the construction of arguments, or in the solution of problems more generally. Laurillard draws our attention to a peculiar characteristic of academic knowledge: that it is 'articulated' knowledge, consisting of other peoples' descriptions of the world. This 'second order' quality distinguishes it from much of the 'first order' knowledge which we acquire through direct experience of the world. Laurillard holds that much of what cognitive psychology can tell us about learning is restricted to the acquisition of 'first order' knowledge through direct experience in naturally occurring environments. Cognitive psychology says little about learning in the artificial environments which higher education must construct in order to help students learn the descriptions of the world devised by others, and to help them in the processes of interpretation, reflection and exposition

Vocationalist view: Through a variety of means and bodies, employers are pressing higher education to attend more closely to what they claim to need in the new graduates they wish to recruit. These demands may include the kinds of specialised technical knowledge acquired by some students on some courses but increasingly they refer to generic competencies. Frequently mentioned generic competencies include literacy, numeracy, communication, foreign language, leadership, teamworking and IT skills.

Lee Harvey's Quality in Higher Education survey data provide some of the most accessible up-to-date evidence on what UK employers feel they need, and are getting, from recent graduates. According to Harvey and Knight, organisations which recruit graduates are looking, above all else, for transformative potential. That is, they want new graduates entering their employ to have the capacity to transform their organisation, not merely to enhance its productivity and competitiveness along current lines. Elements of this transformative potential can be discerned in the six bullet points above and include willingness to learn; ability to deal with change and question assumptions; analytic, critical and problem-solving skills, as well as the knowledge and ideas brought to the organisation. But employers are clearly worried about graduates' difficulties in coming to terms with what might be called the culture of a modern organisation, such as organisations characteristic of growth sectors in a modern, knowledge-intensive, globally-oriented economy.

Critical being and reflexivity: This third conception is best articulated in the writing of Ronald Barnett. Rejecting 'academicist' and 'operational competence' conceptions, Barnett looks to a higher education 'fit for the 21st century'. He argues that individual reflexivity is necessary for dealing with an essentially unknowable modern world. Higher education needs to respond by:

i) *supporting the student in their acquisition of discursive competence*: offering a deep understanding of some discursive realm and an insight into what it is like to handle with confidence the concepts, theories and ideas of a field of thought, to handle complex ideas in communication with others

ii) *encouraging self-reflexiveness*: by framing the student's initiation into a field of thought such that they see its essential openness and how they may be actors in it

iii) *encouraging informed but critical action*: understanding the power and limitations of the field as a resource for action.

All three of these conceptions give an important place to declarative, conceptual academic knowledge: whether as a body of knowledge to be acquired for its own sake, or as a setting in which to develop transferable skills. One cannot learn to communicate without having something to communicate. One cannot be roflexive without having something to be reflexive about. Beyond that, we see agreement about action in the world: whether constructing a logical and informed argument, solving the problems of professional practice, applying discursive knowledge in exploiting strategic organisational opportunities or in advancing one's social projects. Indeed there are a number of convergences in these conceptions which tend to be obscured in their various critiques of each other.

Some aspects of learning to be effective in a work organisation involve processes which are close to learning from direct experience of the world. But much of what distinguishes a novice from an expert worker in a complex organisation is an understanding of aspects of organisational culture — including knowledge objects created in and around the organisation, which are at best only loosely grounded in the 'real world'. An important class of such objects is what might be called the 'organisational fiction'.

The imperatives of efficient, co-ordinated activity within complex organisations create a need for consensual and often implicit simplifications of such things as organisational goals, procedures and resources, or of interpretations of factors in the organisation's external environment, such as competitor behaviour. Such 'organisational fictions' have a strange relation to what we conventionally think of as truth and falsity. They are 'true', in so far as one normally needs to act as if they are true if one is to engage unproblemetically and productively in the day-to-day work and discourse of the organisation. That is, they are part of the taken-for-granted world in which effective action is set: though they need to be learned and they can be questioned. But their constructed status, their artificiality, their 'fictive' quality, is often made explicit. This gives to organisational fictions a status of being both true and false. A more sophisticated epistemology allows one to see that, from time to time, and task to task, one needs to make use of knowledge whose status depends heavily on context and to understand the origins and power of those contextual factors.

Among the generic competencies which graduates will find most valuable if they are to succeed in modern, knowledge-intensive organisations, is a social and epistemological reflexivity which supports them in learning and using organisational fictions and other forms of contingent knowledge. Taking the argument back to the discussion of academic learning, the point is to recognise that students need to be helped in coming to understand the ideas, propositions, theories, etc., within any particular theoretical perspective, but also to understand how that perspective took shape — indeed, to understand what a theoretical perspective is, to understand how theories and other ways of organising ideas within academia are generated, evolve and die. In part, an understanding of the sociology of knowledge production can help them acquire what might be called 'meta-theoretical' perspectives: viewpoints from which they can see how academic workers construct knowledge within their fields of enquiry.

Given the increasing dominance of knowledge work, and knowledge intensive organisations, in late modernity, a convergence between some of the imperatives of academic knowledge production and the exploitation of knowledge in the commercial world is to be expected.

There is insufficient space here for pursuing the implications of this view across a representative range of educational opportunities. Morrison & Collins, referring to the multiplicity of ways in which it is possible to know about things in the modern world, advance an argument for 'epistemic fluency', which they describe as 'the ability to identify and use different ways of knowing, to understand their different forms of expression and evaluation, and to take the perspective of others who are operating within a different epistemic framework'.

MANAGEMENT OF E-LEARNING ENVIRONMENTS

The term 'learning environment' is very widely used yet rarely defined. The term has at least two main usages within the educational research literature. One connotes something rather small scale and relatively self-contained. The other applies in a more holistic and macro-level way, connoting the totality of objects within which learning is situated and/or the totality of resources on which learners can draw. A distinction is sometimes made between the physical and the psycho-social learning environments. This distinction needs some closer scrutiny if we are to be sure what we mean by 'learning environment'. The physical environment consists of material, non-human things. These things can be relatively simple, such as a chair in a classroom, or relatively complex, such as a library building. The science of ergonomics has traditionally concentrated on the design and usability of relatively simple physical things. According to Fraser et al., the psycho-social environment consists of other human beings and, by extension, their activities, including their discourse.

The incursion of ICT enriches, and increases the importance of, the physical environment. A process of reification translates human interaction into objects. For example, tutorial guidance which may once have been given in an informal and relatively unstructured manner by a teacher to his or her students becomes reified in an online study skills booklet. Or face-to-face discussion becomes mediated through electronic mail. Or the expository lecture is recorded on videotape or translated into an electronic book. As education ventures further into the use of open, distance and flexible learning techniques, so the physical environment of computer-mediated communications and networked learning resources displaces face-to-face interaction and reifies its content.

The learning environment is a complex set of nested structures which provide the physical setting for the work of a community of learners. This physical setting can include all sorts of learning resources, including what we conventionally think of as hardware and software but also other knowledge objects produced through interactions between members of the learning community.

In trying to apply techniques from business process re-engineering to the design and management of university learning environments, Ford et al., identified a number of key business processes, business objects and actors. A surprisingly large number of actors, with different roles, need to work together in the design and management of learning environments, especially where the learning environment has a significant ICT component and/or where rapid change needs to be managed. Few of the members of Ford's team felt that their own institution managed these interactions and processes at all well. Academic departments would often engage in innovative developments without informing the library or information systems services. Institutional senior management would fail to link ICT planning with academic planning.

Innovation most often required insulation from the broader institutional setting, rather than integration with mainstream activities and processes. While such fragmentation in the design and management of learning environments is inexcusable now, it is likely to create insurmountable problems as the pace of change in higher education accelerates. Ways need to be found, urgently, of reducing fragmentation and supporting the development of effective co-operation and partnership between the various actors who have responsibility for the learning environment.

The design and management of learning environments, however fragmented, is a responsibility which weighs down hundreds of thousands of academic staff in the universities of Europe. In most international professions, there are methods of sharing experience and of abstracting general 'lessons learned' from particular events. Academics are very accustomed to doing this in their work as researchers, less so in their work as teachers.

Few academics read the specialist literature on learning and teaching in higher education. Even if they did, it is hard to see exactly how the articles in that literature might directly inform their approach to teaching. Paradoxically, this is especially the case with those articles reporting fundamental research on student learning. It can be extremely hard to derive implications for one's own practice from leading edge research on student learning. Of course, it is not just the academic teachers who need to play a part in designing and managing learning environments. Many other kinds of staff are also involved. Some of these staff are even less likely to read the literature on learning and teaching, seeing themselves primarily as specialists in ICT or the management of library resources, and reportedly finding the language and literature of pedagogy impenetrable.

Information is gathered by and about innovative developments in a variety of ways. Three easily recognisable approaches are experimental, summative evaluation and formative evaluation. In the experimental approach, everything is driven by the goal of gathering valid and reliable data which enable the experimenter to reject a hypothesis. Any developmental activity, such as creating a computer assisted learning programme, is subservient to this hypothesis-testing and theory-building goal. This approach is normally deployed in an experimental or quasi-experimental setting.

In the cases of both summative and formative evaluation, development rather than information-gathering is the primary goal. Summative evaluation is carried out at the end of a developmental process, in order to gather information about the success or otherwise of the developed product, resource or teaching method. It may be possible to link the findings of summative evaluation back to the theory or design decisions which underpinned the development — though this is often quite a problematic undertaking. This makes the findings of summative evaluation quite difficult to share, other than at the crudest level of whether the innovation failed catastrophically or not.

Formative evaluation is carried out at key points during the developmental process in order to inform and improve the development process and improve the quality of the product. Draper uses the term 'integrative evaluation' to describe a formative evaluation which focuses on the integration of an innovative product into its context of use. Formative evaluation tends to be very local in its scope: it is primarily concerned with, and is often at its best when sharply focused on, a specific innovative product or activity. Again, the possibilities for generalising the lessons learned through formative evaluation can be quite limited, because of this pre-occupation with local concerns.

On the development methods axis, two influential models are worth describing: linear instructional systems development (ISD) and iterative development. ISD has been the dominant paradigm for the development of complex instructional systems, especially in the USA, for many years. In its canonical form, it favours a linear derivation which works from an analysis of intended learning outcomes, through high level instructional design, detailed design, implementation, testing and embedding. Various commentators have pointed out the difficulties with this model, not least that it often entails a high risk of producing an unusable product because checks on the validity of the understanding of requirements are left too late in the process. This has motivated the adoption of variants of the iterative development approach, in which a prototype is produced as early in the project as possible, in order to validate the project team's understanding of user requirements.

Neither the ISD not the iterative development approach necessarily produces information from which those outside the project team can learn. Much depends on the forms of information gathering that accompany the innovation process. In principle, ISD with good formative evaluation can lead to more systematic accumulation of evidence about the quality of the various sub-processes and interim products involved. The lessons are clearly being learned in the mainstream of information systems development and software engineering, as the growth of participative and user-centered methods testifies. It is time that we sought to apply these insights in higher education. Of course, one can argue that it is permissible for teachers to insist on an identity between task and activity: to insist that students follow a prescribed route. While this may be valid in some contexts, it is clearly inappropriate for contexts in which we want students to take greater control of their own learning activity — whether this be through self-managed independent or group learning, through home-based study using conventional learning resources, or in some kind of 'virtual' classroom.

The main source of requirements and constraints for technology development come not from a specification of the learning task but from an understanding of students' actual activity. In this way, technology is built to support the actual needs of students in their work as learners, not to reify the task definitions of their teachers.

REFERENCES

Bichelmeyer, B. A., Kiggins, E.A., 1998, "Using Web-based Conferencing in Post-secondary Instruction", *Proceedings of the Annual Conference on Distance Teaching and Learning*, Madison, WI, August 5-7, 1998.

Chapin, A. L., "The State of the Internet: 1995", *Telecommunications*, Jan. 1995.

Comeaux, P., 1995, "The Impact of an Interactive Distance Learning Network on Classroom Communication", *Communication Education*, 41(4), pp. 353-361.

Forsyth, I., 1998, *Teaching and Learning Materials and the Internet* (2nd ed.), London: Kogan Page.

Indira Madhukar, *Internet-based Distance Learning*, Authorspress, New Dehi, 2002.

Jonassen, D., Reeves, T., "Learning with technology: using computers as cognitive tools", In D. Jonassen (ed.), *Handbook of research for educational communications and technology* (pp. 693-719). New York: Macmillan, 1996

Paterson K. G. "Student Perceptions of Internet-Based Learning Tools in Environment Engineering Education", *Journal of Engineering Education*, 88:3, pp. 295-304, 1999.

7

The Age of Language Teachers

Today the use of the World Wide Web (WWW) as a resource for language learning materials has gained increasing popularity among language teachers. As the internet keeps expanding, listserves, newsletters, and even journal articles keep listing and pointing out potential web sites that can be used in language learning.

Furthermore, the literature on web-based instruction reveals numerous personal accounts, informally collected student surveys, or occasionally some pilot studies on students' experiences using internet-based resources. As Chun and Plass point out, "the use of networked environment for learning in general, and for second language acquisition in particular, raises many questions regarding the design of these environments that differ from the traditional design of text-based and stand-alone systems".

The internet as a resource can enrich and expand language instruction. There are numerous reasons in favour of integrating the internet into a language curriculum. Chun and Plass mention general capabilities of features of the WWW that have the potential to enhance language learning. These are:

i) the universal availability of authentic materials,
ii) the communication capabilities through networking,
iii) the multimedia capabilities, and
iv) the non-linear (hypermedia) structure of the information.

The WWW has brought the world to the fingertips of each learner. Applying the WWW to foreign language teaching also provides the opportunity to meet the standards in several ways: Competence in more than one language and culture enables people to gain access to additional bodies of knowledge; all students learn in a variety of ways and settings; language and culture education incorporate effective technologies; and using the web is consistent with learning theories about learning to read authentic materials.

There are numerous convincing arguments in favour of integrating internet-based materials into a foreign language curriculum. The internet is not an ideal way of delivering instruction, and there are numerous challenges to overcome. First, there are still many limitations on interactivity and bandwidth. Second, the hyper-linked structure and presentation of information on the internet may easily cause students to get lost. Third, we have no control over the quality and accuracy of the contents of the information. In other words, the use of the internet resources completely depends on reader judgment, which presupposes solid language proficiency and critical reading skills. Fourth, little theoretical and empirical research actually exists that demonstrates how to make use of internet-based materials or how to design tasks that allow the learners to explore these materials and yield expected learning outcomes. In the same vein, little is known about students' attitudes towards the integration of web-based readings in the foreign language curriculum.

The use of the internet as a learning environment requires some technological skills and knowledge. This raises the question on how to take full advantage of the vast amount of internet resources. In particular, what technological skills are necessary and how can learning tasks be designed that make internet-based resources accessible to the learners. By-and-large, little empirical internet-based research exists that provides us with clear guidelines. Student tasks should exploit the associative nature of hypertext or hypermedia so that students can collaboratively discover and construct new connections, which they combine in a coherent whole. Computer-mediated communication activities be experiential and goal-oriented, and that tasks be consistent with principles of situated learning.

Moving from a teacher-centered to a student-centered approach assigns the learners an increasing role in taking charge of their own learning. It promotes the development of learner independence and autonomy, and thus follows principles of communicative language learning. When shifting from teacher-centered to student-centered designs, the students' levels of proficiency play an increasing pivotal role that also need to be taken into account.

The learners need to have a minimal functional proficiency that allows them to explore an open-ended environment as the internet without the intervention of an instructor. Nevertheless, the degree of teacher and student involvement in making decisions regarding the choice of resources, the scope of learning environment, and comprehension tasks closely correspond to the learner's level of language expertise. internet-based reading activities that have gained most widespread attention and popularity among language teachers and students are those in which the instructor provides a set of learning tasks that engage the learners in exploring reading materials in their authentic environments.

The teacher prescreens and selects a set of sites to ensure its contents are appropriate for their pedagogical goals. Through a particular task design, the instructor facilitates the students' reading process and guides the learners to explore a variety of pre-selected resources, thus providing a clear goal to be accomplished by the students. Furthermore, the tasks are designed so they are not so broad that students wander aimlessly through the material yet open enough to provide multiple paths, outcomes, and interpretations, which can form the basis for subsequent classroom interaction. In this way, the teacher controls the navigational scope and the number and kind of internet sites that the students access.

Despite the restriction, the learner has some autonomy as the tasks provide the learner a choice in the sites he or she accesses and explores. Task types usually include comparisons, gathering factual information, descriptions, and short summaries. The outcome of the student assignments is clearly defined, but open-ended. The teacher's role can best be described as a guide and facilitator. The students follow the teacher's lead but get to explore the contents themselves.

Today, Language teachers' trainings are likely to have become familiar with computers as part of their university experience, with the expectation of using, at a minimum, word processing, spreadsheets, and web browsers to do research, writing, and projects. They are likely to be exposed to computer-assisted language learning (CALL), and some may elect to pursue CALL as a major focus. But even those teachers not delving deeply into CALL will be expected by their supervisors, their peers, and, most importantly, by their students to enhance their teaching through technology.

There are too few CALL and SLA (second language acquisition) studies that provide concrete evaluations of specific tools and technologies and how they are used. Before being able to evaluate effectively CALL programmes, teachers need to add to their pedagogical knowledge a fundamental understanding of the workings of computers and networks. To be able to use a word processing programme, for example, one needs to understand the concept of a file and storage media. To use a web browser effectively, one needs to understand about media types and web page delivery.

At a minimum teachers needs to become informed users of technology. This should include not just software use but as well some hardware basics and an understanding of networks (local area and internet). A familiarity with multimedia formats as well as of players is clearly essential for language teachers. Naive technology users are not well suited to make intelligent choices on the selection of CALL materials. Anyone who has used any kind of technology in the classroom also knows how crucial it is to be able to do basic trouble-shooting of technology glitches.

Most US colleges now have computer literacy requirements in place. The requirements vary considerably, but usually are limited to a knowledge of the mechanics of computing. Today, such skills are normally a prerequisite for success in higher education. For students needing training in the use of general purpose software, electronic tutorials have become widely available. Some are available on CD (such as SkillSoft products), others are accessed through the web. In addition to commercial products, some schools have developed their own training materials, like the nice Microsoft Office tutorials from the Florida Gulf Coast University.

One of the useful methods for developing training materials for learning specific software is the use of screen capture software. Such programmes have been available for some time but have become more sophisticated. Programmes from companies like TechSmith and Ambrosia allow not just screen captures but movies of the screen and even sound to be recorded. An instructor can move through successive steps in using an application and have all those steps recorded. Voice-overs can then be added.

An area of obvious interest to prospective language teachers is the use of media in the classroom. The trend towards use of digital media has accelerated in recent years, due to faster processors, increased network speed, cheaper and more flexible storage options, and easier to use software. The slide projector has given way to projected graphics files, web pages, and presentations. All-in-one projectors are displacing LCS panels mounted on overhead projectors. Although still quite expensive, such projectors can now project at high resolutions and are able to show video, sometimes at HDTV quality. They have also become significantly smaller, lighter, and brighter, useable in lit rooms and designed to be highly portable. Getting pictures into a digital format is becoming easier and more affordable. Flat-bed scanners have dropped precipitously in price in recent years, while small portable scanners have become available, useful for travelling and collecting media. Of course, digital cameras can be used for this purpose as well. The close-up mode available in many models allows quite clear pictures to be made of objects such as menus or newspaper clippings. Many models available today offer very high resolution which can show clearly significant detail.

Digital cameras have risen significantly in popularity as prices have dropped and models have proliferated. Options for transfer of images from the camera have increased, with USB connections now standard, and Firewire connectivity available on high end models. Fast transfer is possible with floppy disk or PC card adapters, into which a camera's media card can be inserted. The card then appears on the desktop and images can be easily dragged to the computer's storage device(s). Such adapters now support high capacity media such as the 128 MB SmartMedia card, which can hold hundreds of images.

Software for the transfer, viewing, sorting, printing, and sharing of digital images has improved considerably. Programmes such as Apple's iPhoto are so powerful yet easy to use that they make the manipulation of digital images much faster and more efficient than was possible with earlier software. iPhoto takes advantage of the internet to enable easy sharing of pictures as well as commercial printing in a variety of formats. Teachers using presentation software such as Microsoft PowerPoint generally need little training in its use. Templates make it very easy to develop a good looking slide show. Media incorporation is straightforward as well; graphics, audio, and video can be added from pull-down menus. Some interactivity is possible with presentation software, depending on the product. It is possible in most, for example, to use transitions and sequential display to deliver material in question and answer format or to create simulations. Many teachers are electing to put presentations on the web so that students can review the materials presented outside of class. This can generally be done by using the "save to HTML" option, although the resulting web-based slide show typically lacks some of the features of the original presentation. Software is available which does a better job of converting the presentation to a web format.

An alternative to presentation software is the creation of lessons or presentations directly in HTML. This results in a format which looks the same in class and on the web. It used to be that HTML-created presentations were poor cousins to PowerPoint slide shows. That needn't be the case with the current capability of web authoring. The "dynamic HTML" (DHTML) possible today enables transitions to be added and on-the-fly changes to web pages without reloading. Of course, the learning curve for creating such pages is considerably higher than it is for learning PowerPoint or other presentation software. In addition to knowledge of HTML, creating interactivity in web pages also requires use of JavaScript. Neither poses an insurmountable learning barrier, however, taking that plunge may be more than many teachers are ready to contemplate.

An alternative is to use an HTML editor to create the web pages. Products like FrontPage (from Microsoft) or Dreamweaver (from Macromedia) make the task to creating attractive and functional web pages quite simple. Mastery of HTML or any scripting language is not necessary to use such a product, although some basic knowledge can be helpful in understanding how web pages are put together. Current versions of HTML editors also offer the ability to use some JavaScript or DHTML functionality from pull-down menus. Here, too, some understanding of the underlying scripting systems is helpful in understanding cross-browser and cross-platform issues and what additional functionality might be possible beyond the options offered by the software product.

A basic understanding of what's going on under the hood on web pages is also helpful to teachers who may be using what is generally called a "learning management system" (LMS) such as Blackboard or WebCT. These are products which greatly simplify the task of creating a web site for a class and adding functionality such as discussion forums, chat rooms, and online quizzes. They have become popular options for teachers in higher education and are being increasingly used in secondary schools as well. To use a LMS it is not necessary to have any knowledge of HTML or of web authoring in general. As a consequence, instructors with little or no experiences using the web are able to create a course web site which can incorporate a variety of interactive tools and hold a great deal of course content in electronic format. Also, publishers are making available some textbook content in formats which can be imported into Blackboard or WebCT, including some multi-item question pools.

It is important for teachers to recognise that a LMS can be a powerful teaching tool but also that its use tends to limit choices and options in the design of a course web site. A template-based system necessarily restricts the degree of individualisation. Customisation is possible only up to a point; the basic structure and "look and feel" of the web sites remain the same. Novice teachers also may assume that the tools and functions built into the system are the definitive statement of the functionality that is available for creating course web sites. Given the expense of purchasing and maintaining such a system, institutions are unlikely to provide training beyond the basics of how to use the LMS. This has the unfortunate by-product of discouraging teachers from trying new and creative ways to use the internet, which are not part of the LMS. While a LMS provides significant functions, it is designed for general educational use, not specifically for language learning. A hopeful sign for the future of LMS is the creation of the Open Knowledge Initiative (OKI), a collaborative project to design and deliver an open and extensible architecture for learning management systems. It is being led by MIT and Stanford University but supported by many more US universities.

The goal is to develop open standards for the creation and exchange of tools and learning materials among institutions and faculty. The hope is that the OKI standards will be adopted in future versions of commercial LMS, which should enable the interchange and flexibility lacking today. OKI is working with the long-running IMS (Instructional Management System) project to develop the standards. IMS defines an extensive set of meta-data for identifying and cataloguing learning modules, while OKI is developing an application programming interface (API) specification for a variety of common services. Meanwhile, commercial LMS are beginning to move in the direction of modularity. Blackboard's "Building Blocks" initiative, for example, allows for plug-in modules to be added to Blackboard installations. Third-party developers are beginning to offer such plug-ins. Wimba's voice board, a tool of potential interest to language teachers, is available as a plug-in. When used within Blackboard, Wimba employs the same interface used in creating and managing Blackboard discussion boards.

One of the other issues in using a LMS is content management. Electronic resources teachers make available are grouped together by the LMS, but the content collection is course-specific. The LMS does not provide for sharing of resources or for cataloguing and searching. As teachers accumulate more material electronically, management becomes a critical issue. Even for basic handouts and exams, issues such as version control, sharing with colleagues, and reliable long-term storage are important. These are functions usually associated with digital libraries or content management systems (CMS). Several CMS companies (such as Concord) are now integrating their services into LMS.

The language teachers apply practical experiences from computer-assisted language learning (CALL) coursework to their teaching. It also examines ways in which teachers continue their CALL professional development. Pre- and in-service language teachers should clearly learn about computer use. When integrated appropriately, CALL technologies can support experiential learning and practice in a variety of modes, provide effective feedback to learners, enable pair and group work, promote exploratory and global learning, enhance student achievement, provide access to authentic materials, facilitate greater interaction, individualise instruction, allow independence from a single source of information, and motivate learners.

The promise of computer technologies, supported by both research and practice, underlies the emergence of technology classes across teacher-education programmes and a sharp increase in courses specifically aimed at language teachers. However, the appropriateness of technology for student learning is only one factor in understanding teachers' use of CALL. Teacher educators need to design CALL courses that teach what language teachers really need to know. Course content should also be readily transferable to school settings across language contexts and language teachers should continue to learn and grow in the technology area as practising professionals.

Research in teacher technology use shows that preservice teachers gain confidence in the use of computer technologies through formal teacher-education coursework and that their attitudes towards computers improve through such coursework. Although this research shows changes in perceptions that are often correlated with classroom technology use, it does not explain what preservice teachers take away from the courses and actually use in their classrooms. Galloway stresses the need for research that addresses questions about what computer experience teachers need to gain, how they actually use computers, and how they learn to use and adopt computers. The literature to date that attempts to answer such questions suggests two overarching themes: first, that teachers learn what they actually need to use; and second, coursework does not always address teachers' or students' needs. These two points are explained further.

While the emergence of a great variety of technology courses for teachers suggests a belief that teachers can learn about education technology theory and practice through coursework, some researchers have found that coursework seems to have little or no impact on teacher-education students' beliefs about their abilities or use of what they have learned in their teaching.

Although teachers do learn new skills as a result of instruction, they do not necessarily use those skills in their daily practice or change their instructional practice in the long run. Levy's seminal study suggests that there should be a fit between teachers' philosophies of language teaching and learning and what they see as the capabilities of technology to facilitate teacher use of the technology in their classrooms. Most teachers learned to use computers outside of coursework. While this helps to prepare teachers for CALL coursework in the use and integration of appropriate technologies, it also has other implications for teacher education in CALL.

The most-used computer application among his participants was word processing. This is because teachers use word processing for both personal and professional work. Few teachers actually used telecommunications, hypermedia, or even other business programmes such as databases and spreadsheets because they did not need to use these technologies in their lives outside of the classroom.

The United States Department of Education reports that teachers use technology most frequently to prepare or supplement instruction rather than for instructional delivery, thereby working to save themselves time or to enhance student learning beyond the classroom. Keirns concurs, noting that "the practical experience of learning computer skills which are personally useful has a positive effect" on teacher technology use. This implies that, for CALL coursework to have an impact, it should focus on the needs of individual teachers and their contexts.

A wide range of factors have been found to influence teachers' use of computers. Educators are prevented from using technology in many ways. These include time pressures both outside and during class; lack of resources and materials; insufficient or inflexible guidelines, standards, and curricula; lack of support or recognition for integrating computers; a clash between new technologies at universities and older ones in schools; lack of leadership; and inadequate training and technical support. Other factors that may influence technology use are age, gender, attitudes toward technology, and teaching experience, but the results are mixed as to what extent these variables are related to teacher use of technology.

The rate of technological change poses a barrier to technology use. The top-down implementation of technology by authorities may cause resentment and avoidance by teachers. The lack of perceived legitimacy of the computer as an educational tool has an influence on teacher adoption of the technology. Language teachers do not use computers in their classrooms not because they are technophobes, as some suggest, but because institutions and programmes overlook the importance of training teachers and matching their goals with the tools they hope to employ.

Technology advocates have ignored realities such as the social organisation of classrooms that serve as an inhibitor of classroom technology use. Innovations for solving productivity problems defined by non-teachers invariably were mandated into use by district policy makers, not teachers. Views of teaching and organisational compliance ill-fitted to schools and classrooms and married to feckless strategies aimed at coercing teachers to use the innovation explain limited use of the new technologies. Teachers' attitudes and philosophies toward teaching and technology, regardless of their basis, can both support and prohibit the use of technology in the classroom.

A CALL course should be looked at from a more holistic view than whether or not teachers become computer experts during a course. That is, teachers can learn additional skills after their coursework on their own if they receive a firm grounding in CALL theory through their coursework. It is nearly impossible to cover every piece of technology in a course. However, if teachers understand the underlying theories and perspectives of technology integration, they can continue to learn and develop their materials according to their future needs. Although CALL professional development materials and resources are in the form of books, web sites, electronic discussion lists, journals, and courses exist, it is unclear which of these provide the most effective development and which provide theories and activities that directly transfer to classroom implementation. We may take a cue from the Apple's "Classrooms of Tomorrow" project, where hands-on, active learning by teachers allowed exploration, experimentation, and most important, reflection; these "situated teacher development" activities, in turn, supported many different kinds of change in classrooms.

The technology coursework can change teachers' attitudes toward and confidence with technology and can also provide them with skills that they did not previously have. It also suggests that one course alone is probably insufficient to change teachers' practicc either immediately or over time. Furthermore, it shows that teachers learn many of their technology skills on their own and use technology specifically to support their current teaching practices.

In addition, teachers have different reasons for using or avoiding technology, but those who have more experience in teaching and in technology use, especially in practice, are more likely to integrate technology in their classrooms. More important, teachers need to have specific needs met during their technology learning. Barriers to classroom use may also prevent the professional development of technology-using teachers. Examining the usefulness of a sequence of CALL education courses and experiences, as opposed to one course, could also shed light on this area. Furthermore, we might investigate whether and what theories of learning with technology transfer from coursework to the classroom, and how this is evidenced by the applications that teachers employ.

TECHNOLOGY-MEDIATED LITERACY PRACTICES

Social-cultural activity theory of learning posits that learning occurs through social uses of various tools: language, signs, images, and texts, as well as technology tools. Activity theorists believe that people learn the uses of these tools by learning how they are linked to the objects or outcomes driving a specific activity within an "activity system." Russell defined an activity system as, "any ongoing, object-directed, historically conditioned, dialectically structured, tool-mediated human interaction. Some examples are a family, a religious organisation, a school, a discipline, a research laboratory, and a profession". Central to activity theory of learning is the idea that these tools function to mediate the learning of literacy practices.

Students learn to use a range of tools to engage in these literacy practices. Work in the field of "distributed cognition" posits that certain practices associated with an activity become embodied or "distributed" in tools. For example, navigational instruments are used to capture what is known about navigating the seas. They then serve as tools that guide a ship based on human knowledge about navigation. Similarly, expert computer systems are built on experts' knowledge about a certain phenomena such as diagnosing a particular disease. Tools are therefore used within an activity to function as extensions of certain practices involved in an activity.

One basic literacy practice involves defining intertextual links between texts. Intertextual links are used to define connections between language, images, characters, topics, or themes based on similarities in languages, genres, or discourses. These links reflect connections associated with establishing and reifying institutional power. Intertextuality may also involve connections built on social meanings in which participants make intertextual links in order to build social relationships or connections. For example, participants in conversation may allude to shared experiences to foster a social bond or an insider reference to exclude others.

Participation in online chat exchanges engages early-adolescents in using intertextual links to foster social interaction. Making intertextual links between disparate text types or genres helps students engage in what Semali and

Watts-Pailliotet define as "intermediality": the ability to construct connections between different sign systems, concepts, and technology tools.

Students are engaged in making intertextual links through multi-genre writing about a topic, an approach currently popular in secondary writing instruction. Multi-genre writing involves using a range of different types of genres — reports, poems, letters, diaries, stories, advertisements, field notes, photos, drawings, and so forth — to explore different aspects of and perspectives on a topic. Connecting these disparate genre types requires the ability to determine how different types of texts yield different perspectives on the same topic or phenomenon.

One technology tool that mediates the practice of making these multi-genre intertextual links is hypermedia. Hypermedia functions as a tool by combining hypertext (texts linked together by multilinear nodes) and multimedia (photos, video, art, audio, text, etc.) to produce an interactive media experience for participants. Because hypertext allows participants to choose optional paths through multimedia, participants can both construct and respond to hypermedia interactively. Students often respond positively to hypermedia texts because it is consistent with their everyday experiences with multi-modal environments that combine images, animation, video, music, and texts.

Hypermedia challenges the traditional emphasis in literacy instruction on understanding or producing unified, coherent texts based on a definitive, single perspective. He calls for teaching a "rhetoric of expectations and arrivals" that help students understand where certain links may take them and how they should respond to where they arrive. And, given the important role of graphic representations in hypermedia, he posits the need for often-marginalised art and video-production instruction to help students respond critically to images. Hypermedia can also assist in organising links around central themes or topics in writing instruction. Analysis of first-year college writing class students' construction of hypertexts indicated that students structured information around central ideas and illustrated those ideas through links to other texts or graphics.

Using the hypertext as a tool helped students define links between diverse parts of their hypertext because the links made it visually easier to connect the ideas. In contrast to the essay format that often constrains exploration of alternative, conflicting perspectives, the hypertext format fostered exploration of alternative, conflicted perspectives about an author's life that resisted closure. Analysis of the effectiveness of hypertext or hypermedia production requires going beyond comparisons of linear versus non-linear productions to consider the particular contexts, user characteristics, design options, and types of tasks involved in the production. The quality and nature of hypertext links may be a function of participants' sense of the larger object or outcome driving their participation in an activity.

Another basic literacy practice involves adopting multiple voices and perspectives through making "double-voice" intertextual references or evoking or mimicking the languages or styles from other texts or worlds. Speakers and writers employ these intertextual references to establish social relationships and identities. Through interaction with others, participants construct identities by performing in ways that position them in relation to others' positions —"it is in the connection to another's response that a performance takes shape".

People's utterances reflect their relationships with others' potential, anticipated reactions to their utterances. In participating with a range of diverse perspectives and voices in a computer-mediated context, students learn to consider alternative perspectives different from their own. The more open students are to experimenting with alternative ways of being and knowing, the more open they are to entertaining alternative values, as opposed to a rigid, monologic perspective on the world. Middle-school students engaged in synchronous exchanges employed parodies of peers, teachers, and school discourses, for example, mimicking the pedantic language of textbook "discussion questions".

Constructing the hypermedia production to share with their students involved teachers in a constructivist approach to teaching in that they had to draw on the information about the individual to construct their own interpretation of the person's life through making intertextual links between texts, images, and sounds. This change in learning when using hypermedia sometimes causes problems as learners struggle to integrate information, themes, and stances into a hypertext document. To explore their knowledge as related to their audience, they initially developed concept maps using InspirationTM to represent their knowledge prior to creating the hypermedia production. These concept maps were used as guides to help the teachers choose what links they believed were important as well as what types of media they may have wanted to employ to represent their knowledge in StorySpaceTM. The hypermedia productions were analysed by the investigators in terms of the types of texts — images, written texts, sounds, and so forth — teachers included in their productions, as well as the types of links they employed in connecting these texts.

An asynchronous web-based teacher/student communication site was created to foster communication between the teachers and students during the time when they were not working with each other in school. To address potential security and privacy issues, the middle school students would click on the name of their assigned preservice teacher and then engage in conversation about their projects or personal matters. Only the pupils assigned to the teachers could access those particular teachers. Because the communications were asynchronous, teachers and the middle school students could post and respond to questions relating to their cooperation on the project at any time. These exchanges served to create a sense of "situatedness," commonality, interdependency, and infrastructure essential for creating a computer-mediated community of practice. The middle school students and the preservice teachers were able to participate in the "sociocultural practices of a community", as they were situated in a rich context of practice that involved sharing information about each other while working on completing the biography project. They were therefore sharing in a common activity that required their joint efforts in completing the project. They were dependent on each other: the students providing the materials for the projects and the teachers providing the technical support involved in the hypermedia production. And, they were operating within an infrastructure that involved a sense of accountability to completing the project.

Transcripts of the web-based communications were analysed in terms of the amount of participation as determined by the number of comments employed, defined in terms of a complete "thought unit," a procedure employed in research on online communication. All teachers used digital pictures copied from the internet or scanned from books. Thirty percent of the teachers also used QuickTimeTM movies obtained from the internet that showed the event in detail. As they indicated in their learning logs, teachers believed that these video clips effectively conveyed ideas they wanted to portray about their person. In addition to pictures and movies, 20 per cent of the teachers used sound clips that they prerecorded using SoundEdit Pro TM or that they captured from the internet to add narration to their project.

Hypermedia productions based on the students' writing, the teachers were using multimedia links to model uses of technology for their students as a tool for portraying a range of different biographical elements of their subjects' lives. Because the clips were extracted from related historical or cultural contexts and events, teachers were going beyond simply presenting biographical information to examining individuals' lives as constituted by participation in larger historical and cultural contexts.

The web-based communication served to enhance the quality of teacher/student relationships and provide for frequent collaboration on the project. Through their exchanges, teachers and students were acquiring a number of literacy practices. Analysis of the web-based communication between teachers and students indicated that the teachers initiated all the comments on the asynchronous discussion board. The initial conversations during the first two weeks of the semester typically began with three-to-five sentence personal anecdotes that served to help establish a personal relationship between the teacher and students. The interaction and writing style during these initial exchanges was relatively formal.

Teachers and students were learning the literacy practice of using intertextual links to establish social relationships. In sharing internet addresses, teachers and students were defining ways to establish a social working relationship. Moreover, in formulating their messages rhetorically within an early-adolescent's zone of proximal development, teachers were learning the literacy practice of framing communication in ways that are consistent with their audience's developmental level. Knowing how to communicate in a multi-modal format using computer tools is becoming an essential literacy practice. Students also need to know why they are using these tools to achieve certain objects or outcomes in an activity.

Teachers and students used the web-based communication site as a tool for establishing social relationships and for planning their multi-genre writing projects. This site provided teachers with continuous, on-going interaction with their students, something often lacking in practicum experiences with infrequent school visits. The written exchange allowed teachers to model a range of literacy practices — building personal relationships through intertextual links, mutual planning and development based on shared information and question-asking — practices students then demonstrated in their own responses. There were also marked gender differences, with female teachers eliciting more participation from students than male teachers through uses of "personal" connections, suggesting the need for teachers of both genders to employ such connections. This suggests the need for training teachers to conduct online exchanges as equally important to training in leading and facilitating oral discussions. Such training should examine issues of teacher domination, especially as related to gender. And, the training should help teachers define the range of literacy practices students are acquiring through participation in the interaction.

REFERENCES

Cuban, L. *Teachers and machines: The classroom use of technology since 1920*, New York: Teachers College Press, 1986.

Debski, R., "Exploring the recreation of a CALL innovation", *Computer Assisted Language Learning*, 13(4/5), pp. 307-332, 2000.

Galloway, J. P., "How teachers use and learn to use computers", In *Technology and Teacher Education Annual*, pp. 857-859, 1997.

Johnson, M., "CALL and teacher education: Issues in course design", *CALL-EJ Online*, 1(2). Retrieved November 26, 2001.

Knezek, G., Chiristensen, R., & Rice, D., "Changes in teacher attitudes during information technology training", *Technology and Teacher Education Annual*, 1996, 763-766.

Milbrath, Y., & Kinzie, M., "Computer technology training for prospective teachers: Computer attitudes and perceived self-efficacy", *Journal of Technology and Teacher Education*, 8(4), 373-396.

Reed, W., Anderson, D., Ervin, J., Oughton, J., "Computers and teacher education students: A ten year analysis", *Technology and Teacher Education Annual*, 1995.

8

Changing University Concepts

The educational methods accompanying the new technological paradigm allow of a participatory vision of education by promoting asynchronous learning, a new inter-actor relationship and 'lifelong' education. The internet and the World Wide Web are seen as vehicles for lessening dependence on hardware platforms, but even in this domain there are competing standards and different flavours of web browsers. Educational institutions worldwide spend large amounts of money each year for developing, adapting or acquiring the new learning resources and courses.

The role played by education software in distance education increased in the period from 1985 to 1995 as it gradually replaced learner-controlled approach instruction or programmed education, in which traditional or audiovisual teaching aids were used. By the year 2020, this development process will have been transformed and broadened, relocating learners and teachers, reconstructing the underpinnings of natural course progression, channelling reliable and enriched material through the data transmission networks, combining the necessary documentation with lectures, and enabling teachers, researchers and students to exchange information via electronic mail and forums and thus globalising knowledge.

The current information context is characterised by the mass advent of digital solutions, which are drastically changing established realities, and by a major risk of the hegemony of one single language to the detriment of multilingualism and of one single culture to the detriment of plurality, in particular through the very rapid development of the internet, by the atomised development of the new technologies at different paces in different countries and regions and, finally, by the reduced visibility of non-digitised material for ever-growing communities. And, in parallel, needs are steadily expanding in terms of information and of methods and tools for producing, organising, disseminating and consulting it.

Most of the technical and methodological solutions necessary to this circulation of information, such as the internet and related standards, have their origin in the scientific community, which must now devote thought to its uses and its inescapable penetration of the world of education and research. Past experience will have to be analysed in the light of the impact of the digital, particularly on the circulation and transmission of knowledge. Some consider that the concept of the industrialisation of education is undergoing profound transformation.

Distance education already has a long history of research and achievements, from correspondence courses to systems supported by distance audiovisual aids. The NICT are revolutionising this discipline and should enable it to emerge from arcane debate and the scepticism of educationists, and become a global industry. Whereas the question of the didactic quality of distance education is still the subject of much debate dividing 'traditionalists' and 'specialists', the NICT are beginning to introduce all the factors of what amounts to an educational revolution, in which the teacher-learner and the learner-learner relationship will change radically.

The concepts of 'collaboration' and 'asynchronous education' should gradually become established, more because they reflect the necessities of the evolution of society than for purely educational reasons. This change contains a veritable educational revolution in embryo, in which the traditionally rigid space-time-hierarchy structures will be shattered. The main argument in favour of this change is, of course, economic;

but it must be borne in mind that distance education fees are still as high as those charged for traditional education, since the mass economies that will offset an initial outlay higher, in every respect, than that involved in traditional education, have not yet been achieved. This will change radically as the mass application of this technology becomes established — which could be the case after a transition period of several years. There are, of course, still many challenges to be faced:

i) the use of various technologies in appropriate proportions and applications,

ii) the question of the evaluation of learners and teachers,

iii) the question of intellectual property where educational material is concerned,

iv) and the major bottleneck: training (particularly for teachers) in the skilled use of these new tools.

A large number of different terms and expressions are used in the context of distance or virtual education warrants semantic examination so that they can be classified, misunderstandings can be avoided and the major past and future trends highlighted.

i) *Distance teaching/distance learning/distance-teaching university*: characteristic of the audiovisual (televised) stage of distance education and facing a serious threat from the novel contribution of the NICT.

ii) *The open university*: places emphasis on the collaborative and global aspects.

iii) *The collaborative or co-operative university:* places emphasis on the aspect of collaboration, both between teachers and learners and between education partners.

iv) *Asynchronous education*: places emphasis on one of the fundamental aspects of the new style in education which technology has made possible, i.e. studying at one's own pace with no constraints as regards time.

v) *The global university*: places emphasis on the geopolitical vision.

vi) *Computer-mediated education and distributive learning are used by technology specialists.*

vii) *The internet university:* technological and commercial. Often a 'meta-university' which sells logistic apparatus with which the purchaser can produce educational material intended for distance distribution.

viii) *The virtual university*: characteristic of the advanced technology approach. Sees itself as an integrative concept of the new paradigm, in which physical space and the need for synchrony disappear. One could add a semantic restriction towards higher education, however, whereas in the new paradigm the education field tends to reduce the boundaries between the various types of studies.

The concept of the virtual university is the most widespread at the present time. It meets traditional universities' need to provide new services and to find new modes of relating to learners. Following are the ingredients of success:

i) use of the NICT and a combination of the various technological tools 'in proportion' with a view to radically changing the equation of the cost of education;

ii) teaching which accompanies the new technological paradigm and makes possible:

iii) asynchronous learning;

iv) a new inter-actor relationship;

v) continuing education;

vi) a participatory vision of education; the virtual university is where three areas intersect:

a) the area of possibility;

b) the technology area;

c) the teaching area.

In the technology area, the NICT are at the top of the hierarchy, but it must be realised that unless these technologies are applied with the appropriate teaching methods, they will add nothing to education but confusion and mistaken objectives. If, on the other hand, they are mastered, the change of paradigm which they will bring will allow of nothing short of a revolution in teaching, marked primarily by the abandonment of the vertical form of education in favour of a ring structure, in which the teacher becomes the facilitator of a process which is focused on the learner and on his or her ability to discover knowledge at his or her own pace and in collaboration with other learners and facilitators.

As the result of an asynchronous mode of operation, this new form of teaching will ease the constraints of space and time. By losing its verticality, learning becomes a process of collaboration and partnership among various groups. The teaching area is undergoing far-reaching changes. Some recent inputs have been disqualified to a certain extent by technological change, and concepts are currently being revised from the point of view of means and objectives. The major challenge is to devise a new form of teaching which is based on and transcends technological devices without adopting the attitude of a technologist or mythifying technology. The challenge appears to be less contradictory whenever the sociological aspects accompanying the technological revolution are emphasised.

After several years of slow and difficult progress, this discipline has entered a 'push technology' phase, which could come to maturity in less than two years and could give way to a new global market-driven phase, in which market shares will grow significantly in less than five years. We are in a situation similar to that of the internet in 1992; we are going through a two- to three-year period of transition, which will be followed by a period of tremendous expansion.

The following are the three key factors in the 'push technology':

i) the necessary change in teaching methods, and in the student-teacher and student-student relationship in particular;

ii) the key ingredients for the change in teaching methods: the pursuit of group interactiveness and proactiveness;

iii) determination of the judicious proportion of technological facilities.

The distance factor will no longer be a constraint. The student can take part in education without needing to be present in person at the university. The pedagogical investment for modern distance education is certainly greater than that of the traditional model, whether in terms of initial outlay or the investment connected with delivering the education. There are two factors, however, which will reduce the overall cost in factors of scale:

i) the reduction of needs in terms of area and premises;

ii) the appreciable increase in the size of the virtual class.

The traditionally vertical teacher-student relationship will evolve towards a more horizontal model, in which the teacher becomes a facilitator, expert or colleague and the learner becomes naturally active. In this evolution of roles the group will gain importance as a place for consultation, dialogue and collaboration. Through this mechanism the education is 'received' by the individual in interaction with a group, of which the teachers constitute only one element. Roles are thus completely redefined, and the dynamism of the new roles requires a new student.

The internationalisation of the education market and the emergence of new entities placed deliberately in the commercial area will intensify competition between educational establishments. In parallel, collaboration and strategic alliances on the part of universities will become imperative as the appropriate response to change.

The traditional concepts of student assessment based on results will have to be adapted to new methods in which the assessment of the process will gain more importance so that the measuring of assimilated knowledge can be circumvented and factors more sensitive to the equation of the new professional can be integrated: ability to carry out research, to adapt, to communicate, to collaborate, etc. The distinctions drawn between the various types of education (primary, secondary, technical, university, vocational) will become less important, and the emphasis will be placed on continuing education.

As this trend develops, the distinction between 'attendance-oriented' and distance education will become blurred, and the foregoing concepts will also apply to 'local' forms of education. The advent of the NICT in the years that lie ahead raises the question of how the teaching profession can prepare for these radical changes. Structurally, distance education is much more demanding as regards teaching ability. The 'new teachers' will have to master this new NICT environment and be mentally prepared for a radical change of role while adding to and updating their knowledge of their special subjects.

The new teachers will emerge from the isolation of the classroom and receive considerable logistical support, and it is up to them to be able to co-ordinate and use it: they must have production specialists at their disposal for both audiovisual means and the web, so that they can achieve high-quality results as regards form and can concentrate on content, i.e. on the educational material. The realisation by university authorities of the need to provide teachers with a set of support functions is a key factor in successful educational production.

The production of interactive multimedia as personal learning tools complementing network-based tools seems to be reserved for industry for the time being, and distance universities are slow to apply themselves to this field. Yet there is basically no economic reason for this. Web-based educational sites are to be observed which have excellent graphic models but response speeds which are too low to serve as an educational tool — a fact which argues in favour of producing interactive CDROMs and implementing intranets rapidly. Moreover, the emergence of digital radio (DAB) has made it possible to found new hopes on the mass dissemination of knowledge at low cost and in acceptable conditions. This technology is particularly suited to developing countries.

UNESCO recommends that 'design templates' be created for educational software. Thus, the suppliers of course material will be able to offer programmes in the language of their choice, regardless of the region of the world. Each producer will be supplied with a compendium of examples of good practice in using NICT-related software. This action should enable the countries of the South to develop good-quality open and distance education rapidly.

Information is becoming globalised; it is becoming an inescapable market framed by strict laws. The need is growing for measures to defend freedom of access to information in the form of a universal public service intended for the research and education sector in particular. Considerable efforts to put informal literature, reports and theses on line are becoming a matter of priority. The same applies to free software designed according to the ideas of the producer groups; the LINUX operating system and the CDS-ISIS documentary software can be quoted as examples.

Multilingualism is an important point in the defence of cultural pluralism as opposed to the monolingualism of information. Automatic translation tools must be implemented rapidly.

The purpose of virtual reference libraries and electronic libraries is to provide all scientists, researchers, teachers, and students with a virtual information site through which they can access all the products necessary to their education, training and research work.

The human factor is one of the major factors curbing NICT penetration of higher education. Before any technological action can be taken, training programmes need to be defined at various levels for various target groups. Plans must be made for training technicians and engineers to back up technology within institutes of education and research, for training teachers, and for training decision-makers. The latter is a *sine qua non* if the NICT are to enter the scientific world. It is essential to convince the political and institutional authorities that these technologies are justified as a factor of development and modernity.

Various factors must be taken into account when the NICT are being introduced into higher education — an undertaking which is not without risks. The economic imbalance between the countries of the North and those of the South disqualifies the latter. There are several factors which determine this imbalance:

i) universities do not all have flat-rate connection;
ii) it is paradoxical that the poorest countries should be those where the cost of telecommunications is highest;
iii) computers are still expensive and heavily taxed in those countries, although the states are beginning to pursue incentive policies;
iv) universities are undergoing a reorganisation whose contours are still vague and not yet fully understood;
v) there is a risk of cultural uniformisation unless diversity — linguistic diversity in particular — is assured;
vi) there is a gap between the academic world and the industrial world;
vii) there is a risk of de-skilling in the case of teachers who cannot or do not want to adapt to the new circumstances;
viii) de facto technological imperialism entails the risk of cultural imperialism if only one part of the world produces material and the other consumes it.

Today universities are in a position to take up the challenge of the new information and communication technologies. To do so they must launch a process of collaborative work in which the least developed countries have an important place. The scientific excellence of the industrialised countries will have to irrigate the poorest countries according to a co-development rationale. The risk of 'infopoverty' is one of the factors curbing development, and it is therefore essential that universities should be the predominant sources of the circulation of knowledge in the service of shared collective intelligence. They must be prepared for the validation of acquired skills and knowledge and the awarding of diplomas, for which the procedures will have to develop further, with a view to achieving 'transnational knowledge'.

Most of distance learning programmes were developed and deployed by traditional educational institutions and these institutions are leading the way in adopting the internet to its service. Commercial educational institutions are concomitantly expanding in several directions. Commercial universities are growing at an unprecedented pace. Commercial organisations assuming an ever greater role in the administration of private and state educational institutions. Traditional institutions of higher education are consigning one aspect of their administration after another commercial corporations: food services, laundry services, book stores, some aspects of the registrar's office are currently being run by privately owned corporations. Presumably universities are incapable of administering the operations successfully.

Electronic distance education is worrisome because it is vastly superior to traditional video distance learning. It is interactive so that teacher and student can communicate in real time to visual representations of each other. Video conferencing is possible on- and off-campus and in all universities. But this is not even the central issue in electronic distance education. The fact that the computer is involved means that the interaction between teacher and student can be much more complicated than in a conventional classroom. The lines between lecturing, answering questions, testing and grading break down completely.

The online exercise does more than test. It provides the student with immediate feedback in the form of hints to help him learn the rules and principles he is being tested for. It can only be replicated in a classroom with a teacher but the teacher can administer this interactivity to only one student at a time. The tool here is a powerful interactive tool that duplicates an important part of teaching on an enormous scale without a teacher other than that the compiler of the exercise.

Electronic distance education is a very powerful educational delivery system allowing interaction between teacher and student impossible any other way. In addition to this advantage we must remember that courses by the world's best teachers, edited and improved infinitely, can be made available on this network in perpetuity. Students who choose education by this vehicle ten years will have no need to make allowances for mediocre teaching in some of their courses in order to take a few excellent ones. All electronic distance education courses will be excellent, exciting, proven effective, and endorsed if not created by the most famous teachers and textbook writers in the world.

Corporate educational institutions pose a greater threat as their numbers grow since they combine an economically operated campus with a vast electronic network. Corporations are concurrently assuming more and more of the responsibilities of operating state and private universities: food services, dormitory operations, book stores, even the registrar's office has recently become the target of the more parsimonious hand of corporate managers.

If private and state universities concede they are incapable of managing their own operation, it is only a matter of time beforc corporations begin offering assistance in instruction. Indeed, publishers already provide most the materials we use and the course we teach is to a large extent dependent upon those materials. So over recent decades we have seen the expansion of commercial universities and a growth of commercialisation in private and state university administrations.

In the most valuable commodity in the information age is — information. If follows that the source of reliable information is also extremely valuable. The academic community is the largest creative source of reliable information on earth. Commercial institutions, therefore, can be expected to pay a premium for what educators have been donating to society in exchange for modest living expenses over the past millennium. Corporations have a growing expertise in our business. Many corporations have been educating their employees for decades, teaching them not only the business, but skills we often fail to instill: writing, reading, and thinking skills. Now corporations and some educational institutions are joining forces to bring graduate education and training to the web. These new informational conglomerates will combine residential campuses with worldwide reach.

The roles for a modern university are easily reduplicated by electronic systems. They are:

i) education and professional training,
ii) credentialing, i.e. certification,
iii) the selection of academic elites,
iv) fostering a worldwide community of scholars, and
v) the transfer of knowledge.

There are certainly differences between education and professional training. The latter has been conducted by distance learning since the end of the 19th century. What distinguishes education from training is certainly one or more of the intangibles we are looking for. The distinction usually turns on the ability to think critically, the ability to discover faults in data and in the interpretation of data. Acquiring this ability is difficult without thoughtful conversations with a master whose primary mode of thought is critical thinking. The scientific method is difficult to learn without some sort of laboratory experience. That is why all universities require a laboratory experience of its undergraduates. The appreciation of art and music is difficult without a knowledgeable guide and direct experience with real art. Certainly, no one can learn a foreign language without speaking it, or a sport without participating actively in it. These are certainly some of the intangibles that distinguish education from training.

The first virtual university, Jones International University, was recently accredited by the North Central Association, although not everyone agreed with the decision. The degree one receives from a university currently is the most important part of their credentials for the rest of their lives. Employers attach widely differing weights to certification from different universities.

Universities are the guarantors of levels of intelligence and ability in those who rule and are ruled. The academies have a long and generally lustrous history of distinguishing the great intellects of our time and providing them with the facilities and wherewithal to pursue their ideas. We simply do not know if genius would be lost without residential universities. We do know that a lot of genius is being invested in the web and that computers are the most important tools genius has ever had at its disposal. Certainly, e-mail and the web currently contribute far more the to the intellectual community than have bricks and mortar if the plethora of lists and user groups is any indication. Information, if not knowledge, is transmitted at least as well electronically as in the space between a lecturer and his audience.

The roles played by universities are more or less reproducible in cyberspace and look more intensely at the four remaining roles, roles that seem less amenable to electronic transmission. These are:

i) the creation of knowledge,

ii) social integration,

iii) providing a venue for 'rites of passage', and

iv) networking.

Current universities are playing some roles that may be difficult to reproduce online. A the internet progresses and a wider variety of online and off-line educational opportunities emerge, even these roles may not save residential education as we currently know and love it. The role are:

i) *Knowledge assessment and creation:* Knowledge assessment is certainly possible on the web. There is a security issue surrounding online testing but it will eventually be resolved. Testing does require a physical place today, but even today it does not require four years of internment. Knowledge creation is another matter. The research function of universities, ironically, will probably be a strong force holding them together unless that function is ultimately assumed by industry. Basic research by its very nature is expensive and wasteful, and not profitable. While this role may justify residential universities, we must remember that undergraduate enrollment supports this research in those institutions not underwritten by the states. This role thus does not speak directly to the issue of residential education since it could more efficiently be conducted by research centers supported by federal and state governments.

ii) *Social integration:* Universities provide a unique place where people peacefully interact across multiple social boundaries: wealthy students willingly support poorer students and students of all social classes, of all national origins, intermingle with little attention to caste, race, or, indeed, age. If students come to universities for this experience with diversity, it certainly militates against study at home but not against study at a corporate for-profit university with a diverse student population. The diversity argument is a new one, coming at a rather odd time: a time when highly diverse multinational countries are disintegrating. Students imbued with tolerance will cast away any inherited affinities for social intolerance. Some universities are taking positive steps in the direction of imbuing their students with a sense of tolerance, but this does not strike us as a fundamental mission of educational institution. It is one of those moral missions we have inherited from a disintegrating religious institution.

iii) *Rites of passage:* The vast majority of higher education institutions around the world are not residential; indeed, most are specialised. The residential colleges may in fact delay maturation because, rather than half-way houses between childhood and adulthood, more recently they have taken on the appearance of post-secondary day-care centers where their charges are encouraged to extend their childhood. Most universities today are struggling with the problem of irresponsible drinking and property damage, often related, and students who prefer athletic games and social get-togethers to study.

iv) *Networking:* Since colleges came into existence, they have provided life-long friendships and initial career connections important in the lives of our graduates. They are equally credentialed, usually find similar jobs, and have similar tastes. Networking also occurs in church, at work, at play, and in the various social organisations we participate in. Networking also occurs on the campuses of corporate universities and it is a benefit they could offer their students. Indeed, even if someone is taking courses over a distance education network, they are not prevented from networking by e-mail, chatrooms, telephone, and video conferencing. Currently, we do not currently trust relationships established over the internet; we are more secure with recommendations of college acquaintances, church acquaintances, and the like.

The nature of the world itself is changing radically. It follows that the positive frenzy among young people to get into residential universities may not survive the next three decades as more and more alternatives arise before them. In order for a university to survive, it must do two things: it must physically and financially survive and it must remain a university. If it remains, even grows, but becomes a social club, it has not survived but transformed.

In order for a university to remain a university, extracurricular activities cannot become co-curricular activities; sports must remain secondary to study, and the interest in knowledge must hold steady, if not regain its historical luster. We cannot sustain a university if social organisations become more attractive than the business of the classroom or if sports take precedence over that business.

Educational institutions driven primarily by the profit motive consider students customers. In most successful businesses the customer is always right. Such commercialised institutions would be much more likely to provide more nonacademic activities than academic ones, if that tack produced a stronger revenue stream, while giving the customer what he or she wants in the classroom: easy, entertaining courses with a high grade for dessert.

Historically, noncommercial educational institutions have treated students as apprentices told what to do and how to do it. The result should have been widespread dissatisfaction but, in fact, the result has been just the opposite. Yet many independent educational institutions are succumbing to childish whims that delay passage to adulthood, expanding the powers of extracurricular activities, already called 'cocurricular' activities in some quarters. This term is a dangerous point for the faculty of an independent educational institution to concede, for it voluntarily moves us closer toward a commercial enterprise that poses a threat to our traditional roles.

In this infoage, we are facing a social revolution, a challenge to legitimate authority at all levels that will shape much of the character of the next century. Since the educational enterprise is based principally on the authority of knowledge, the technological revolution driving these social changes deserves our full attention. Decades ago Marshall McLuhan explored the evidence of human irrepressibility. McLuhan argued that we humans cannot endure the containment of the flesh, and that is why we invented automobiles—then airplanes—to extend our feet, telephones to extend our ears, and television to extend our eyes. The computer now extends the most characteristically human of all the animate modalities, the mind. It provides the mind with perfect, limitless memory, perfect recollection of unlimited sounds and images arranged in whatever fashion we can conjure or invent, it can respond to sophisticated questions, evaluate answers, gather information on its own and distribute it very extensively, quickly, and inexpensively. The computer can run machines and conduct business. Now that we have networked all our mental extensions in one cybernetic system, we have in fact converted the world into an encyclopedia even beyond Tesla's dreams.

The world has in fact become an enormous and yet-growing encyclopedia of itself. Millions of people are archiving enormous amounts of information on every topic from the personality of the webmaster to the top secrets of the tobacco industry. To the extent the inhabitants of cyberspace accumulate as much information, and interpret it at least as well, universities may well lose their relevance in the early moments of the third millennium. There are already hundreds of corporations with their own universities, teaching their employees skills that they failed to master in high school and college—how to read, write, and think. Now, the largest state universities are moving hand-in-hand with the corporate world to develop libraries of distance-learning courses to be administered over the web. Educational institutions will be changed by networked computers in the way they administer themselves, the way they teach, and the way they conduct and publish research. Catalogs, course guides, course schedules, and syllabuses will all be on line and linked to each other. The distinction between these university publications will eventually vanish.

Online interactive syllabuses will contain colour graphics and photographs, motion pictures, and sounds of various sorts. Background music, entire symphonies, foreign language conversations, animal calls, interviews—all will be part and parcel of the syllabus. The syllabus will hold the course together. Students will use it 24-hours a day, 7 days a week; professors will project it onto a flat screen behind him or her in the classroom so that the maps and illustrations studied by students at home will be identical to those used in class. Lecture notes and examples will also be projected in class rather than scribbled on blackboards. The blackboard, or better, smartboard, will be reserved for the occasional addendum that occurs to the instructor during the course of a lecture. The smartboard will automatically save these addenda as part of the lecture notes to be projected the next time the lecture is read.

Online, projected lecture notes will dramatically reduce note-taking in class, and the time wasted writing examples or outlines on the board or while students copy them down. Misunderstandings arising from note-taking will be obviated. When we catch up with the technology, all that time spent copying to and from the blackboard will be reconverted to the original activity of academy—human colloquy between experts and novices that guide the novices toward a capacity to use the opulent endowment of information we now have in critical analysis and thinking. The 'net generation' will have the same profound economic, social, and political effect on the 21st century that the baby boomers had on the latter half of the 20th century. It will take its toll on education once again, too. Young people already learn much of what they know about the world from motion pictures, television, radio, and interaction with peers and adults outside the academy. We really don't know to what extent the university's importance has been dimmed by other such sources of knowledge, we only know that it occurs. We need to know more about other sources of knowledge that compete with the educational system.

Traditionally, universities have survived by providing knowledge not available on television or radio, learning not encouraged in the media. The new worldwide encyclopedia will change that. Out-of-work PhDs and enthusiastic specialists who learn from experience will be providing massive amounts of in-depth information on all topics, even electronic colloquy via e-mail, for free. Students will arrive at the university knowing more than ever and even more about how to find knowledge and information quickly and reliably. Two questions bearing on universities and the academics who manage them are quickly rise to mind. First, how will these changes affect the academy, its mission and conduct? Second, how should universities and colleges react to these changes? The internet revolution offers a wide range of hazards for educators who prefer technology-free colloquy and opportunities for educational entrepreneurs who will take advantage of it. The question is whether the entrepreneurs will remain on campus or take their expertise and educational skills the new commerce that is currently attracting so many of our students.

State universities and city and community colleges share in common large numbers of non-resident students, a growing number of part-time and adjunct teachers, career-oriented student bodies, and a general disdain for teaching and teachers. The growing predilection for adjuncts is itself a concession that practical experience can substitute for education in a teacher and the increase in part-time instructors, indeed, the very use of teaching assistants, is a concession that the teacher less important that most of us would prefer to believe. State universities, in addition, are saddled with many courses with enrollments in the hundreds, where the student has little or no contact with the instructor and is lucky to have a graduate assistant to converse with about the subject matter. All these conditions make them very vulnerable to virtual universities and distance learning.

The internet offers a different set of opportunities and hazards for small colleges and universities. We are defined more by high quality teaching, close teacher-student relationships, and the "collegiate" residential experience—extracurricular activities that complement academic studies—than are the larger research institutions. Research does not absorb as much of our time and this leaves more time to devote to teaching and advising.

Unlike large institutions, it is commonplace for full professors with stellar publication records to teach undergraduate courses and advise undergraduates at smaller colleges and universities, and visiting and adjunct professors are laid on sparingly and only with cause. The residential experience accounts for much of the attractiveness of smaller institutions.

Distance learning should not represent any serious threat or opportunity here. However, we need to keep in mind the current experience that most of the distance-learning students are, in fact, in residence. The methods and flexibility of web-based courses are appealing and effective, and it is to our benefit to take advantage of that attraction rather than to cede it to corporate education. Face-to-face learning with experienced, full-time PhDs is an important attraction at smaller universities. They offer more opportunity to participate in extracurricular activities such as intramural and intercollegiate athletics. They offer a multitude of fraternity, sorority, service club, and other activities that students feel contribute positive practical experience to their character.

Until the rise of theweb, there was no alternative to university education. Now there is. As a result, educators are faced with a rich array of opportunities and hazards. The web represents less a threat to small residential colleges than to the large research institutions where the quality of teaching has already eroded. In order for small universities to survive, they must survive as universities. The danger for small residential institutions is that the residential experience itself may rescue them rather than the intellectual experience of fact-to-face interaction with experienced academics. To assure that this does not occur, the faculties of these institutions are obliged to take advantage of the technology toward two ends.

First, they must use this most powerful intellectual tool to free them from such classroom drudgery as writing to the blackboard, worrying about student note-taking, and shifting from one traditional technology to another, i.e. overhead, VCR, projector, tape recorder. The time saved by using a web-based course must then be converted to time spent in more meaningful face-to-face colloquy.

Second, the web-based courses used in small institutions must be as rich in resources and creatively contrived as the distance-learning courses with which they will inevitably compete. That is, courses in residence must reflect all the advantages of distance-learning courses plus direct access to a master teacher, inside the classroom and outside.

Academics can provide general and specific information about the world for the internet and manage that information better than any other social class. Indeed, academics will perform this function; the question is whether they will do it for academic institutions or for corporations that pay much more. Universities should be moving much more swiftly to establish information resources, e-journals, data bases, and the like before corporations do. Knowledge and information should not be a commodity bought and sold by commercial interests; it should be a freely available intellectual resource provided by and associated with universities.

At the very outset of this new age of higher education, the lines have already been drawn in the struggle which will ultimately determine its shape. On the one side university administrators and their myriad commercial partners, on the other those who constitute the core relation of education: students and teachers. It is no accident, then, that the high-tech transformation of higher education is being initiated and implemented from the top down, either without any student and faculty involvement in the decision-making or despite it.

The major change to befall the universities over the last two decades has been the identification of the campus as a significant site of capital accumulation, a change in social perception which has resulted in the systematic conversion of intellectual activity into intellectual capital and, hence, intellectual property.

There have been two general phases of this transformation. The first, which began twenty years ago and is still underway, entailed the commoditisation of the research function of the university, transforming scientific and engineering knowledge into commercially viable proprietary products that could be owned and bought and sold in the market. The second, which we are now witnessing, entails the commoditisation of the educational function of the university, transforming courses into courseware, the activity of instruction itself into commercially viable proprietary products that can be owned and bought and sold in the market. In the first phase the universities became the site of production and sale of patents and exclusive licenses. In the second, they are becoming the site of production of — as well as the chief market for copyrighted videos, courseware, CDROMs, and web sites.

The first phase began in the mid-1970's when, in the wake of the oil crisis and intensifying international competition, corporate and political leaders of the major industrialised countries of the world recognised that they were losing their monopoly over the world's heavy industries and that, in the future, their supremacy would depend upon their monopoly over the knowledge which had become the lifeblood of the new so-called knowledge-based industries. This focus upon intellectual capital turned their attention to the universities as its chief source, implicating the universities as never before in the economic machinery. In the view of capital, the universities had become too important to be left to the universities. Within a decade there was a proliferation of industrial partnerships and new proprietary arrangements, as industrialists and their campus counterparts invented ways to socialise the risks and costs of creating this knowledge while privatising the benefits. This unprecedented collaboration gave rise to an elaborate web of interlocking directorates between corporate and academic boardrooms.

The result of the first phase of university commoditisation was a wholesale reallocation of university resources toward its research function at the expense of its educational function.

Class sizes swelled, teaching staffs and instructional resources were reduced, salaries were frozen, and curricular offerings were cut to the bone. At the same time, tuition soared to subsidise the creation and maintenance of the commercial infrastructure that has never really paid off. In the end students were paying more for their education and getting less, and the campuses were in crisis.

The second phase of the commercialisation of academia, the commoditisation of instruction, is touted as the solution to the crisis engendered by the first. Ignoring the true sources of the financial debacle - an expensive and low-yielding commercial infrastructure and greatly expanded administrative costs - the champions of computer-based instruction focus their attention rather upon increasing the efficiencies of already overextended teachers. And they ignore as well the fact that their high-tech remedies are bound only to compound the problem, increasing further, rather then reducing, the costs of higher education.

This second transformation of higher education is not the work of teachers or students, the presumed beneficiaries of improved education, because it is not really about education at all. The foremost promoters of this transformation are rather the vendors of the network hardware, software, and content, who view education as a market for their wares.

Corporate training advocates view online education as yet another way of bringing their problem-solving, information-processing, just-in-time educated employees up to profit-making speed. Beyond their ambitious in-house training programmes, which have incorporated computer-based instructional methods pioneered by the military, they envision the transformation of the delivery of higher education as a means of supplying their properly-prepared personnel at public expense.

The university administrators see it as a way of giving their institutions a fashionably forward-looking image. More importantly, they view computer-based instruction as a means of reducing their direct labour and plant maintenance costs -

fewer teachers and classrooms — while at the same time undermining the autonomy and independence of faculty. At the same time, they are hoping to get a piece of the commercial action for their institutions or themselves, as vendors in their own right of software and content. University administrators are supported in this enterprise by a number of private foundations, trade associations, and academic-corporate consortia which are promoting the use of the new technologies with increasing intensity.

Universities throughout western countries are rapidly being overtaken by commercialisation. There are the stand-alone virtual institutions like University of Phoenix, the wired private institutions like the New School for Social Research, the campuses of state universities like the University of Maryland and the new Gulf-Coast campus of the University of Florida. On the state level, the states of Arizona and California have initiated their own state-wide virtual university projects, while a consortia of western "Smart States" have launched their own ambitious effort to wire all of their campuses into an online educational network. In Canada, a national effort has been undertaken, spearheaded by the Telelearning Research Network centered at Simon Fraser University in Vancouver, to bring most of the nation's higher education institutions into a "Virtual U" network. The overriding commercial intent and market orientation behind these initiatives is explicit, as is illustrated by the most ambitious US effort to date, the Western Governors' Virtual University Project, whose stated goals are to expand the marketplace for instructional materials, courseware, and programmes utilising advanced technology, expand the marketplace for demonstrated competence, and identify and remove barriers to the free functioning of these markets, particularly barriers posed by statutes, policies, and administrative rules and regulations.

The use of interactive technology is causing a fundamental shift away from the physical classroom toward anytime, anywhere learning — the model for post secondary education in the twenty- first century. This transformation is being made possible by advances in digital technology, coupled with the protection of copyright in cyberspace.

The implications of the commoditisation of university instruction are two-fold in nature, those relating to the university as a site of the production of the commodities and those relating to the university as a market for them. The first raises for the faculty traditional labour issues about the introduction of new technologies of production. The second raises for students major questions about costs, coercion, privacy, equity, and the quality of education.

With the commoditisation of instruction, teachers as labour are drawn into a production process designed for the efficient creation of instructional commodities, and hence become subject to all the pressures that have befallen production workers in other industries undergoing rapid technological transformation from above. In this context faculty have much more in common with the historic plight of other skilled workers than they care to acknowledge. Like these others, their activity is being restructured, via the technology, in order to reduce their autonomy, independence, and control over their work and to place workplace knowledge and control as much as possible into the hands of the administration. As in other industries, the technology is being deployed by management primarily to discipline, de-skill, and displace labour.

Once faculty and courses go online, administrators gain much greater direct control over faculty performance and course content than ever before and the potential for administrative scrutiny, supervision, regimentation, discipline and even censorship increase dramatically. At the same time, the use of the technology entails an inevitable extension of working time and an intensification of work as faculty struggle at all hours of the day and night to stay on top of the technology and respond, via chat rooms, virtual office hours, and e-mail, to both students and administrators to whom they have now become instantly and continuously accessible. The technology also allows for much more careful administrative monitoring of faculty availability, activities, and responsiveness.

Once faculty put their course material online, moreover, the knowledge and course design skill embodied in that material is taken out of their possession, transferred to the machinery and placed in the hands of the administration. The administration is now in a position to hire less skilled, and hence cheaper, workers to deliver the technologically prepackaged course. It also allows the administration, which claims ownership of this commodity, to peddle the course elsewhere without the original designer's involvement or even knowledge, much less financial interest. The buyers of this packaged commodity, meanwhile, other academic institutions, are able thereby to contract out, and hence outsource, the work of their own employees and thus reduce their reliance upon their in-house teaching staff.

Once the faculty converts its courses to courseware, their services are in the long run no longer required. They become redundant, and when they leave, their work remains behind. In Kurt Vonnegut's classic novel Player Piano the ace machinist Rudy Hertz is flattered by the automation engineers who tell him his genius will be immortalised. They buy him a beer. They capture his skills on tape. Then they fire him. Today faculty are falling for the same tired line, that their brilliance will be broadcast online to millions. Perhaps, but without their further participation. Some skeptical faculty insist that what they do cannot possibly be automated, and they are right. But it will be automated anyway, whatever the loss in educational quality.

The new technology of education, like the automation of other industries, robs faculty of their knowledge and skills, their control over their working lives, the product of their labour, and, ultimately, their means of livelihood. That learning via multimedia is more efficient than studying textbooks with only text and graphics by now is a truism. Humans have more than one type of intelligence capable of learning and multimedia exploits more than one simultaneously. We can no longer ignore multimedia learning tools because the 'net generation' demands them. This generation will not only be computer literate but computer- and internet-sophisticated.

Teachers who are not themselves internet sophisticated will appear incompetent before students who can find the similar courses with interactive multimedia elsewhere on the internet. Again, teachers will have to think in vastly different ways about their subject matter if they are to create successful multimedia applications.

The spread of effective online multimedia instructional techniques has already improved students' ability to visualise problems and develop some of the other intelligences. Developing these applications will require a kind of visual imagination not usually associated with all disciplines.

When the web first emerged, an immediate concern was whether education would be undermined by the disorganisation of hypertext. The advantage of a book is that everything in it is sequentially ordered, page after page, and it is easy for the author to control the reader's thinking. Hypertext, on the other hand, is filled with hyperlinks leading to topics of varied relation to the main text: background information, supplementary material, peripherally related topics. It is virtually impossible for the author of a hypertext web page to control the progression of ideas in the mind of the reader without eliminating hyperlinks, a step that would defeat the very purpose of websites. The application of a bit more imagination to this vice, however, converts it into a virtue. Human do have multiple intelligences, multiple ways of learning and sequential learning is but one such possibility.

The impact of the web as a publication outlet for university faculties has so far been minor but that will not continue indefinitely. Placing teaching materials online publishes them—either for a limited audience such as a class or for everyone in the world interested in the topic. The web, of course, will be the great leveller in publication. Because access is equal, the web will not be prejudiced in favour of faculty at large, research institutions as are the presses. Those of us at smaller institutions, indeed, high school teachers and students, will have an equal opportunity to publish and be read. Indeed, we will have to publish online, for the process will be student-driven by the net-generation. These changes will transform attitudes toward course materials themselves. A major advantage to having course materials online is to allow one instructor to link to the materials of others at several institutions in order to enrich his or her courses. Eventually this will become such a widespread practice, that it will have to be considered in faculty evaluation. Faculty will hence be judged to an increasing extent, not on what they borrow from others and incorporate in their course materials, but what they contribute to the common pool.

EDUCATIONAL PHILOSOPHY IN CYBERSAPCE

Educational philosophies evolve in response to the needs of each era and in harmony with available technology. The ancient Greek image of the teacher facing a single student while sitting on opposite ends of a log seems quaint and appealing, although inadequate in a modern context. The common practice of medieval students' copying manuscripts or compiling mathematical tables is now seen as insufficiently creative. The industrial age teacher standing in front of classroom with rows and columns of separated desks seems orderly, but possibly too rigid. Mid-century scenarios of computer-based instruction or TV-based lecturing have never been fully realised but they are still useful supplements.

The effectiveness of online learning tasks depends on the way they generate interaction. Interactivity is a "necessary and fundamental mechanism for knowledge acquisition" and interactivity is the "key to successful online learning." Interaction can occur at different levels and in different ways. The terms 'interaction' and 'interactive' are now ubiquitous, but the intention is often not matched by the result. There are two sorts of interaction to consider; social and cognitive interaction. Obviously, online learning will be most effective when these are integrated. An example of a pedagogical approach that incorporates both social and cognitive forms of interaction is given by Schneiderman who uses collaborative team projects that result in publication of valuable, peer-critiqued, products under the rubric 'Relate-Create-Donate'.

As technology evolves, teachers, students, administrators, and parents busily re-negotiate to shift the methods and goals of education. Academe requires students to acquire facts, information, knowledge, and wisdom, but a holistic view also includes the preparation for participation in family, community, work, and national structures. Additional goals could be personal growth, self-actualisation, communication skills, and increased capacity for learning, critical thinking, and creative problem-solving. To respond to these goals, teachers need a guiding philosophy that they can adapt to their personal style, course contents, student population, and available technology. The three-component philosophy called relate-create-donate which stresses:

i) *Relate*: work in collaborative teams
ii) *Create*: develop ambitious projects
iii) *Donate*: produce results that are meaningful to someone outside the classroom.

The *relate component* emphasises team efforts to develop communication, planning, management and social skills. The modern workplace demands proficiency in these skills, yet students are often taught to work on their own. Research on collaborative learning indicates that in the process of collaboration students are forced to clarify and verbalise their problems, thereby facilitating problem solution and anchoring/assimilating/accommodating novel information in the student's ideational structure. Collaboration has dangers, but when managed well, it generates intense motivation from many students, encourages learning from peers, and reduces drop out rates.

The *create component* points to a fusion between learning and creative work. In creating substantial and appropriate individual and team projects, students will learn many things that serve the goals of education. Similarly, learning is useless if it does not prepare a student to be creative. Successful students create to learn, and learn to create.

The *donate component* stresses the benefits of having authentic, service-oriented projects that will be meaningful and useful to someone outside the classroom. Having an outside "customer" generates intense motivation, helps clarify goals, and provides training for future professional work. Outside customers might be employers for student's who have part-time jobs, managers at volunteer organisations or campus groups, curators at local museums, or administrators at nearby schools.

Any definition of a teaching philosophy is merely a starting point for teachers, who adopt, adapt, and apply it in their own creative way. Variations on the relate-create-donate philosophy have existed for thousands of years.

The historical path of technology in education is filled with controversy. Even books and paper faced resistance because they reduced human memory skills. Although they are powerful tools in fostering learning, their contents and usage are shaped by prevailing philosophies of education. Powerful technologies change our expectations and curricula. Paper has an even more potent role than as a store house of knowledge. It achieves remarkable power when it is a blank sheet that invites student creativity. But the transformational insight that students should be more than copiers took centuries to emerge, and must have been difficult to promote.

Contemporary educational philosophies and teachers assume that students should write as well as read. Listening to radio and records, or watching TV and videotapes have been proposed as educational panaceas, but they too have become only components for constructing a pedagogical framework. These are largely passive media, with limited capability for students to be creative, unless educators shift their focus to student generation of these media. Advocates of more interactive approaches oversold computer-based instruction, and promoters of "intelligent tutoring systems" still portray them as having the potential to solve educational problems. Some technology cheerleaders and national leaders focus on installing computers in classrooms as a measure of success in transforming education.

However, even if there were one computer available for each student, with appropriate software and network access, there is no assurance that education would improve. The technology alone can never be a solution, but in the hands of a knowledgeable teacher, appropriately designed technology can become a useful tool. The Wweb cannot be a solution to educational needs unless the creative component is included. We have to do more than teach kids to surf the net, we have to teach them to make waves.

Knowledgeable teachers provide challenge, guidance, and evaluation. They build a motivating and supportive environment while attending to the diverse needs of each student. Creating a trusting relationship between the teacher and each student begins with the first encounter. The successful teacher conveys enthusiasm for and competence in the subject and the process of instruction, earning trust by presenting the right level of challenges for each individual and team. As the relationships mature through constructive guidance and thoughtful evaluations, students joyfully seek greater challenges, eagerly pursue proficiency in the subject, and willingly take greater responsibility for their education. Appropriate design for educational technology supports the teacher-student relationship by enabling teachers to propose more ambitious challenges, tailor guidance to individual student and team needs, and give more detailed evaluations.

Let us discuss how relate-create-donate works in realistic educational settings.

Relate—collaborative teams: Extensive descriptions of collaborative teaching methods reveal the rich set of possibilities available to teachers. Collaborations can be as simple as a two-minute in-class exercise involving pairs of students or as elaborate as a two-year project-oriented curriculum involving dozens of students. Collaborative team projects have the potential to raise motivation, reduce drop-out rates, and develop job-related skills, but collaborative methods are not commonly used. Most teachers have little experience with collaborative methods and team management, since they were likely to have been trained by lecture methods. Lectures can be effective, and technology can help improve them with presentation software and online demonstrations, but more active teaching strategies with collaborative teams offer appealing possibilities.

Term-length or shorter team projects done outside the classroom seem more acceptable to teachers, maybe because they minimally disrupt a lecture-oriented course plan. Students who work together on substantial team projects learn a great deal about project management, leadership styles, and efficient use of time. They often need to be trained in making a modular work plan, setting schedules, reviewing each other's work, and resolving differences. College-level collaborative projects are typically organised around half-hour meetings, separated by 2-10 hours of individual work. Adding class reports from project teams is an appealing way to give students a chance to develop presentation skills. Team sizes typically range from 2-6 students. As the team size grows, more attention should be paid to management strategies.

Teachers are more familiar with in-class collaborations for laboratory science and studio art classes, but these methods can be effective in any discipline. Math students can work on problems, English students can write or review each other's poems, and computer science students can compose or debug a programme. In-class collaborations may take 2-120 minutes and often take longer than anticipated because of the high degree of student engagement. Pairs of students are easy to arrange, but getting 3-10 students to work together during class takes creative planning and flexible seating arrangements.

In many situations, groups of two students per computer produces superior educational outcomes than one or three. Pairs of students verbalise potential solutions; typically, one student deals with the computer while the other focuses on the problem. Regularly switching roles ensures balanced learning. High variance in problem solving times is disruptive, because the quick students are eager to move along, while others need more time. Verbalisation by pairs overcomes hurdles and reduces the discouraging situation of individual students who cannot solve a problem even after 15-20 minutes.

Computer-rich networked classrooms enable a variety of collaborations. Students can create on their computers and show to the whole class for discussion with a large-screen projector or by copying to every student's computer. By rapidly reviewing student work, everyone can see the range of good to bad work and can sharpen their reviewing skills. With appropriate software, classroom brainstorming among dozens of students can, within minutes, produce an amazing variety of comments, which can then be discussed or saved for review. Anonymous inputs encourage diverse and creative suggestions. Rapid class voting on brainstorm results or on any list of alternatives typically leads to a spirited discussion.

Collaborative methods may be novel for teachers and for students, so some resistance is likely and it may take a teacher several attempts to create successful collaborative projects. Students need experience and guidance in working together. Often they are busy with other courses, extra-curricular activities, jobs, and family responsibilities; and then they must add the complexities of arranging team meetings on a tight commuting schedule. Teams often meet briefly before and after class, coordinate through e-mail discussions, and occasionally hold longer meetings. But by working in teams students learn efficient time management and realistic expectations of how long each task takes.

E-mail is a fundamental collaborative tool, and its low cost plus high payoff should make it useful in almost every course.

Similarly listservs, newsgroups, or bulletin boards should be established automatically for every course, even before the first face-to-face meeting. These tools are wonderful for sending hints on assignments to an entire class or messages to individual students commenting on their work, especially when the next class is 3-4 days away. Students can also initiate questions at any time to the entire class, to individual students, or to the teacher. This 24-hour classroom approach has the potential for creating an intense environment that may be overwhelming to some students and teachers.

Experience is accumulating in many disciplines and educational settings, but many questions remain open: What size team in optimal? Should team membership be assigned or should students be able to chose their partners? Is uniform skill and motivation helpful? How does a teacher intervene when a team member consistently fails to perform? Should grades be assigned individually or to the team? Research on collaborative teaching/learning continues with the promise of deeper understanding and refined guidance for teachers.

Create—ambitious projects: The formulation of team projects and in-class collaborations challenges many instructors, especially since textbooks provide only modest help. Computers and the web have opened new possibilities for resources and for projects. Access to digital libraries with remarkable primary resources expands the opportunities for students to perform research projects in many domains. The web can publish student projects, making them available for anyone. In-class projects range from simple questions with factual or open-ended answers to design projects that may involve teams working across several class meetings. Careful use of class time dictates thoughtful choice of challenges and constructive discussions that are beneficial to many students.

Donate—service-oriented authentic projects: The rewards of doing good by helping others are especially sweet when you are also helping yourself. This can be the case when students work on service-oriented authentic projects for clients outside the classroom. Students have skills that can be highly beneficial in many situations, and students benefit by having an actual client whose needs can promote advanced learning.

The philosophy of relate-create-donate is still fresh and needs refinements to suit diverse settings. A central problem is how to deal with the resistance to change, especially among teachers, but also among administrators and occasionally among students. Teachers are often unfamiliar with the variety of short and long-term collaborations so they are unsure about what to do. They may also hesitate because of bad experiences or negative expectations. A gentle start is advisable with a simple in-class exercise or a limited team project out of class.

FEATURTES OF CYBER CURRICULUM

The electronic revolution is proceeding at an unprecedented tempo, much more like that of larger, genuine revolutions. It was only in 1981 that Bitnet and Usenet went on line to make e-mail between government, universities, and corporations a reality. For twelve years prior to that Arpanet connected government offices with a few departments at universities. Just as it began to grow in 1975, the same year Bill Gates founded Microsoft; it was taken over by the Defense Department. This forced those interested in a worldwide network to come up with a new idea. The new idea was Bitnet. Bitnet's popularity surprised its inventors, who had not foreseen the necessity of e-mail. So, the internet as a worldwide network of computers began only about 20 years ago; its growth has been stunning.

Even more remarkable has been the growth of that part of the internet known as the web. The first web browser appeared, in 1993. As of September 27, 1996, 611,860 individuals, organisations, and businesses have established a web presence, a web site. The latest versions of the web browsers are, in fact, internet browsers for they are capable of accessing everything on the internet: formatted e-mail, voice mail, FTP and gopher sites, Usenet's, and telephonic communications including teleconferencing. Not only has communication become faster and simpler, we now have access to amounts of information greater than ever before at a moment in human history when we are already overwhelmed by information.

The internet revolution brings two questions to bear on universities and those of us in academia. First, how will these changes affect the academy, its mission and conduct? Second, how should universities and colleges react to these changes? Some of the effects of the shift in publishing are obvious from previous remarks. Educational institutions will be changed by networked computers in the way they administer themselves, the way they teach, and the way they conduct and publish research. Catalogs, course guides, course schedules will all be online and linked to each other. The distinction between them will eventually vanish. Opening the university catalog you will be able to bring up the course syllabus, the instructor's homepage with his qualifications, schedule and e-mail address. Much if not all of the materials for the course will be built into the electronic syllabus: the readings, animated graphics, videos and sound bites—eventually, entire videos, and interactive exercises in which students cause things to happen and see the possible results.

Every bit of information necessary to evaluate and select courses will be available around the clock every day of the year. The admissions page will contain an online application that may be filled out in complete privacy. Applicants will type or read in their credit card number to cover the application fee, attach the essay they previously dictated, and instantaneously submit the application. Receipt of the application will be immediately acknowledged with a personal video note from the admissions office. No paper, postage, typing, envelop-stuffing or -opening, or filing will be involved.

Courses will be taught from interactive online syllabuses. These syllabuses will contain everything current syllabuses contain but much more. They will contain a complete set of lecture notes, illustrations, interactive exercises, and examples for the course. They will contain hyperlinks to information in government bureaus, museums, universities, libraries, corporations, and private web sites around the world.

Interactive online syllabuses will also contain self-administered exercises and quizzes, so that students may test their knowledge of the concepts of each segment of the course before taking the examination that counts. Concepts, including foreign language vocabulary, will be tested by electronic flashcards. These present the students with the concept to define or the definition to identify with a name. They may work with these exercises until they are confident of their mastery.

Even the tests that count toward the grade will slowly move to the internet. Tests will be taken under security conditions and the results e-mailed to the instructor. Students will not have a single date for an examination, but a broader 3-5 day period over which they may take it. They can then schedule all their quizzes and examinations so that none fall on the same day and so that study time may be optimised for each quiz or test. Look out—grades will go up again.

An implication of the changes both in teaching and research is that the internet is a great equalizer, providing equal access to all the resources, which it offers. The equality of the internet makes affiliation less important, providing an immense opportunity for small colleges and universities located in beautiful, tranquil settings. Being physically in a department with the best minds of a discipline is unimportant so long as you are connected to their websites and can communicate with those minds almost instantaneously via discipline-oriented listservs and e-mail. The prestige of the great institutions will eventually erode as prestige is redistributed among individuals rather than institutions. Current search engines on the internet are of limited use. They require minor programming knowledge to filter out irrelevant and filter in the relevant targets. Search engines like Logos, Magellan, Web Crawler, and Yahoo are already beginning to break up the resources they link into broad categories.

The internet has already become the most enormous encyclopedia the world has ever known. In fact, through the internet, the world is becoming an encyclopedia of itself. The telephone extends our ears; television our eyes. The computer extends our minds with knowledge, images, sounds, and emotions. It is the most human and self-expressive of all our inventions. Now it unites us in an enormous democratic family without race, colour, gender, handicap, or physical disfiguration.

Cyberspace is without location or physical direction; men and women of all nations express themselves freely on websites and communicate instantaneously with each other. The enormity of it all, and its popularity, inevitably calls for intellectual management. That is where we come in. Without leaving the geographical location of our choice we not only can become the intellectual entrepreneurs of the future and at least some of us must. Academics can provide general and specific information about the world for the internet and manage that information better than any other social class. The intellectual entrepreneurs of today will be the new authorities of the coming age, an age ruled by information rather than production, individuals rather than historical prestige.

REFERENCES

Aronowitz, S., *The Knowledge Factory: Dismantling the Corporate University and Creating True Higher Learning*, Boston: Beacon, 2000.

Beard, Robert, "Will the 21st Century Need Universities." Paper presented at Haverford College, 8 p.m., on the evening of April 23, 1998.

Jansen, D. G., and Lewis, W. B., 1996, "Creating High-levels of Interaction in Distance Education Courses", *ATEA Journal*, 24(1), pp.8-9.

Kirby, E., "Building Interaction in Online and Distance Education Courses", *Paper presented at the Society for Information Technology and Teacher Education International Conference*, 10th, San Antonio, TX, February, 1999.

9

Communication

Communication is derived from the Latin word "communis" which means common, sharing ideas in common. Communication is the process of transmitting ideas or thoughts from one person to another for the purpose of creating under standing in the thinking of the person receiving the communication. This emphasis on understanding focuses attention on the effectiveness of communication rather than simply on the mechanics of transmitting information.

Earlier communication was considered to be a phenomenon more associated with the business management, but with changing times, its importance and need in other fields including the field of education has become more prominent. In fact the masses of people in the world today cannot manage without the access to information whether through written word, electric media, films, live performances or other forms of communication. The purpose of information may be varied, to inform, to enlighten, to educate or simply entertain but its requirement is more or less universal.

Communication can be defined as passing on of information ideas or instructions from one person to another by choosing an appropriate media and seeing that it is understood in the same sense as it was conveyed. Message/instructions conveyed should exactly be identical to the message understood. Any deviation between the two calls for remedial measures.

Communication can also be expressed as a process by which meanings are exchanged between individuals through a common systems of symbols. It also means a technique for expressing ideas effectively; There is communication:

i) When you talk or listen to someone;

ii) When you read a book, the author communicates his thoughts;

iii) When you watch T.V/film/; the script writer communicates with you.

But communication does not merely mean oral/ written messages, In fact it includes everything that may be used to covey meanings from one person to another, i.e. wave of hand, movement of lips, and; even the lack of communication may also be a form of communication.

A manager, irrespective of the level at which he is operating has to perform all functions, i.e., Planning Organisation, Direction, Staffing, Co-ordination and Control, Reporting and Budgeting (PODSCORB). Though all the functions are important, the most important of all is direction which includes four components i.e.

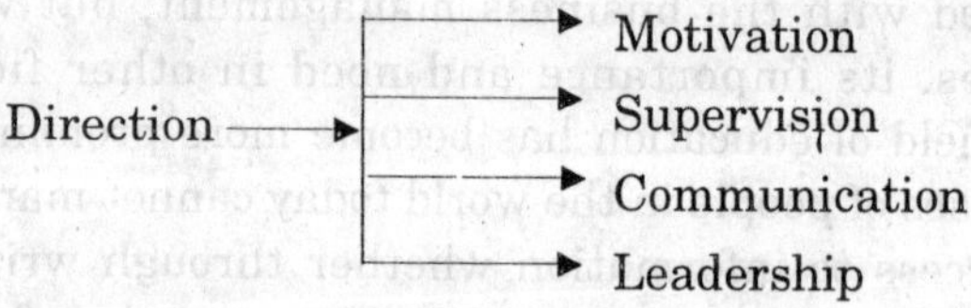

All four components include a common ingredient of skill of imparting knowledge and guidance, a skill of communicating at different levels. Manager/ Educational manager is a director under whose guidance and supervision all have to work, this first executive function is "to develop and maintain a system of communication".

DEFINITIONS

According to Mockler, "Communication is the process of passing information's, ideas or even emotions from one person to another".

"Communication is an exchange of facts, ideas, opinions or emotions by two or more persons".

Newman, Summer and Warren

"It is the interchange of thought or information to bring about mutual understanding and confidence or good human relations".

The American Society of Training Directors'

"Communication is the sum total of all things one person does when he wants to create understanding in the mind of another. It is a bridge of meaning. It involves a systematic and continuing process of telling, listening and understanding".

Louis A. Allen

"Communication is the process of passing information and understanding from one person to another, communication, fundamental and vital to all managerial functions, is the process imparting ideas and making oneself understood by others.

Theo Haimann

Effective communication takes place when the received message is understood in the same sense by the receiver as it was conveyed by the sender.

NATURE/ FEATURES OF COMMUNICATION

Following are the important features of communication:

i) *Two parties*: Communication is a process which involves two parties- a sender and a receiver. Sender is also known as 'communicator' and the receiver 'Communicatee'.

ii) *Two-way process*: It is a two way process. It includes sending of a message and responding to the message.

iii) *Pervasive function:* Communication is a pervasive function as it is required at all levels and in all departments. It is the key to establish networking and enables effective coordination and control.

iv) *A continuous process*: It is a continuous and ongoing process and managers have to be in regular touch with their subordinates and superiors.

v) *A circular process*: The process of communication is a circular process. A message sent is followed by a reaction/ response/feedback from the receiver which requires another message, unless the senders message matches the receivers end.

PROCESS OF COMMUNICATION

Communication is a process which involves two parties — the sender and receiver. It is a process of transmitting meaning between individuals. This is vital for the progress of society. In ancient times man communicated through symbols and gestures and later on the spoken word in the form of language was used for communication. As technology developed written words and other media were used in addition to the symbols gestures and spoken words. Every symbol and gesture had a meaning in the primitive times and even today carry meaning and has an important place in the communication process.

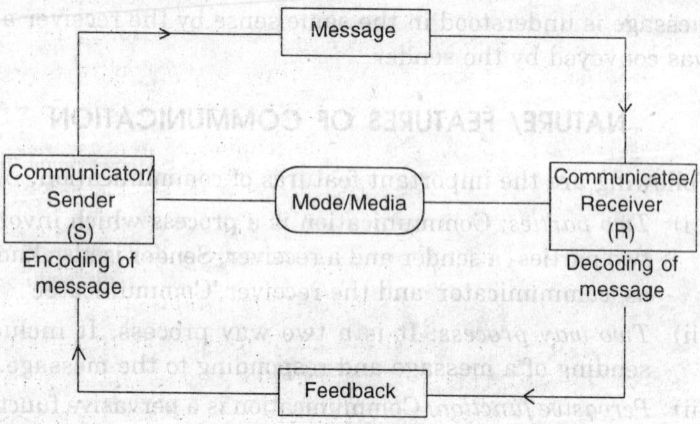

Figure 1. Process of communication

Communication process is complete through the following phases:

i) The sender formulates an idea or something to communicate

ii) Idea/information/ message is translated by him in to words, symbols or some other form which he expects the receiver to understand as desired by the sender.

iii) He selects mode/ media/ method to send the message i.e. he may decide to send a letter, a report, talk on phone or even communicate face to face.

iv) Message is received by someone (communicatee)

v) The receiver of the message decodes (interprets) i.e. translates the message into ideas as understood by him.

vi) The message is acted upon (Remedial measure)

vii) The circular process of communication continues until reaches algebrically i.e., $\frac{S}{R} = 1$

There is another method/ way of explaining the communication process, which is commonly used in the "Extension work" i.e community of development and extension programme. Generally in educational extension activities, the importance of communication is intended to bring behavioural modification of the learner. The following flow diagram will help in under standing the communication process.

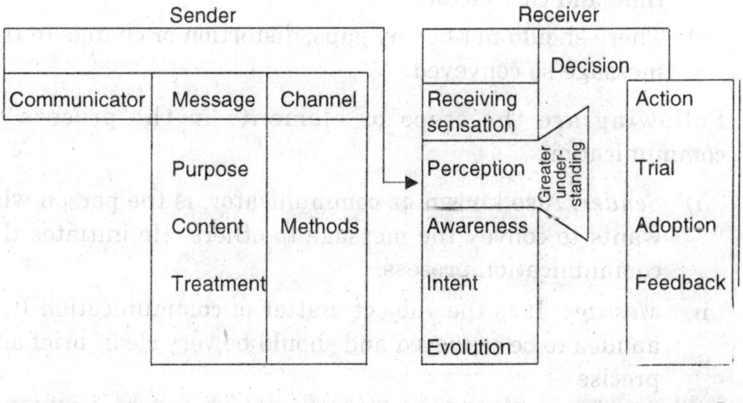

Figure 2. Process of communication (used mostly in extension work)

It is through this process that the aims and objectives of the programme are to be widely disseminated to the people and useful information to solve their problems. This necessitates that extension workers should have a through understanding of the communication process (see Figure 2)

The extension worker cannot expect to bring about change unless he is able to communicate effectively. He has to create a conducive situation where information can be transmitted with greater impact on people. For example the new knowledge acquired through research has to do disseminated to effect change in the methods of farming. The central challenge therefore, to the extension worker, is to help people to adopt innovations for increasing the production of crops livestock, the better the communication earlier will be developments in the desired direction.

Key elements in the process of communication can thus be — Communicator, Communicatee, Message, Communication Channels, Response/Feed back.

While framing the message, the following should be kept in mind:

i) Message must have substance and a sense/ purpose.
ii) It should be clear and precise.
iii) It should be sent through proper channel keeping in mind time and cost factor.
iv) There should not be any gaps, distortion or change in the message so conveyed.

Following are the steps or elements in the process of communication:

i) *Sender*: Also known as communicator, is the person who wants to convey the message to others. He initiates the communication process.
ii) *Message*: It is the subject matter of communication It is an idea to be conveyed and should be very clear, brief and precise.

iii) *Encoding*: The idea is to be expressed in to words, symbols, pictures or any other form which will make the receiver understand the message. It is called encoding.

iv) *Communication channel*: Channel is the media/ mode through which the message is sent by the sender to the receiver it may be formal or informal and written or oral.

v) *Receiver*: He is the person who receives the message. He may be a listener, viewer or reader. The communication process does not get completed till the receiver understands the message in the same sense as it was conveyed by the sender.

vi) *Decoding*: The message is decoded by the receiver to understand it. After decoding the message, the receiver interprets it. Without understanding the message no appropriate action can be taken.

vii) *Feedback*: A message sent is followed by a reaction/ response from the receiver which requires another message to be communicated by the sender and soon the reaction/ response is known as 'feedback'. Thus the procured transmission and communication are not complete without feedback.

FORMS OF COMMUNICATION

There can be different forms of communication. A distinction typically is made between formal and informal communications. Also communication can flow in various directions. Methods used for communication can also take various forms.

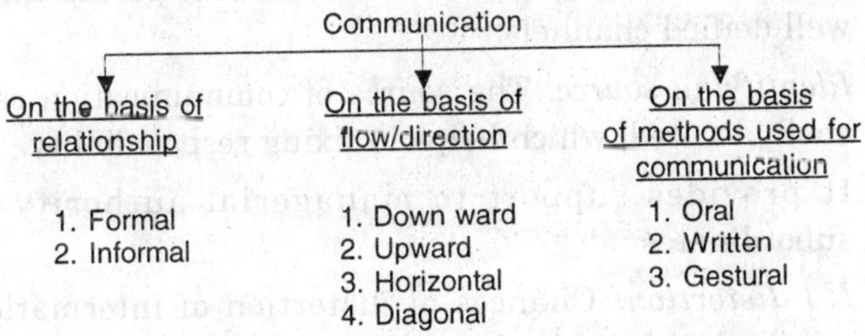

Figure 3. Forms/Types of Communication

The different types of communication can be categorised as under.

I. On the Basis of Relationship

On the basis of relationship between the communicator and the communicatee, communication can be:

1. Formal communication

Formal communications recognised communication system. It is said to be formal when it is transmitted through the officially established chain of command in the organisation structure. The organisation structure reflecting superior - subordinate relationship determines the flow of formal communication. Formal communication normally takes the form of written communication such as note, memos, letters, reports and statements etc. It is the formal type of communication with which the supervisor and administrators are vitally concerned in any department for guiding and motivating their subordinates. e.g instructions, order, commands, guidelines all flow from top to bottom through a strict level of hierarchy in any formally structured organisations with people placed at various levels also is an example of formal/official communication.

Advantages of formal communication

i) *Systematic:* Formal communication is systematic and ensures orderly flow of information as it passes through well deified channels.

ii) *Identifying source:* The source of communication can be easily located; which helps in fixing responsibility.

iii) It provides support to managerial authority over subordinates

iv) *No distortion:* Chances of distortion of information is minimal as formal communication normally is in written form.

v) *Helps in better co-ordination and control:* It is helpful in the process of co-ordination and control co-ordinating various levels which ensures effective controlling. It provides feedback without which effective control is not possible.

Disadvantages of formal communication

i) *Slow:* Formal communication is a slow moving process as the formal communication follows the scalar chain of authority.

ii) *Impersonal:* It is conveyed mostly in an impersonal manner and thus lacks personal warmth the involvement.

iii) *Rigid*: It has very less scope of flexibility as it has to strictly follow the hierarchy.

iv) *Inaccurate information:* Sometimes, employees don't transmit accurate information for fear of their image and unfavourable consequences of the reporting.

2. Informal Communication

Informal communications are those that are outside the formal recognised communication system such as the conversations between and among subordinates arising from their social relationships. It takes place independently of the formal line of authority. The necessity of such communication arises among people to satisfy their social needs. The network of informal communication is also known as grape vine. It often leads to rumours...... and spread very fast through informal channel. The origin and direction of the flow of informally communicated messages cannot be easily traced as in case of 'vineyard' it is commonly called as 'grape vine' which often leads to rumours which is the information without any adequate evidence. Rumour is an untrue part of the grapevine. Since they are distorted and twisted depending upon the interest and perception of the sender and receiver, rumour are thus undesirable and therefore should not be allowed to spread.

Advantages of informal communication

Informal communication is helpful to the members of the organisation in the following ways.

i) *Satisfaction of social needs:* Exchange of ideas and information through informal channels helps the employees in developing friendly relations and derive social satisfaction. It may arise due to be the common place of work, common interests, same area they come from, or emotional attachments etc.

ii) *A substitute channel:* It serves as substitute channel where formal communication is not possible. The matters which cannot be communicated through official channels, can be transmitted through informal channel.

ii) *Communication between persons hawing no official link.* It is a means of communication between persons, who are not linked through official chain of command.

Informal communication may be useful to management in the following ways:

i) *Speedy transmission:* It can be used for speedy transmission of massage in emergency and under exceptional circumstances, as it follows no formal channels.

ii) *The gap in formal communication*: For management it serves to fill the gaps in formal communication. It helps in communicating those messages which cannot be communicated through proper channels.

iii) *Understanding employees attitudes and reactions.* Through informal contacts and interactions, managers can understand the attitude of employees and their reactions an certain policies and programme.

iv) Cordial human relations: It provides an outlet for emotions and reduces tension in labour management relations as it has a personal touch.

Disadvantages or limitations of informal communication

Following are the limitations of informal communication:

i) *Distortion of message*: There is greater scope of distortion of message as it passes to different persons with different interpretations. Informal communication is usually oral and has a greater possibility of distortion.

ii) *Unsystematic and unreliable*: It is unsystematic and cannot be relied upon for regularity and timeliness. It often carries rumours and distorted facts

iii) *Lack of secrecy*: informal communication, at times is not good for management as there is a greater risk of confidential information being leaked through informal channels. Management should take care and precautions, while using these channels.

II. On the Basis of Direction

On the basis of direction communication can be classified in four type:

i) Downward communication;

ii) Upward communication;

iii) Horizonal communication;

iv) Diagonal communication.

Downward Communication

Downward communication refers to the flow of communication from the top management downwards to the operating level. Thus communications from superiors to the subordinates at different levels of organisation are known as downward communication. Downward communication refers to organisational plans, policies, strategies, by the management at top. At the middle and lower levels such communications include orders and instructions rules and procedures etc. These communications may take form of, oral or written.

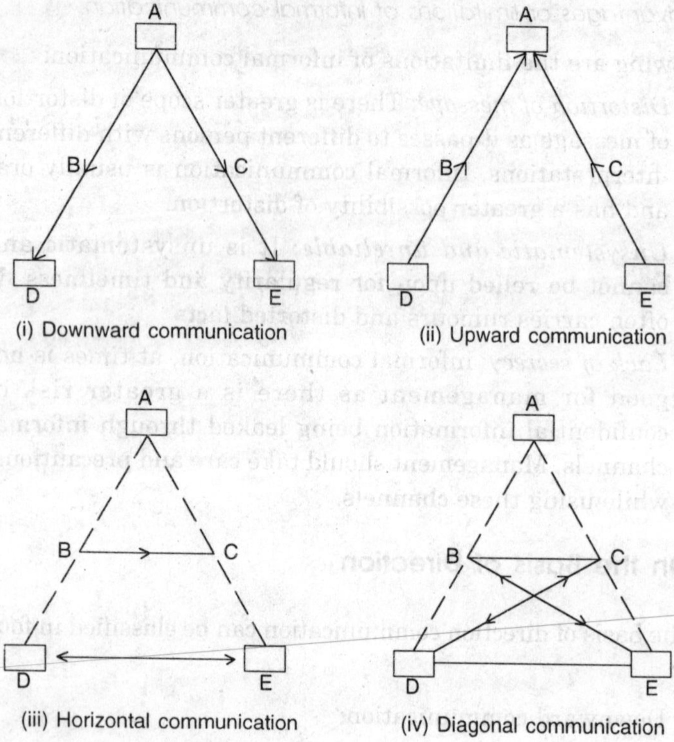

Figure 4. Types of communication

Upward Communication

The upward (from subordinate to superior and downward (from superior to subordinate), How of information is vertical in direction. The upward communication flows from subordinate to his superior in the hierarchy. It may consists of information related to:

i) Subordinate's work performance;
ii) Problems faced by them relating to work; and
iii) Opinion grievances /suggestions etc.
iv) Reports (routine reports, special reports necessitated by special events, commissioned reports by the subordinates etc.)

It may also relate to clarification needed with regard to instructions, procedure and methods of work or statement of personal problems. Upward communication not only keeps management informed about the progress of work and the performance of subordinates but also helps managers to take necessary remedial steps to overcome the problems relating to work, to settle grievances, clarify instructions rules etc., and to offer advise to employees regarding their personal problems as well. Free flow of upward communication helps in maintaining cordial human relations in the organisation

Horizontal Communication

The direction of communication is said to be horizontal when the messages are passed across the organisation as from people to others on about the same level. Communication takes place, say from one section officer to another in a ministry / organisation and is generally more effective because of near identity in status and prestige of the sender and the receiver.

Hence flow of communication between persons holding positions at the same level of the organisation is known as horizontal communication. Exchange of information between managers of equal rank are examples of horizontal communication. This type of communication usually becomes necessary to co-ordinate different activities or to resolve interrelated problems of two or more departments.

Diagonal Communication

It refers to the transmission of information between persons of different departments and of the different levels, such communication is speedy but violate the principle of scalar chain such practices are generally not encouraged.

III On the Basis of Methods used for Communication

Communication can also be either oral written or gestural:

Oral Communication

It refers to messages transmitted orally or verbally. It includes face to face contact, interview, joint consultations etc. It usually takes place where superiors give instructions to subordinates or when discussion is held in meetings, seminars. Conferees etc.

Advantages

Major advantages of oral communication include the following:

i) *Takes less time*: Oral communication takes less time if message is brief.

ii) *Permits clarification of doubts*: It permits detailed explanations and clarification of doubts.

iii) *Gives personal touch*: Oral communication gives a personal touch

iv) *Useful operative level:* Oral communication is particularly useful at operative level i.e. giving instructions at lower level e.g. handling of a particulars job/machines or in case of emergencies, time is saved by communicating orally.

v) *Immediate reaction / feedback*: Oral communication is especially useful when the sender wants to know the reaction of the receiver quickly Immediate feedback helps taking of fast remedial actions.

Disadvantages

The major disadvantages of oral communication include the following

i) *No verification*: No verification is possible afterwards in case of oral transmission, since no records are kept.

ii) *Time consuming:* It may be time consuming as it happens in meetings, seminars and conferences.

iii) *Not taken seriously:* Oral communication may not be taken seriously by the parties involved.

iv) *Difficult to act*: It may be difficult to act on oral communication if details are missing or forgotten.

v) *Costly for distant places:* Oral communication is more costly for distant places and even the media used may also be responsible for distortion or filtering of message.

Written Communication

It refers to message transmitted in written form. Some of the more common types of written communication include memos, memoranda, letters reports, proposals training and job manuals, newsletters etc. Visual media such as charts, photographs, drawings and colour coding are also used to make written communication more effective. The advantages generally associated with written communication are that information conveyed through such message is authentic, accurate, permanent and wide in coverage as it can be duplicated and distributed to all individuals who should receive it.

Advantages

Major advantages of written communication are as under.

i) *Lengthy communication:* Written communications are ideal in case the subject matter to be conveyed is too lengthy.

ii) *Record:* Written communications can be safely preserved for long periods of time and they can be referred to in future also.

iii) *Repeat value*: A written communication can be used again and again which is not possible in case of verbal communication e.g. rules and regulations, codes of conducts, instructions, etc.

iv) *Facilitates verification:* Written communication can be verified from written records.

v) *More economical:* It is more economical specially when the subject matter/ to be conveyed is lengthy or where it is intended to be conveyed to a large number of persons.

vi) *Taken seriously*: It is taken more seriously by the parties involved.

vii) *Only means for distantly placed persons*: Written communication serves as the only means of exchange of ideas and information where the sender and receiver are separated by long distances.

viii) *Precise terms*: written communication can be expressed in precise terms after due thought and preparation.

Disadvantages

The major disadvantages include the following:

i) *Takes more time:* Transmission of written communication takes more time especially when sender and receiver are placed far away from one another.

ii) *Expensive:* It is very expensive especially when lengthy messages are to be sent by telegram or fax.

iii) *No personal touch*: Written communication lack personal touch and are more formal.

iv) *Secrecy difficult:* It is difficult to maintain complete secrecy about a written communication.

v) *Not permits immediate feedback:* It is not useful when sender wants to know the reaction of the receiver quickly.

Gestural Communication

It refers to the communication by actions. Communication through gestures include gestures by hands, movement of eyes, facial expressions etc. It is important to develop and maintain interpersonal communication It may take place in form of:

i) Facial expressions;

ii) Movement of hands;

iii) Movements of head;

iv) Movement of lips;

v) Movement of eyes etc;

MODES OF COMMUNICATION

The selection of appropriate mode whether audio, audio-visual, is one of the precondition for effective communication. According to Burton, "Audio- visual aids are those aids which help in completing the triangular process of learning i.e motivation, classification and stimulation.

Edger Dale states: Audio visual aids are those devices by the use of which communication of ideas between persons and groups in various teaching and training situations is helped, these are also termed as multi - sensory materials.

Table 1. Types of modes of communication

1	2	3	4	5	6
Graphic aids	**Display boards**	**Three dimen tional aids**	**Projected aids**	**Audio aids**	**Activity aids**
(Photographs pictures posters, flash cards strip, diagrams, maps, cartoon, comics etc)	(Black board flannel board bulletin board magnetic board, peg board)	(Model, specimen puppets, objects etc)	{Films film strips, Slides)	(Radio, Tape)	Dramatics Demonstraions tours, field trips etc.

16 mm film projectors,. Episcope, tape-recorder microphones, T.V, computers, internets etc, so many new modes are increasing in this constant flux of time where the education to society are changing everyday. Modern modes/ means of communication are available which makes the communication attractive, fast and consumer friendly. Selection of appropriate mode lies in time, economy and utility factors.

Edgar Dale's Cone of Experience

According to Edgar dales cone of experience the use of direct to indirect experiences help in meaningful learning. Moving from direct and purposeful experience to the visual and verbal symbols show the usefulness and effectiveness in learning and communication process.

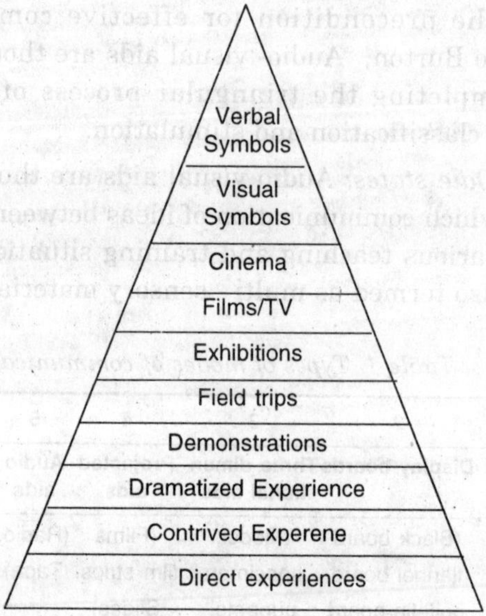

Figure 5. Edges Dale's cone of experience

The focus of his cone of experience is on the learning through senses. Various modes have been shown various levels, how it imparts effective learning.

The base of come, 'Direct purposeful experience' focuses on the concept of 'learning by doing' e.g learning to ride or repair enables one to learn permanently. All senses are active when one learns by direct experiences.

IMPORTANCE OF COMMUNICATION

For effective communication in any set up, a good communication network not only increases productivity but stimulates people to work harder without increasing unhealthy working conditions. The importance of communication can be stated as follows:

i) Communication enables top management to formulate comprehensive plans and policies on scientific basis.

ii) Effective communication of policies and decisions to those who have to put them into action results in accurate and able performance.

iii) It becomes the strong determinant of direction and leadership

iv) Constant communication with personnel or working force helps the management to be informed of their problems, difficulties and grievances. Appropriate timely steps and remedial measures can be taken.

v) Effective communication network also helps to reduce and resolve the conflicts as generally conflicts arise because of communication gap.

vi) Communication is quite essential for co-ordination which is the essence of effective management of any institute.

vii) It brings about mutual understanding between personnel at all levels and fosters the spirit of co-operation.

viii) Transmission, interpretation and adoption of policies will lead to concerted action.

ix) Planned sequence of operations will not be disturbed if proper communication network is there in the institute

x) Communication helps in securing largest possible participation or consultation is decision making, planning and general administration This gives democratic character to managerial process and strengthens the morale of the employees. The importance of communication, in brief, can be stated as follows:

— Aid to performance
— Aid to understanding
— Aid to leadership
— Aid to co-ordination
— Aid to job-satisfaction
— Aid to economy in time and effort.

BARRIERS TO EFFECTIVE COMMUNICATION

Barriers to effective communication are the obstacles which create confusion, misunderstanding and may even lead to breakdown of the communication process. Communication is impeded by three broad type of barriers:

i) *Physical barriers*: Physical barriers are environmental factors that present or reduce the sending and receiving of communication. They include physical distance, distracting noises and similar interference.

ii) *Personal barriers (social psychological barriers)*: Personal barriers arise from the judgments, emotions and social values of people. They are similar to the physical distances as mentioned. Psychological distance may entirely prevent a communication, filter part of it out, or simply cause misinterpretation. Emotion acts as filters in all communications. We communicate our interpretation of reality instead of reality itself.

iii) *Semantic barriers*: Semantic barriers arise form the limitations of the symbolic system itself symbols usually have a variety of meanings and sender has to choose one meaning from among many.

The other major barriers to effective communication are given below:

i) *Multiplicity of organisational levels*: Information in a multiple level organisation in the hierarchy may be withheld at a particular level or passed on with changes. This happens particularly when communication of correct information is likely to have an adverse impact.

ii) *Language barrier*: The language used for communicating a message may also be an obstacle in effective communication. This happens when the pronouncement of words for example is not clear in verbal communication or words are not clear in written communication or words having different or more than one meaning have been used. Ambiguity in any form in language used may result in faulty communication.

iii) *Status quo:* The difference in the status of sender or receiver may also an obstacle to effective communication. For example subordinates often withhold or pass on distorted information to please their superiors or a boss may suffer from ego or his status position to ask the subordinate for clarity or advise. These are the obstacles arising out of the status positions in the hierarchy of any organisation.

iv) *Lack of organisational facilities*: People generally fail to communicate effectively due to lack of organisational facilities/ forum such as meetings, conferences, complaint or suggestion boxes, open door system etc

v) *Organisational rules and regulations*: The rigid organisational rules and regulations also act as an obstacle to effective communication when these rules restrict the flow of certain messages, prescribe the subject matter to be communicated and also the channel through which it is to be communicated leaving no scope of flexibility or personal discretion.

vi) *Inattentiveness*: In attentiveness of the receiver also act as an obstacle to effective communication. The purpose of communication is defeated when the receiver shows the inattentiveness to the message conveyed.

vii) *Over burdening or lengthy communications*: When too much content or lengthy communications are sent, at one point of time, there are chances of it being filtered or not comprehending it fully.

viii) *Defective selection of media*: The communication also gets affected when the media so selected has problems i.e. telephonic long distance call may distort the message due to mechanical barrier.

STEPS TO IMPROVE EFFECTIVENESS OF COMMUNICATION

Removal of the barriers to effective communication goes a long way in improving the effectiveness of communication, some of the other steps that are helpful in further increasing the effectiveness of communications are listed below:

(i) It is better to communicate information little by little over a period of time than all at once. Further logical and sequential presentation of ideas facilitates interpretation and understanding of messages.

(ii) Short sentences, familiar words standard gestures and active verbs help to make communication both understandable and effective

(iii) Repeating a communication obviously prolongs its influence and increases the impact of the message

(iv) In the practice of communication, receiver is continuously making attempts at identifying the role played by sender and his actual status. It is thus helpful for the sender to clarify his ideas before communicating and put them across in a way so as to minimize the chances of his role being misconceived.

(v) Feedback is vital part of any communication as it helps in correcting the errors and misunderstanding between sender and receiver. Timely remedial measure and action is only possible through a sound feedback mechanism in any communication network.

(vi) The use of audio-visual aids and taking help of more than one medium whenever possible, also improve the effectiveness of communication.

(vii) Both sender as well as receiver must be good and active listeners.

PRINCIPLES OF EFFECTIVE COMMUNICATION

The principles which can be followed to make the communication effective is given below:

i) Principle of readiness
ii) Appropriate use of language
iii) Principle of lucidity
iv) Principle of precision
v) Unity of thought

Principle of Readiness

Communication is a two way process, where the readiness or preparedness of both the parties is essential. One must be ready to hear or receive the message and respond or give feedback so that the purpose of communication is achieved. In order to make the message effective, the recipients, attention should be drawn to the message communicated. Each one is different in behaviour sentiment and emotions, which determines the degree of attention and readiness. For this purpose, the superior must note that he himself should not expect from his subordinates what he himself does not practice. So the golden rule is prepare your audience to hear you or make them attentive and ready to receive for having effective communication. Readiness exercises i.e. contexualising, stating with some interesting activity, game narratives, past references brainstorming, debates, discussions can be initiated to make them involved in the process. Whenever any organisational change takes place subordinates have to be prepared for accepting such changes as any change mects with strong resistance in initial phases.

Principle of Appropriate Use of Language

Language used in any form of communication: i.e. oral or written, is very powerful tool in the hands of communicator.

In oral communications specially use of appropriate language which expresses ideas in clear terms leaves powerful impact in bringing about the desired response. Vague expressions should be avoided. Researches have shown that oral communications together with written versions are more effective. The sender must use the language with which the receiver is familiar.

Principle of Lucidity

Also known as principle of clarity states that the idea or message to be transmitted should be clearly worded so that it may be interpreted by the receiver in the same sense in which it is communicated. It should be noted that the words do not speak themselves, but the speaker gives them meaning. Hence the idea to be communicated should be very clear in the mind of the sender. If message is lucid, transparent and clear if would invoke an appropriate response from other party. It is also necessary that the receiver must be conversant with the languages, the inherent assumptions and the mechanics of communication.

Principle of Precision

Principle of precision means the exactness or accuracy in communication process. The information should be adequate and complete in all respects. Inadequate and incomplete information may delay action and destroy understanding and create confusion e.g. communication should always be consistent with policies, plans, programmes and objectives, and not in conflict with them. They have to be stated very precisely without being inconsistent with the policies plans of organisation. Otherwise if may lead to prove detrimental to the organisations health. In oral as well as written communication the principle of precision plays a very pivotal role in developing an effective communication network in any organisation. Even in oral communication, the precision in speaker's speech is appreciated and well received by the audience. The desired feedback /response is invoked when the idea/ message so communicated is precise and accurate.

Unity of Thought

For communication to take place, there has to be two parties- the sender and receiver or communicator and communicated. But despite this, there has to be a cordial relation for the communication process to complete If one is communicating and the other person is not listening or receiving properly, there is bound to be a communication gap and the purpose of communication will be forfeited in the absence of desired feedback or response by the receiver. There has to be 'unity of thought' a common sharing of interest to invoke desired response. For this, the management should promote the participative approach in management. The subordinate should be invited to participate in the decision-making process. It should seek co-operation from the subordinates and reduce communication barriers. Even in oral communications, to make it effective the receiver and sender (speaker us audience), should reach same wavelength and commonality of interest then only it will be well received by audience. The desirable response is only invoked when there is unity of thought and sharing of common interests.

There are other principles like principle of timeliness, principle of feedback and principle of communication net work which also contribute to effective communication.

Principle of timeliness. It emphasizes the importance of timely communications as any delay in communication message serves no purpose except to make them merely historical document as it loses its importance. Timely action cannot be taken due to the delay and it may result in deadlocks, losses or other delays in interrelated tasks or assignments.

Principle of feedback: The communication must have feedback information from receive to know whether if has been understood in the same sense in which sender has meant it or whether subordinates agree or disagree with the contents of the message; It also helps in understating the attitude of the people.

Principle of communication network. Communication network implies the routes through which the communication travels to its destination. A number of such network may exist in an organisation at a given point of time; but the management should consider the effectiveness of communication network in the given situation, and its effects on the behaviours of the recipient before it finally chooses the net work.

The above principles, if followed will make the communication effective An effective communication system when installed in any organisation promotes healthy organisational culture/climate and better interpersonal relations resulting in increased productivity and commonality of interest.

Thus conditions for effective communication can be put as under:

1. Think before you speak;
2. Define the purpose of communication;
3. Know your audience;
4. Use right words for the right occasion
5. Get your facts straight;
6. Show interest in others development;
7. Be sure to follow up;
8, Follow up communication with action;
9. Communicate for tomorrow as well as today;
10. Polish your listening skill
11. Relationship between the people who are comminuting must be vital sound and healthy

12. Be direct;
    (a) don't be evasive
    (b) don't be ambiguous
    (c) don't hold back things you know

Some times one faces barriers to communication or hurdles, be it physical barrier or noise barriers arising from motives, attitudes of people, improper state of mind, love for status quo hasty conclusions, lack of attention or interest one must find ways to first diagnose the nature of barrier and the remove it with proper line of action.

Few steps can be followed for diagnosing communication problems:

i) Select concept to describe current communication practices and procedures.
ii) Implement technique of reporting on "The state of system".
iii) Develop 'criterion measure' (policies for evaluation)
iv) Implement programmes to correct deficiencies in communication patters.

COMMUNICATION IN EDUCATION

The importance of communication in education i.e. teaching-learning process cannot be over-emphasised, the communication skills empower the speaker in communicating his ideas effectively. The use of Mass Communication in Education is proving very useful and effective in this era of modern technology and increasing use of new modern means of acquiring knowledge. Some of the importance of mass communication can be listed below:

i) It enables students to sensitise themselves about the realities of life. T.V. and radio serve as powerful means to get varied informations which is not possible in closed/confined walls of classrooms.

ii) It give the primary source of information, student can see and hear the programmes of their our choice.

iii) For developing language skills, they provide a very effective and powerful means, the talks, debates, panel discussions, news items etc.

vi) National integration and communal harmony can be achieved by showing in an attractive package of programmes, serials, songs, debates dramatisations etc.

Mass communication systems are powerful tools for bringing revolution in the field of education. In many other areas like modernisation of education, community participation, adult and informal education, Human resource development, economise development, vocationlisation of education etc, the means of communication prove to be very useful and affective.

Appendix

UNESCO Report: "Towards a Culture of Peace"

Pursuant to General Assembly resolution 50/173 of 22 December 1995, the Director-General of UNESCO submits herewith a report on educational activities in the framework of the UNESCO transdisciplinary project entitled "Towards a culture of peace". The report is set within the framework of United Nations actions for peace-building, including the United Nations Decade for Human Rights Education and the United Nations Year for Tolerance.

INTRODUCTION: THE CHALLENGE OF A CULTURE OF PEACE

With the end of the cold war, the international community was challenged to regain the initiative towards the achievement of the great objectives of the Charter of the United Nations for peace and security. In conjunction with the substantial increase in peacekeeping and peace-building operations of the United Nations, a new and comprehensive vision of United Nations action for peace was formulated in the report of the Secretary-General to the Security Council in 1992 entitled "An Agenda for Peace".

In accordance with its fundamental mission of peace-building as defined in its Constitution, UNESCO celebrated in July 1989, at Yamoussoukro, Co^te d'Ivoire, the International

Congress on Peace in the Minds of Men, from which the concept of culture of peace emerged. The organisation is mandated by its Constitution to promote "collaboration among the nations through education, science and culture in order to further universal respect for justice, for the rule of law and for human rights and fundamental freedoms". In fact, from the time of its founding, UNESCO has worked to ensure the free circulation of ideas, the development of understanding and solidarity among individuals and cultures, respect for human rights, and the effective exercise of the democratic principles enshrined in the Constitution.

In 1992, the Culture of Peace Programme was proposed by UNESCO as a contribution to peace-building as outlined by "An Agenda for Peace" and by the Yamoussoukro Congress. Peace-building, at that time, was limited to situations following violent conflict when peacekeeping operations had been undertaken, and was described as "comprehensive efforts to identify and support structures which will tend to consolidate peace and advance a sense of confidence and well-being among people".

The concept of "peace-building" has evolved since its formulation in the context of peacekeeping operations in post-conflict situations. In "An Agenda for Development", presented by the Secretary-General to the General Assembly in 1994, the scope of peace-building was expanded. It was said that "peace-building is a matter for countries at all stages of development", including countries emerging from violent conflict, countries in transition, and countries of wealth and power which should engage in demobilisation and defence conversion. Further, in the "Supplement" to "An Agenda for Peace", published in 1995, peace-building was proposed not only in post-conflict situations associated with peacekeeping operations but also as preventive action in situations with the potential for violent conflict.

The Culture of Peace Programme includes specific activities in the fields of competence of UNESCO in both pre-conflict (prevention) and post-conflict (national reconciliation) situation. The first national culture of peace programmes were developed in post-conflict peace-building situations. They were launched in 1993 and 1994 in El Salvador and Mozambique as a complement to United Nations peacekeeping operations. In 1995 and 1996, national programmes and related activities were initiated in Burundi, Congo, Guatemala, Philippines, Rwanda and Somalia, among others, in situations that could be considered as much preventive as post-conflict.

The fundamental principle of a culture of peace was put in practice in the initial programmes in El Salvador and Mozambique: the transformation from conflict to cooperation through a process of dialogue leading to cooperation for shared goals of human development. This principle, although originally employed in post-conflict situations, is equally valid for conflict prevention. In fact, it is a fundamental finding of social psychology, replicated in various types of contexts, that the most effective means to end or avoid a conflict is the engagement of the contending parties in collaboration for a shared higher goal. The scope of the programme has been elaborated in a series of international forum and consultative meetings, including the First International Forum on a Culture of Peace, hosted by El Salvador in February 1994, and the Second International Forum, hosted by the Philippines in November 1995.

The culture of peace addresses the deep roots of conflict. As formulated in An Agenda for Development, "pulling up the roots of conflict goes beyond immediate post-conflict requirements and the repair of war-torn societies. The underlying conditions that led to conflict must be addressed. As the causes of conflict are varied, so must be the means of addressing them. Peace-building means fostering a culture of peace."

At this moment of history, when it is for the first time possible to plan and take action towards the general disarmament of nations, so too it is both feasible and necessary to disarm people's minds. People may begin to transform the shared aspects of their cultures that have been shaped by war and violence to the sharing of a culture of peace. This means that in the place of violence, there must be dialogue and respect for human rights; instead of enemy images, intercultural understanding and solidarity; instead of secrecy, the sharing and free flow of information; and instead of male domination, the full empowerment of women. This means that resources and knowledge must be better shared in order to include the excluded—through life-long education—and to reach the unreached—by means of learning without frontiers.

As set forth in An Agenda for Development, peace-building is a vast and comprehensive project to replace the institutions of war and violence by other alternatives based upon non-violence and respect for fundamental rights and freedoms. Therefore, peace-building is linked intrinsically to development based on justice and the full exercise of democratic principles.

"Development is the most secure basis for peace", as "without development, there is no prospect for lasting peace". Sustainability of development is only possible in a framework of justice and freedom of expression. It requires the "intellectual and moral solidarity of mankind", as phrased in the Constitution of UNESCO. Reciprocally, peace is a fundamental dimension of development as there is no development without stability and security. Development must preserve the environment in a "true partnership ...between humanity and nature".

Justice—there is no justice without freedom—is essential to peace-building. Injustice lies at the very roots of conflict and without justice there can be no peace. Peace-building activities reduce poverty and disease and provide for skills and education that facilitate active life, not only in the developing world and countries in transition but even in the richest countries where many are excluded from their basic political, economic and social rights.

Peace can only be sustained through democratic participation and good governance. This requires not only fair elections but citizen participation through a continuous process of dialogue, discussion and agreement on the decisions that affect their lives. And there is no participation without citizenship, which includes full empowerment through education. "Education for All" is the key for democracy in everyday life. For these reasons, it is more important, particularly in societies in transition, to assist in the solid construction of justice and democratic values which provide a basis for good governance and to avoid the imposition of routine democratic models.

In addition to institutions, the minds of men and women must undergo change. Their values, attitudes and behaviour must go through a process of transformation so that instead of supporting and perpetuating the institutions of war and violence, they create and sustain the relationships and structures which make up a culture of peace. As phrased in the Constitution of UNESCO, "since wars begin in the minds of men, it is in the minds of men that the defences of peace must be constructed".

The culture of peace project is dedicated mainly to this transformation of mind and behaviour. It is a complex process taking place on many levels, and linked to learning through collective action. Rather than taking place in isolation, it must develop as an integral part of peace-building activity.

Recognising the broad and long-term scope of this task, the General Conference of UNESCO, at its twenty-eighth session in 1995, expanded the Culture of Peace Programme into a transdisciplinary project, beginning with the biennium 1996-1997 and involving all of the programme sectors of the organisation both at headquarters and in the field. The project is a coordinated effort to contribute to a global movement from a culture of war and violence to a culture of peace. It comprises four units, as follows.

Unit 1—Education for peace, human rights, democracy, international understanding and tolerance: (1) promotes educational policies, plans and programmes; (2) fosters the elaboration of manuals, textbooks and teaching aids; and (3) reinforces networks of institutions active in education for peace, human rights and democracy.

Unit 2—Promotion of human rights and democracy; struggle against discrimination: (1) contributes to better understanding and recognition of all human rights; (2) contributes to the prevention and elimination of all forms of discrimination based on racial, national or ethnic origin, language, religion or belief, or any other ground; (3) promotes the effective application of the principle of the equality of law of men and women; (4) ensures the follow-up to the United Nations Year for Tolerance; and (5) contributes to the consolidation of democracy.

Unit 3—Cultural pluralism and intercultural dialogue: (1) consolidates cultural pluralism in multicultural societies; (2) promotes values that may help to consolidate intercultural dialogue with a view to peace; and (3) creates, through intercultural projects, new opportunities for dialogue and exchange between cultural areas.

Unit 4—Conflict prevention and post-conflict peace-building: (1) promotes the search for effective methods of conflict prevention; (2) provides emergency assistance during conflicts; and (3) supports post-conflict peace-building.

As requested in General Assembly resolution 50/173, emphasis is placed in this report on education, which is the leading modality to promote a culture of peace. This includes, especially, the long-term actions of UNESCO for education in peace and human rights, including those within the framework of the United Nations Decade for Human Rights Education and actions taken within the framework of national culture of peace programmes and related projects. Further, the final section of this report describes how the transdisciplinary project is intended to contribute in a coordinated way to peace-building in cooperation with the entire United Nations system.

EDUCATION: THE LEADING MODALITY TO PROMOTE A CULTURE OF PEACE

Education, seen broadly, is the most important process by which people gain the values, attitudes and behaviours of a culture of peace. By this is meant learning, formal, informal and non-formal, not only in schools but also in the family, through the mass media and in other social institutions, not as an isolated process but as part of a shared global experience of learning by doing. The key, as expressed in the recent report to UNESCO by the International Commission on Education for the Twenty-first Century, is "learning to live together". It is in this sense that education may be said to be the leading modality in the struggle to create a culture of peace.

The Basic Principles of Education for Peace and Human Rights

Since its inception, UNESCO has taught and promoted the basic principles of peace and human rights and disseminated the international conventions of human rights in order to make their provisions known to the widest possible audience. The organisation continues to work in accordance with the principles adopted in its 1974 Recommendation concerning Education for International Understanding, Cooperation and Peace, and Education relating to Human Rights and Fundamental Freedoms. These principles include, among others:

a) Understanding and respect for all peoples, their cultures, civilisations, values and ways of life, including domestic ethnic cultures and cultures of other nations;

b) Awareness not only of the rights but also of the duties incumbent upon individuals, social groups and nations towards each other;

c) Readiness on the part of the individual to participate in solving the problems of his community, his country and the world at large.

The 1974 Recommendation was recently reviewed and its principles confirmed by the International Conference on Education at its forty-fourth session, held at Geneva in October 1994. At the Conference, education ministers from around the world committed themselves to a Declaration and Integrated Framework of Action on Education for Peace, Human Rights and Democracy.

The education ministers stressed their intention to strive resolutely "to take suitable steps to establish in educational institutions an atmosphere contributing to the success of education for international understanding, so that they become ideal places for the exercise of tolerance, respect for human rights, the practice of democracy and learning about the diversity and wealth of cultural identities". They also pledged to give special attention to improving curricula, the content of textbooks, and other educational materials, including new technologies with a view to educating caring and responsible citizens, open to other cultures, able to appreciate the value of freedom, respectful of human dignity and differences, and able to prevent conflicts or resolve them by non-violent means. The recommendations of that Conference were adopted by the twenty-eighth General Conference of UNESCO, meeting in Paris in October-November 1995.

In 1993-1995, the international community adopted a number of other plans and programmes which are the basis of UNESCO activities in education for peace, human rights and democracy: the World Plan of Action on Education for Human Rights and Democracy (Montreal, 1993); the Declaration and Programme of Action of the World Conference on Human Rights (Vienna, 1993); and the Plan of Action for the United Nations Decade for Human Rights Education, 1995-2004.

The World Plan of Action conceives human rights in their broadest senses to include, inter alia, learning about tolerance and acceptance of others, solidarity, participatory citizenship and the importance of building mutual respect and understanding. Accordingly, the Plan calls for the global mobilisation of energies and resources to educate individuals and groups about human rights. The Plan has been disseminated widely by UNESCO particularly through the bulletin Human Rights Teaching. In its follow-up to the Plan, UNESCO is aided by an Advisory Committee on Education for Peace, Human Rights and Democracy.

The Vienna Declaration and Programme of Action requests States to develop specific programmes and strategies for ensuring the widest human rights education, taking into account the Montreal World Plan of Action. UNESCO and its member States are committed to its implementation, with an emphasis of provisions for fostering mutual understanding, tolerance and peace, full development of human personality and promotion of values related to peace, democracy, development and social justice. This commitment has been strengthened through an exchange of letters between the Director-General of UNESCO and the Secretary-General of the United Nations and by UNESCO Executive Board decision 144 EX/5.1.2, inviting the Director-General to ensure the highest possible standard of UNESCO activities to implement the Vienna Declaration and Programme of Action.

B. Actions at the Global Level

To put these principles into practice, UNESCO engages in a variety of activities, including the publication and dissemination of educational materials in many languages. A list of these materials which present and explain the various normative instruments and declarations promoting human rights and a culture of peace is provided in the appendix to the present report.

Emphasis is placed on textbook research and revision with a view to the improvement of textbooks as instruments of peace, human rights, democracy, tolerance, international and intercultural understanding. UNESCO works with the Georg-Eckert Institute on Textbook Research of Germany within the framework of the International Textbook Research Network and in bilateral and multilateral consultations with member States, including the preparation of guidelines on the most effective procedures and methodologies for textbook writing and revision.

The teaching of peace, justice, solidarity and intercultural cooperation is the priority of the UNESCO Associated Schools Project (ASP), which links over 3,700 schools and teacher training institutions in 129 countries. Students and teachers take part in the production of ASP materials; thus, the new brochure "No to violence" is composed of contributions from ASP schools in Brazil, Estonia, Germany, Haiti, Sri Lanka and Zaire. Materials promoting a culture of peace are also being produced by the students and teachers who participated in the regional culture of peace festivals which took place in Cook Islands, Costa Rica, Greece, Grenada, Jordan, Thailand and Zimbabwe. The festivals were organised in 1995 by ASP and the UNESCO Culture of Peace Programme to mark the fiftieth anniversary of UNESCO and the United Nations. Among the initiatives of ASP taking place in 1996 are the "Global Teach-in" workshops in 11 countries, the International Conference on Peace and Tolerance at the Jewish Arab Institute in Israel, and the International Forum for Solidarity against Intolerance, for a Dialogue of Cultures, in Georgia. Solidarity is an important aspect of ASP activities. As an example, the German ASP network has campaigned since 1994 to raise support for schools in Bosnia and Herzegovina.

The UNESCO LINGUAPAX project is designed to promote peace, human rights, democracy, tolerance and humanistic values through the teaching of mother and foreign languages, with special attention to the linguistic and cultural rights of minorities. In addition to the publication and dissemination of materials, the project will hold regional seminars in Bolivia, Burkina Faso, Japan, Luxembourg and Spain in 1996-1997.

UNESCO cooperates closely with the academic community in the promotion of human rights education. Annual meetings of directors of human rights institutes provide an opportunity for discussing new modalities of action for human rights education at institutional levels. UNESCO Chairs in human rights, democracy and peace promote an integrated system of research, training and information activities and facilitate subregional and regional cooperation between university researchers and teachers. In addition to Chairs already established in 19 countries of Africa, Europe, the Arab States and Latin America, new Chairs are being established in 1996 in Madagascar, Mexico, Morocco and South Africa. A regional Culture of Peace Chair is being set up in the Latin America and the Caribbean region, embracing various universities and academic institutions, to mobilise and renew curricula dealing with preventive diplomacy and peace-building. With the College of Mexico, a "virtual" Culture of Peace Chair has been established beginning in 1996.

Exemplary actions for the teaching of human rights and peace are recognised through the biennial UNESCO Prize for the Teaching of Human Rights and the annual UNESCO Prize for Peace Education. The Prize for the Teaching of Human Rights was awarded in 1994 to the Philippine Commission on Human Rights for its training of Filipino armed forces and police, and to Mr. Jose Zalaquett Daher of Chile for his teaching of human rights in the context of Amnesty International. The Prize for Peace Education was awarded in 1995 to the Austrian Centre for Peace and Conflict Resolution Studies and the European University Centre for Peace Studies. In addition, UNESCO launched a prize of Mayors for Peace at the United Nations Conference on Human Settlements, held at Istanbul in June 1996. The prize will recognise cities which have contributed to peace by means of various activities, including exemplary actions in education, particularly civics education, and to combat exclusion and promote intercommunity dialogue. The establishment of a data bank of "best practices" is foreseen.

An Ibero-American meeting of Human Rights Ombudsmen was held recently in Antigua, Guatemala. The participants signed a declaration committing themselves to promote justice and respect for human rights and established a network of Human Rights Ombudsmen for a culture of peace.

The main objective of the United Nations Decade for Human Rights Education, 1995-2004 is to make an assessment of needs and the formulation of effective strategies for the furtherance of human rights education. The Executive Board of UNESCO, recognising the organisation's role and responsibility in the Decade, urged member States and National Commissions to participate actively in developing national plans of action for human rights education as foreseen in the Plan of Action for the Decade. The Plan of Action stipulates UNESCO cooperation with the United Nations Centre for Human Rights to assist the High Commissioner for Human Rights in a preliminary survey and evaluation of existing human rights education programmes and initiatives. A memorandum of cooperation, signed between the High Commissioner for Human Rights and the Director-General of UNESCO in October 1995, provides the framework for further developing and strengthening cooperation to that effect.

With the framework of the Plan of Action for the Decade, UNESCO conducted in 1995 a preliminary country survey and evaluation of human rights education in nine countries in different regions of the world. A prototype was developed by means of a workshop in collaboration with the Indian Institute of Advanced Study, which surveyed the Indian national experience. The final report includes: (a) the legal and policy framework of human rights education; (b) human rights at different levels of education—primary, secondary and higher education; (c) minorities and human rights education; (d) the role of the media in education for human rights and democracy; and (e) education for democracy.

A separate report has been submitted by UNESCO in its capacity as lead agency for the United Nations Year for Tolerance (in response to General Assembly resolution 49/213 of 23 December 1994, and before the General Assembly under item 110 (b) of its agenda in document A/51/201). However, note should be taken here of the significant contribution of these activities to education for peace, democracy and human rights. Taking into consideration the many regional conferences and local meetings held within the framework of the United Nations Year for Tolerance, the General Conference of UNESCO, at its twenty-eighth session adopted the Declaration of Principles on Tolerance. The Declaration defined tolerance as 'an active attitude' and a "responsibility that upholds human rights, pluralism (including cultural pluralism), democracy and the rule of law". It commits the member States to "support and implement programmes of social science research and education for tolerance, human rights and non-violence". They commit themselves to putting this into practice by "devoting special attention to improving teacher training, curricula, the content of textbooks and lessons, and other educational materials, including new educational technologies, with a view to educating caring and responsible citizens open to other cultures, able to appreciate the value of freedom, respectful of human dignity and differences, and able to prevent conflicts or resolve them by non-violent means".

In the recent report to UNESCO by the International Commission on Education for the Twenty-first Century, four pillars of education are proposed—learning to know, to do, to be and to live together—with the greatest weight placed on the fourth. This represents the management of conflict by working together on common projects. As elaborated by the Chairman of the Commission, Mr. Jacques Delors, in his introduction, people may learn to live together "by developing an understanding of others and their history, traditions and spiritual values and, on this basis, creating a new spirit which, guided by recognition of our growing interdependence and a common analysis of the risks and challenges of the future, would induce people to implement common projects or to manage the inevitable conflicts in an intelligent and peaceful way.

Under the specific circumstances prevailing for many people today, it is not enough to confine learning to the traditional schooling situation. Therefore, taking full advantage of modern technology, UNESCO has expanded its educational activities, through its new programme "Learning without frontiers", in order to meet the learning needs of the unreached and to respond to the challenge of lifelong learning. Through programmes of training, professional exchange, policy development, development and promotion of affordable technology use, and the organisation of partnerships and networks, both academic and vocational education is made increasingly available to everyone. Designed to eliminate the barriers of space, time, age and circumstance which have prevented access to education, the programme is considered by the organisation to be a vital contribution to the establishment of a culture of peace. It includes intensive audiovisual learning of basic skills for illiterates in their mother tongue as an essential first step for those who have been demobilised from war, who live in dispersed human settlements, or who for other reasons have not had access to the educational mainstream.

In any society with the phenomenon of street children, one finds either open or latent violence. Urgent measures must be adopted worldwide to eradicate this shameful effect of social injustice. For its part, UNESCO is developing the capacity of the member States to provide education to street children in the context of its programme "Education for All", thus promoting their reinsertion into society.

Under the leadership of the United Nations Drug Control Programme (UNDCP), UNESCO participates fully in education to prevent drug addiction, which affects the lives of young people so severely and even irreversibly. The Culture of Peace Programme contributes to a better understanding of the reasons underlying the problem of drug addiction and to providing the values and hope required to overcome it. It is indispensable to prevent not only demand but also trafficking, which involves money-laundering and the financial interests of hundreds of billions of dollars.

Specific educational content for peace is encouraged and disseminated by UNESCO in special messages from opinion leaders and authorities, such as religious representatives, scientists and women leaders.

Representatives of different religious traditions adopted the Declaration on the Role of Religions in the Promotion of a Culture of Peace at a meeting sponsored by UNESCO in Barcelona, Spain, in 1994. In that Declaration, the participants committed themselves to resolve or transform conflicts without using violence, and to prevent them through education and pursuit of justice. They placed emphasis on education for peace, freedom and human rights, and religious education to promote openness and tolerance.

Scientists, too, have spoken out from their expert knowledge on the bases for education for a culture of peace. Meeting in Seville, Spain, in 1986, at the request of the Spanish National Commission for UNESCO, an international team of scientists issued a Statement on Violence countering the commonly believed myth that war is inherent in human nature. The Statement was adopted by the General Conference of UNESCO in 1989. Speaking from the relevant disciplines of animal behaviour, psychology, brain research, genetics and anthropology, the scientists rejected the idea that war is genetically programmed into human nature or inherited from animal ancestors. They concluded that "the same species who invented war is capable of inventing peace. The responsibility lies with each of us."

Education for a culture of peace was taken up by participants in the Fourth World Conference on Women, convened by the United Nations in Beijing in September 1995, and integrated into the Platform for Action. The UNESCO Statement on Women's Contribution to a Culture of Peace, emphasising that "efforts to move towards a culture of peace must be founded in education", was signed by eminent participants at the Beijing Conference. Keeping in mind that "girls and women constitute a large majority of the world's educationally excluded and unreached", it called for equality in education as the key to meeting other requirements for a culture of peace. It is important to tap the full capacity of women for leadership, as they can be the "source of innovative and much-needed approaches to peace-building". Specific recommendations for education towards a culture of peace, as a follow-up to the Beijing Conference, have been set forth in the report of the Commission on the Status of Women, at its fortieth session in March 1996.

Education in National Culture of Peace Programmes

Education is key to the task of reconciliation and reconstruction undertaken by national culture of peace programmes. This incudes non-formal and informal education by means of the mass media and other systems of communication as well as formal systems of schooling.

In keeping with the basic principle of national culture of peace programmes, projects are planned and implemented through a process involving all sides of the conflicts from which the country is recovering. National forums and dialogues to launch such programmes have been held in a number of countries, including El Salvador (1993), Burundi (1994), Congo (1994), Somalia (1995) and Sudan (1995, 1996).

In the El Salvador programme, the first major project to be carried out is the production of daily radio broadcasts and non-formal education campaigns for the most needy and neglected women in the country. Not only was the project planned by representatives of the Government, the Farabundi Marti National Liberation Front (FMLN) opposition and the radio stations, but even the technical committee which does the day-to-day work of the project is composed of representatives from all three.

The radio programmes, broadcast daily by 24 stations by the beginning of 1996, deal with the legal rights of women, violence against women, sharing of domestic work and women's values and self-esteem. The radio programmes are participatory; their contents are gathered by a network of community correspondents coming from diverse sectors of Salvadorian society. A second stage of the project will launch non-formal educational campaigns on related themes for women, beginning with visits to radio listeners by one of 1,500 female and male campaign promoters.

Similar involvement of both formal educational systems and non-formal education through the mass media have characterised the development of national culture of peace programmes in Burundi, Mozambique and Rwanda. In each case, the guidelines are set forth in a national forum or by a national steering committee, and the projects involve all sides to the conflict in their planning and implementation. In Mozambique, the programme sponsored the First National Conference on Culture of Peace and Human Rights, at Maputo in January 1996; the participants included high-level government officials, leaders of opposition parties, non-governmental organisations, media representatives and parliamentarians who debated on the legal system, education for peace, social communication, women's issues and traditional culture. The Conference was covered extensively by television, radio and the printed press.

In Rwanda, a UNESCO plan of action was signed by the Director-General of UNESCO and the Minister of High Education, Research and culture involving a total value of US$ 2.6 million. A wide range of actions are foreseen, following recommendations from the National Consultation on a Culture of Peace held at Kigali in January 1996. These include a contribution to reform the educational system, rehabilitation and reorganisation of the judicial system, and training of media professionals.

In Burundi, the programme is run from the "House of the Culture of Peace" established by UNESCO in conjunction with other United Nations and international agencies and staffed with national specialists in education, communication, culture and human rights for peace. The first action was the National Forum in December 1994, which brought together the full range of government and non-governmental actors to make recommendations for activities to facilitate the process of peace and reconciliation. On the basis of these recommendations, there have been a series of seminars and educational initiatives. In July and September 1995, in collaboration with UNDP, the United Nations Centre for Human Rights, government organisations and the Burundian Association of Journalists, UNESCO organised two seminars on the role of the media in promoting peace in Burundi. In collaboration with the Ligue ITEKA, a local non-governmental organisation for human rights, UNESCO provided training for the teaching of human rights and democracy in secondary schools, in which about 60 teachers from 13 secondary schools participated. Two workshops on peace and human rights were organised in October 1995 in collaboration with the Ministry of Youth, with the support of the delegation of the European Union; the workshops were attended by 111 youth counsellors. In December 1995, training seminars on human rights for local government officials were held in two provinces, organised in collaboration with UNDP and the Ministry of Interior.

A million-dollar, multidisciplinary UNESCO Plan of Action for Burundi, 1996-1997, was announced by the Director-General of UNESCO in March 1996. The plan includes, among its many provisions, rehabilitation of school infrastructure damaged during the conflict, support to the creation of a research and training centre for peace education and conflict resolution, programmes of culture of peace training for women, support to youth associations for peace, and training of media professionals.

Education and communication are central to the activities being carried out in the countries of Central and Eastern Europe and Central Asia within the framework of the International Forum for Solidarity against Intolerance, for a Dialogue of Cultures, held at Tbilisi, Georgia, in 1995. Among these initiatives are the foundation of a UNESCO Culture of Peace Teachers Association, which is engaging in teacher training in the context of a multinational society, and a series of television broadcasts on education for tolerance and peace by the Russian Federation television programme "Obvious yet Incredible", with more than 10 million viewers in the region.

An important contribution to the reconciliation has been made through UNESCO support for the independent media in a number of regions. In the former Yugoslavia and Rwanda, where radio had been used in some cases to promote enemy images of other ethnic groups, UNESCO, in collaboration with non-governmental organisations and other international organisations, has supported the development and sustainability of the independent media which bridge ethnic divisions and promote reconciliation. Similarly, UNESCO support for independent and community radio is making possible the use of the media by the people themselves for peace and reconciliation in Haiti and the Palestinian autonomous territories.

In recognition of the many UNESCO programmes to support the independent media in the region, the United Nations, in its revised consolidated Inter-agency Appeal for former Yugoslavia (January-December 1996), decided that UNESCO would be the lead agency for assistance to the independent media, indispensable for the establishment of democratic society. In this respect, UNESCO and the authorities of Bosnia and Herzegovina have agreed on the following priority projects: creation of a private network of independent radio and television broadcasters, rehabilitation of RTV Bilt and RTV Pale as public service broadcasters; training for media professionals; and drafting of new media legislation.

School programmes, which include education for peace, conflict resolution and multiculturalism, have been elaborated by UNESCO for Bosnia and Herzegovina, in coordination with other international agencies. It is planned to train teachers and students in the needed skills, to reach all schools in the country with materials on tolerance and international understanding and to stimulate exchanges of experiences in conflict resolution at faculties of philosophy in other countries of the region, including Croatia, the former Yugoslav Republic of Macedonia, and the Federal Republic of Yugoslavia.

In Rwanda, where radio was used to broadcast the propaganda of violence during the genocide in 1994, UNESCO, in cooperation with a French non-governmental organisation, supported the establishment of Radio Gatashya (literally, "the swallow that brings good news") to provide independent information to Rwandan refugees in nearby countries. With the help of another non-governmental organisation, over 3,000 portable radios were dispatched to refugees so that they could listen to the station. Within Rwanda, assistance is being given for the development of the independent media, including transformation of the national radio-television into a public service station with an editorial policy independent from political and ethnic powers.

A similar programme of information for a culture of peace to be broadcast by radio is being planned as a key part of a new programme in Somalia. This is based on the recommendations of a UNESCO-sponsored symposium held at San'a, Yemen, in 1995 on the culture of peace, which brought together Somali intellectuals from all sides of the conflict in that country.

The education of demobilised soldiers receives special emphasis in national culture of peace programmes. The demobilised, in many cases, have missed out on basic education as a result of being forced into military service. Their reinsertion into civil society can be a key component of the process of post-conflict reconciliation and reconstruction, and with education, rather than being a liability, they can serve as important actors in the peace process. In this regard, UNESCO is sponsoring an international conference of demobilised soldiers' organisations at Maputo in December 1996.

Training is a key component of national culture of peace programmes. In order to facilitate the process of cooperation in the development process between former enemies, a priority is placed on the training of "peace promoters", who help them jointly design and implement projects of human development which can produce results of benefit to all. These peace promoters, who may be teachers, journalists, social workers or development workers, are trained to use local as well as universal methods of mediation and conflict resolution. They function for a culture of peace in the same way that literacy promoters are at the heart of literacy campaigns.

TOWARDS THE FUTURE

In establishing the transdisciplinary project "Towards a culture of peace", the General Conference of UNESCO, meeting in October/November 1995, placed it at the heart of the organisation's Medium-term Strategy for 1996-2001, which emphasises the "two objectives common to the United Nations system as a whole, namely, development and peace". Seeing these objectives as inseparable, UNESCO member States called for renewed approaches and determination to achieve them through the promotion of a culture of peace. With education as the key modality in this enterprise, the General Conference set a long-term goal of "a comprehensive system of education and training for peace, human rights and democracy ... that is intended for all groups of people and embraces all levels of education, whether formal or non-formal".

The General Conference formulated a strategy of broad and extensive partnerships for the realisation of the project: "the organisation's strategy will consist in mobilising both individuals and institutions (Governments, educators, the media, families, parliaments, businesses, trade unions, non-governmental organisations, etc.) so that everyone may receive an education and appropriate training". Hence, much of the initial emphasis of the project has been to contact and engage potential partners from all of these sectors in common action for a culture of peace. For example, in June 1996 the new educational programmes for a culture of peace were shared with mayors meeting at the United Nations Conference on Human Settlements at Istanbul and with parliamentarians at the Inter-parliamentary Union Conference on Education, Science, Culture and Communication on the eve of the Twenty-first Century held at UNESCO headquarters in Paris.

Within this framework, UNESCO plans to launch an interregional project for culture of peace and non-violence in educational institutions. The guidelines for the project were developed in Sintra, Portugal, in May 1996, at an international forum of educational experts from around the world, many of them coming from schools located in areas of urban violence and war-torn societies. The project will establish a network to facilitate exchange of experiences and to provide recognition and resources to those working for a culture of peace and non-violence in schools, with an emphasis on regions of the world that suffer from violent conflict. Pilot projects are expected to have a multiplier effect through training, curriculum development, research and wide dissemination of results. The project will be linked closely to the work of the UNESCO Associated Schools Project.

These new educational initiatives for a culture of peace are linked to and extend those of national culture of peace programmes in Africa and Central America. They extend to a global level the principle developed in these programmes, which is to transform conflict into cooperation for human development. Therefore, they are characterised by the participation of the entire educational community. Educational institutions located in areas of conflict, rather than being avoided, are the first choice of pilot projects and for attention.

It is essential that educational activities for a culture of peace be integrally linked to peace-building activities of the society as a whole. In order to build a culture of peace in the next generation, young people need to be involved in the full range of peace-building activities, including sustainable development, justice and democracy. Schools should nurture, through organisation and practice, tomorrow's citizens capable of democratic participation. They should be centres where the community, including students, plan and implement actions for human development.

The process must not be limited to schools, but extended to the full range of non-formal educational activities. As seen in national culture of peace programmes, the mass media and other non-formal communication make possible the full participation of the community, including all sides of conflicts, in peace-building. In this regard, a meeting of Latin American journalists, for a culture of peace will take place in December 1996. It is hoped that this will contribute to a process by which the media become fully involved in peace-building actions.

Special emphasis is being placed on the involvement of the miliary and its educational institutions. The end of the East-West confrontation, the shift from violence between nations to violence within nations, the increase in United Nations peacekeeping operations—all these dramatic changes lead to a new concept of security, prompting the military to reconceptualise its role and retrain its personnel. Training in human rights and non-violent conflict resolution, the fundamentals of a culture of peace, is becoming part of the order of the day. At the same time, it is increasingly appreciated that the skills and resources of the military, with appropriate coordination, transparency and education, can make great contributions to peaceful social change. A number of recent meetings have unanimously supported the contribution of the military to peace-building and conflict resolution: the seminar "Security for Peace: Peace-building and Peacekeeping" held at the Inter-American Defence College in Washington D.C., in April 1995; the Central American Military Forum for a Culture of Peace, held in El Salvador in June 1996; and the international symposium "From Partial Insecurity to Global Security" organised jointly by UNESCO and the Institute of Advanced Studies of National Defence of France, in Paris, in June 1996. The symposium involved the directors of defence institutes and high-level representatives of the armies of more than 40 countries.

What is needed today is a global training effort for non-violent social change that transforms conflict into cooperation for human development. Through both formal schooling and the popular media, people need to learn the skills of dialogue, negotiation and consensus. These skills might be called the "second literacy" which, in its own way, is as important for future generations as reading and writing. While the contents of the educational messages must be based on universal principles, they must at the same time develop out of the traditions and experiences of the people concerned as they struggle to make development democratic and participatory. UNESCO is prepared to take the lead in coordinating such a global training effort, fulfilling its mandate to construct the defences of peace in the minds of men and women. In the past it has contributed to make available at the global level the universal principles of justice that have been elaborated in the Universal Declaration of Human Rights and many subsequent standard-setting instruments. Now it is prepared to extend the process of training in conflict transformation to everyone through the linkage of educational and media systems to the process of participatory development.

The linkage of actions for a culture of peace to the process of development ensures that they will contribute to the drastic reduction of poverty and exclusion which most often lie at the roots of violent conflict. Through imaginative new modalities of action, such as micro-credits, the promotion of women's handicrafts and other productive activities, the economic situation of the poor and the quality of rural life can be improved, thus decreasing migration to urban slums.

By promoting a culture of peace, the process launched by An Agenda for Peace can be extended from peacekeeping to the prevention of violent conflicts. Prevention is the key, as problems are more difficult to solve after they have reached a stage of crisis. Although action taken to prevent conflict is often invisible and unrecognised, in the long term it is more economical and sustainable, and it is a necessary condition for the advances in human development, justice and democracy on which our common future depends.

Bibliography

Alcord, B., and Wittgen, A., "The Authority to Think: The Student-centred Classroom", *Contemporary Education*, 61(2), 1990.

Auter, P. I., Hanna, M. S., "The Challenge of Developing Online Courses", *Paper presented at the Annual Meeting of the Speech Communication Association*, San Diego, CA, November 23-26, 1996.

Ackermann, E., *Tools for Teaching: The World Wide Web and a Web Browser*, 1996.

Beare, P.L., "The Comparative Effectiveness of Videotape, Audiotape, and Telelecture in Delivering Continuing Teacher Education, *American Journal of Distance Education*, 3(2), 57-66, 1989.

Bell, D., "The Social Framework of the Information Society", In Forester, I (ed.), *The Microelectronics Revolution*, Blackwell, Oxford, 1980.

Berge Z. L., 1999, "Interaction in Post-secondary Web-based Learning", *Educational Technology*, 39(1), pp. 5-11.

Bichelmeyer, B. A., Kiggins, E.A., 1998, "Using Web-based Conferencing in Post-secondary Instruction", *Proceedings of the Annual Conference on Distance Teaching and Learning*, Madison, WI, August 5-7, 1998.

Braun Ludwig, "Computer-aided learning and the Microcomputer Revolution", *Programmed Learning and Educational Technology*, vol. 18, No. 4, 1981.

Brindley, L.J. (ed.), 'The electronic campus: an information strategy', *Library and information research report 73*, London, British Library, 1989.

Chapin, A. L., "The State of the Internet: 1995", *Telecommunications*, Jan. 1995.

Clayes, L., Vander Perre, "Innovative Education through the Use of New Technologies: Reflections from the Field", *Educational Media International*, Vol. 34, No. 3, pp. 144–52, 1997.

Cohen, J. A., Castner, M. H., 2000, *Technology and Classroom Design: A Faculty Perspective*, in L. Lloyd (ed.), *Teaching with Technology, Rethinking Tradition*, Medford, NJ: Information Today, Inc.

Comeaux, P., 1995, "The Impact of an Interactive Distance Learning Network on Classroom Communication", *Communication Education*, 41(4), pp. 353-361.

Cuban, L. *Teachers and machines: The classroom use of technology since 1920*, New York: Teachers College Press, 1986.

Debski, R., "Exploring the recreation of a CALL innovation", *Computer Assisted Language Learning*, 13(4/5), pp. 307-332, 2000.

Dede, C. J., "The Future of Multimedia: Bridging to Virtual Worlds, *Educational Technology*, 1992.

Dick, W., and Carey, L., *The Systematic Design of Instruction* (3rd ed.), Glenview, IL: Scott, Foresman, and Company, 1990.

Doulai, P. and Mandel, M., "Computer and Information Literacy Skills for Professional Engineering Educators", In *the Proceedings of Australasian Universities Power Engineering Conference*, Melbourne, 1996.

Duhaney, D., 2000, Technology and the Educational Process: Transforming Classroom Activities, *International Journal of Instructional Media*, 27(1), pp.67-72.

Duffy, T., Jonassen, D., (eds.), 1992, *Constructivism and the Technology of Instruction: A Conversation*, Hillsdale, N., Lawrence Erlbaum Associates.

Ferrington, G. and Loge, K., "Virtual Reality: A New Learning Environment", *The Computing Teacher*, 1992.

Foa, L., Schwab, R., Johnson, M., "Introducing Technologies into the Schools: Triumph or Train Wreck?", *NEA Technology Brief*, No. 13, 1998.

Forsyth, I., 1998, *Teaching and Learning Materials and the Internet* (2nd ed.), London: Kogan Page.

Galbreath, J., 1995, "Compressed Digital Videoconferencing", *Educational Technology*, 35(1), pp. 31-38.

Galusha, J. M., 1998, *Barriers to Learning in Distance Education, Interpersonal Computing and Technology*, 5(3-4), pp. 6-14.

Galloway, J. P., "How teachers use and learn to use computers", In *Technology and Teacher Education Annual*, pp. 857-859, 1997.

Gilbert, S. W., 1997, *Teaching, Learning, and Technology*, Change, 217, 4 6. Guernsey, L., and Young, J. R. 1998, June 5.

Graham, S.W., and Wedman, J.F., 1989, "Enhancing the Appeal of Teletraining", *Journal of Instructional Psychology*, 16(4), 183-191.

Guha, A.S., "Student-cetred Open Learning", *University News*, November, 27, 2000.

Harasim, L. (ed.), *Online Education*, New York: Praeger, 1990.

Hawkins, J., "Technology and the Organisation of Schooling (Technology in Education)", *Communication of the ACM*, Vol. 36, May 1993.

Heamshaw, D., 1998, "Capitalising on the Strengths and Availability of Desktop Videoconferencing, *Active Learning*, 7, pp. 52-9.

Hiltz, R. S., *The Virtual Classroom*, Norwood, NJ: Ablex, 1995.

Holmberg, B., "Communication in Distance Study", In *Status and trends of Distance Education*, Lund, Sweden: Lector Publishing, 1985.

Ho, M. S., *Learning and Teaching in Cyberspace: An Empirical Investigation of Computer-assisted Instruction for Geography*, Academic. exercise, Dept. of Geography, Faculty of Arts and Social Sciences, National University of Singapore, 1996.

Huges, K., *Entering the World-Wide Web: A Guide to Cyberspace*, Enterprise Integration Technologies, 1994.

Hawkridge David, *New Information Technology in Education*, Croom Helm, London, 1983.

Indira Madhukar, *Internet-based Distance Learning*, Authorspress, New Dehi, 2002.

Information Technology and its Impact on American Education, Office of Technology Assessment, US Congress, Washington DC, 1982.

Jonassen, D., Reeves, T., "Learning with technology: using computers as cognitive tools", In D. Jonassen (ed.), *Handbook of research for educational communications and technology* (pp. 693-719). New York: Macmillan, 1996.

Johnson, D. W., 1981, "Student-Student Interaction: The Neglected Variable in Education", *Educational Researcher*, 10(1), pp. 5-10.

Johnson, M., "CALL and teacher education: Issues in course design", *CALL-EJ Online*, 1(2). Retrieved November 26, 2001.

Kearsley, G., 1995, "The Nature and Value of Interaction in Distance Learning, In M. Koble (ed.), *The American Centre for the Study of Distance Education Invitational Research Conferencing Distance Education: Toward Excellence in Distance Education*, University Park, PA: Penn State University.

Kerr, E. Hiltz, S., *Computer-Based Instruction*, 17(1), 1982.

Kirby, E., "Building Interaction in Online and Distance Education Courses", *Paper presented at the Society for Information Technology and Teacher Education International Conference*, 10th, San Antonio, TX, February, 1999.

Knezek, G., Chiristensen, R., & Rice, D., "Changes in teacher attitudes during information technology training", *Technology and Teacher Education Annual*, 1996, 763-766.

Kumarasamy, K., Teacher Education in the Twenty First Century, *University News*, November, 27, 2000.

Lochte, R.H., *Interactive Television and Instruction*, Englewood Cliffs, NJ: Educational Technology Publications, 1993.

Maddox, C. C., 1997, *The World Wide Web and School Culture: Are they Compatible?*, in D. L. Johnson, C. D. Maddux, and L. Lieu, (eds.), *Using Technology in the Classroom*, New York: The Haworth Press.

Madhu Parhar, "Surfing Through Web—Exploring a New Educational Resource", *University News*, November, 20, 2000.

Milbrath, Y., & Kinzie, M., "Computer technology training for prospective teachers: Computer attitudes and perceived self-efficacy", *Journal of Technology and Teacher Education*, 8(4), 373-396.

Minoli, D., *Video Dialtone Technology, Approaches, and Service: Digital and Services: Digital Video over ADSL, HFC, FTTC, and ATM, New York: McGraw-Hill*, 1995.

Martin, B. L., "Using Distance Education to Teach Instructional Design to Preservice Teachers", *Educational Technology*, Vol. XXXIV, No. 3, March 1994.

McHenry, L., and Bozik, M., 1995, "Communicating at a Distance: A Study of Interaction in a Distance Education Classroom", *Communication Education*, 44(4), pp. 362-371.

Osberg, K. M., "Virtual Reality and Education: Where Imagination and Experience Meet", *VR in the Schools*, 1995.

Pantelidis, V. S., "Virtual Reality in the Classroom", *Educational Technology*, 1993.

Paterson K. G. "Student Perceptions of Internet-Based Learning Tools in Environment Engineering Education", *Journal of Engineering Education*, 88:3, pp. 295-304, 1999.

Patil, V.T., *Virtual Education: Dimensions of Educational Resources*, Authorspress, New Delhi, 2002.

Phye, G., 2000, "Engaging Technology and Learning Opportunities: Technology Assessment Tools", *Paper presented at the Annual Meeting of the American Educational Research Association*, New Orleans.

Pisapia, J., Coukos, E., Knutson, K., 2000, "The Impact of Computer on Teacher Capacity, Attitudes, and Behaviours in Elementary Schools", *Paper presented at the Annual Meeting of the American Educational Research Association*, New Orleans.

Reed, W., Anderson, D., Ervin, J., Oughton, J., "Computers and teacher education students: A ten year analysis", *Technology and Teacher Education Annual*, 1995.

Reid, K. A., *Impact of Technology on learning effectiveness. AT&T CEDL Newsletter*, 1995.

Regan, K., and Tuchman, S., 1990, "The Importance of Authority and Peer Relations on the Educational Process of Onsite and Online Students: An Exploratory Investigation", *Paper presented at the International Conference on Technology and Education,* 7th, Brussels, Belgium, March 20-22, 1990.

Roberts, L., 1996, *A Transformation of Learning: Use of the NII for Education and Lifelong Learning*, In D. P. Ely & B. B. Minor (eds.), *Educational Media and Technology Yearbook 1995/1996*, pp. 50-66, Englewood, CO: Libraries Unlimited.

Schuemer, R., 1993, *Some Psychological Aspects of Distance Education*, Hagen, Germany: Institute for Research into Distance Education.

Stenerson, F., 1998, "Systems Analysis and Design for a Successful Distance Education Programme Implementation", *Journal of Distance Learning Administration*.

Stuart, R. and Thomas, J. C., "The Implications of Education in Cyberspace", *Multimedia Review*, 1991.

Tapscott, D., 1998, *Growing up Digital: The Rise of the Net Generation*. New York: McGraw-Hill Book Company.

Tiffy J., "The Search for the Virtual Class", *The Virtual University Symposium: A report,* D. Baird (ed.) UltiBASE http://ultibase.rmit.edu.au/Articles/maher1.html, 1996.

Verduin, J.R., Clark, T.A., 1991, *Distance Education: The Foundations of Effective Practice*, San Francisco, CA: Jossey-Bass Publishers.

Velayo, R. S., "Supplementary Classroom Instruction via Computer Conferencing", *Educational Technology*, 1994.

Whitelock D. and Scanlon E., 1996, "Motivation, Media and Motion: Reviewing a Computer Supported Collaborative Learning

Experience, In *Proceedings of the European Conference on Artificial Intelligence in Education*, P. Brna, a. Paiva and J. Self (eds)., Euro AIED, Lisbon, 1996.

Williams, M., and Paprock, K., 1994, "Instructional Design in Distance Education", *The ED Journal*, 7(4), 1994.

Willis, B., 1993, *Distance Education: A Practical Guide*, Englewood Cliffs, NJ: Educational Technology Publications.

Wilson, A., 1994, "Instructional Multimedia in the Math Classroom and Beyond", *Paper presented at the Annual Conference of the American Mathematical Association of Two-year Colleges*, Tulsa, OK, November 3-6, 1994.

Yucha, C. 8., 1996, Interactive Distance Education: Improvisation helps Bridge the Gap, *Journal of Biocommunication*, 23(1), pp. 2-5.

Wentworth, N., "Educational technology: From curriculum course to the classroom", *Technology and Teacher Education Annual*, 335-358, 1996.

Work, Colin, 'The future development of campus-wide information systems: towards the virtual campus', *Journal of Information Networking* 1(1), 1993.

Index